# By Scalpel and Cross

Archibald G. Fletcher, MD

# By Scalpel and Cross

*A Missionary Doctor in Old Korea*

Donald R. Fletcher

Foreword by
Sung-Deuk Oak

RESOURCE *Publications* • Eugene, Oregon

BY SCALPEL AND CROSS
A Missionary Doctor in Old Korea

Copyright © 2016 Donald R. Fletcher. All rights reserved. Except for brief quotations in critical publications or reviews, no part of this book may be reproduced in any manner without prior written permission from the publisher. Write: Permissions, Wipf and Stock Publishers, 199 W. 8th Ave., Suite 3, Eugene, OR 97401.

Resource Publications
An Imprint of Wipf and Stock Publishers
199 W. 8th Ave., Suite 3
Eugene, OR 97401

www.wipfandstock.com

PAPERBACK ISBN: 978-1-4982-9237-5
HARDCOVER ISBN: 978-1-4982-9239-9
EBOOK ISBN: 978-1-4982-9238-2

Manufactured in the U.S.A.

To Arch and Jessie,
and to the people of Korea, named and unnamed,
who are part of this story.

# Contents

*List of Illustrations* | ix
*Foreword by Sung-Deuk Oak* | xiii
*Acknowledgments* | xv
*Abbreviations* | xvii

Chapter 1   Suddenly at War | 1
Chapter 2   Roots in Ontario and Nebraska | 6
Chapter 3   "To Any Available Post" | 11
Chapter 4   The Beginning of Protestant Mission | 19
Chapter 5   Bewildering Assignments | 31
Chapter 6   Taegu Station | 41
Chapter 7   The Scourge of Leprosy | 46
Chapter 8   A Brief and Furtive Courtship | 57
Chapter 9   Would God Ever Bring Them Back? | 66
Chapter 10  Laid on the Shelf | 78
Chapter 11  A Hospital Preaching Society | 84
Chapter 12  "The Doctor is Safe, and All of the Children" | 92
Chapter 13  A Quiet World, and Small | 100
Chapter 14  *Romance, Tragedy and Opportunity of Leprosy Treatment* | 111
Chapter 15  Treatment Stations—a Bright Hope Eclipsed | 121
Chapter 16  Our Last Family Furlough | 129
Chapter 17  Crowning Achievement | 137

Chapter 18   "Dr. Fletcher, Praise, Grace Pavilion"  |  148

Chapter 19   Sorai Beach  |  155

Chapter 20   Donkey Egg  |  161

Chapter 21   A Heartbreaking Mess  |  169

Chapter 22   Sayonara  |  178

Chapter 23   Thirty-Eighth Parallel  |  190

Chapter 24   Quonset Huts on a Hill  |  199

Chapter 25   A Stone Tablet Set Up Again  |  204

*Postscript*  |  207

*Illustrations*  |  209

# Illustrations

Frontispiece: Archibald G. Fletcher, MD

Photo 01: Arch Fletcher (left) with younger brother Dave, Ontario, c. 1888 | 209

Photo 02: Fletcher children, top left to right: Gordon, Tom, Arch; bottom: Olive and Dave, Ontario, c. 1898 | 210

Photo 03: Fletcher brothers in Nebraska, top, Tom and Gordon; bottom, Arch and Dave, c. 1905 | 210

Photo 04: Archibald and Gordon Fletcher, together in medical practice, Nebraska, c. 1906 | 211

Photo 05: Archibald G. Fletcher, MD, age 26, Sioux City, Iowa, 1908 | 211

Photo 06: Jessie Rodgers (left) with sister Elsie, Philadelphia, Pennsylvania, c. 1908 | 212

Photo 07: Archibald G. and Jessie Rodgers Fletcher, with children Arch Jr., Donald, and Elsie, 1920 | 212

Photo 08: Archibald G. Fletcher, MD, in his medical coat, Korea, c. 1910 | 213

Photo 09: The Presbyterian Hospital, Taegu, 1937 | 213

Photo 10: One of the seventy three rural churches established by the Taegu Presbyterian Hospital by 1937 | 214

Photo 11: Hospital Evangelist preaching in a village, 1937 | 214

Photo 12: The Rev. K. W. Kim, first Christian and first pastor of North Kyeung Sang Province, 1938 | 215

x

ILLUSTRATIONS

Photo 13: Part of the Taegu Leprosy Hospital compound in winter, c. 1937 | 215

Photo 14: View of the Taegu Leprosy Hospital in the hills outside Taegu, c. 1938 | 216

Photo 15: One of the dormitories, Taegu Leprosy Hospital, c. 1938 | 216

Photo 16: Dr. A. G. Fletcher urges a mother with leprosy to allow her children to enter the home for disease-free children | 217

Photo 17: Taegu Leprosy Hospital, 1 ½ miles outside Taegu, providing care in modern dormitories for 660 men, women, and children in 1938 | 217

Photo 18: Hog house and dairy barn of the Taegu Leprosy Hospital, providing fresh meat in the production of hogs, rabbits, pigeons, and chickens, 1938 | 218

Photo 19: Black Berkshire boar at the animal husbandry facility, Taegu Leprosy Hospital, 1938 | 218

Photo 20: Farmer Pak, an enterprising farmer and active church member, Taegu, 1938 | 219

Photo 21: Korean child, giving the church the gift of a goat, from his grandmother, 1938 | 219

Photo 22: Dr. A. G. Fletcher and a group of healthy children whose parents are being treated for leprosy, c. 1938 | 220

Photo 23: Dr. and Mrs. A. G. Fletcher, in Korean dress outside the Guest House, built with contributions from leprosy patients to honor their 25th anniversary in Korea, photo c. 1937 | 220

Photo 24: Presbyterian Hospital in Taegu, established 1899, grown to a seventy-five-bed hospital by 1938 | 221

Photo 25: Dr. Fletcher and hospital staff making ward rounds, Taegu, c. 1937 | 221

Photo 26: The x-ray department of Taegu Presbyterian Hospital took 1,307 images and gave 1,231 examinations and treatments in 1937 | 222

Photo 27: Medical technicians' course, Taegu Presbyterian Hospital, c. 1938 | 222

ILLUSTRATIONS  xi

Photo 28:  Students in the laboratory, Taegu, c. 1938 | 223

Photo 29:  Laboratory technicians' course, Taegu, c. 1938 | 223

Photo 30:  Free night clinics as outreach of Taegu Presbyterian Hospital, c. 1938 | 224

Photo 31:  Taegu Hospital Baby Clinic Nurse Li Yoo-boon and Mothers' Club president, c. 1938 | 224

Photo 32:  Graduates of the Baby Clinic wellness program, c. 1938 | 225

Photo 33:  A. G. Fletcher in Taegu with visiting Toyohiko Kagawa, the famous Japanese social and labor activist and Christian leader, November 1939 | 225

Photo 34:  Portrait of Archibald G. Fletcher, MD, around the time of his presentation of medical papers in Tokyo, 1931 | 226

Photo 35:  Dr. L. W. Whong and family, Taegu, c. 1953 | 226

Photo 36:  Dr. L. W. Whong and Mrs. Whong at his Ordination ceremony, Taegu, 1955 | 227

Photo 37:  Dr. Archibald G. Fletcher serving the Board of Foreign Missions in New York, after his retirement from the Korea Mission, c. 1960 | 227

Photo 38:  Archibald G. and Jessie Rodgers Fletcher in retirement, New York, 1963 | 228

Photo 39:  Archibald G. and Jessie Rodgers Fletcher at Westminster Gardens, California, 1968 | 228

Photo 40:  Dongsan Medical Center today, with the original "fireproof" hospital seen in the lower left, Taegu | 229

Photo 41:  Stone tablet in modern-day Aerakwon, recovered and re-erected to commemorate the ministry of Dr. Archibald G. Fletcher | 229

# Foreword

THIS IS A RARE page-turning book on a medical missionary, Dr. Archibald G. Fletcher, in Korea from 1909 to 1942 and then from 1946 to 1952. He was one of some missionaries who served the Korean people for more than 40 years. Under his leadership the Taegu station would have one of the largest mission hospitals, with a hospital and center for lepers.

So far, some descendants of missionaries to Korea have published academic books, biographies, or transcribed collections of documents of their parents and their works in Korea. Yet the literary dexterity of the author, a son of Dr. Fletcher, goes beyond just a historical biography and a fictional hagiography of a missionary. The book magnificently combines conscientious and detailed historical research on the archival mission materials with literary imagination and humor. It contains not just detailed historical information on a medical missionary's lifelong work, but is filled with profoundly inspiring stories of love for the suffering, joy in healing their bodies and souls, perseverance in the pilgrims of faith on earth, and hope for eternity from the author's memories, his parents' experience, and missionary communities' delightful secrets.

Thus, it is my great honor and pleasure to recommend this book to any serious student of mission studies, as well as any Christian who is interested in the wonderful works that God has been doing through devout missionaries, especially, a surgeon and his family in a foreign land.

Sung-Deuk Oak

Dongsoon Im and Mija Im Chair
Associate Professor of Korean Christianity
Department of Asian Languages and Culture
University of California, Los Angeles

# Acknowledgments

ALMOST SIXTY YEARS AGO I set out to write this book, for which my father had accumulated copies of letters, reports, and a few old photographs. My family and I were living in Mexico City at the time, as my position with the Presbyterian Church entailed travel among several countries of the Caribbean area. My parents, being retired, came to spend some months near us, and I devoted such time as I could find to long talks with them, while roughing out a narrative of their missionary experience that I had known from a child's perspective while growing up with them in Korea. Disappointingly, the book never took adequate form, and in time was pushed aside.

Now, rather recently, my daughter Sylvia came across copies of pages of that old version, which she had found and squirreled away. Encouraged by her, I went to work on it, re-writing and amplifying, and here it is. I gratefully acknowledge my debt to her, both for reviving the project and for lending dedicated support through each step of seeing it through. Appreciation goes also to the rest of my family: to my late wife, Martha, who shared in the Mexico City phase, but, for her Alzheimer's, was not able to share in its revival, and to our other five children, giving constant encouragement along the way.

A particular debt of gratitude that I wish to pay is to Prof. Sung-Deuk Oak of the University of California, Los Angeles, who, out of his broad knowledge of Korean history, culture and affairs, and particularly, Korean Christianity, has generously provided the Foreword, as well as comments on the historical material in chapter 4.

For both technical and personal assistance, I wish to acknowledge the invaluable help of Roger Williams, of Washington, DC, my literary advisor and friend, who has invested lively and persistent effort in seeing the book finished and helping to find its publisher. Wipf and Stock Publishers, once taking me on, have been both efficient and unfailingly courteous; with special appreciation due their staff member Matthew Wimer, my personal contact.

The reader will see that I have drawn on source material that my father brought together, permitting me precise quotations from letters and other papers. At the same time, in my wish to convey the vigor and immediacy of the story I am telling, I have, in some scenes, created dialogue and personal reflection for these people whom I knew well. It is their personhood and their life that I hope we may re-live.

Donald R. Fletcher

Voorhees, New Jersey
May 1, 2016

# Abbreviations

| | |
|---|---|
| Ave. | Avenue |
| c. | circa |
| cc | cubic centimeter |
| DC | District of Columbia |
| DD | Doctor of Divinity |
| Dr. | Doctor |
| MD | Medical Doctor |
| Mr. | Mister (Master) |
| Mrs. | Missus (Mistress) |
| MSc | Master of Science |
| Penn | University of Pennsylvania |
| PhD | Doctor of Philosophy |
| Rev. | Reverend |
| RN | Registered Nurse |
| US | United States |
| USA | United States of America |

# 1

# Suddenly at War

Ned Adams paused at the door. He had just let in a swirl of night air with the light chill of early December. Let in, too, was the distant barking of a dog and other muted night-sounds of Taegu, Korea, still a small city in 1941.

As he turned to add a last comment, Ned closed the door again—it was important to be conserving heat. "It's hard to imagine that even the warlords in Tokyo would take on more than China just now—but remember, Japan has built up a fine navy and never had a chance to use it."

With that he said goodnight. Jessie and Arch stood watching him go down the walk into the shadows, off toward his house on the low hill a quarter mile away.

Jessie said, "Arch, it's just the three of us here now, with all of the other houses empty and everyone gone—even Sue Adams with Jack. How lonely it must be for Ned! And how much longer may it be now for Ned and for us?"

"Are you worried, dear?" Arch patted her arm. He was like that, affectionate—always a bit restrained, but deeply, genuinely affectionate.

"Yes, I guess so, a little. I'm glad the mission and the board let me stay, though; I wouldn't want to leave you here. And I believe in what we're doing, what we were called to do."

"Then we'll keep on doing it, just as long as we can." That was the way he put it—Archibald Grey Fletcher, MD—and his voice sounded deep and strong.

"All right," Jessie responded. "The Lord knows and cares. The Lord knows that Ned wants to keep the Boys' Academy running and is ready to stay behind, alone, to do it, and the Lord knows how much the hospital needs you and means to you—to all of your people, who are my people, too."

They were back in the dining-living room now. Jessie let the talk stop there, while she busied herself with clearing cups and teapot and what else was left from their Sunday evening supper. For his part, Arch was glad to think about tomorrow, whom he needed to talk to and what further steps ought maybe to be taken at the hospital to be sure it could keep functioning, even without him. He knew—all of his Korean staff knew—that the clouds were darkening.

In Europe, from what they could read, Hitler's war machine kept gaining ground, and Japan had allied itself formally with Germany with an eye toward grand military conquest. How far might Japan decide to go, pursuing her expansionist designs on the Asian mainland?

The Koreans had a huge stake in this. For just over thirty years, since 1910, their country had been occupied and totally dominated by Japan. Christian missions and Western missionaries, already there when Japan took over, had been tolerated and allowed to expand, as long as they did not represent a political danger. Arch, in his single-minded effort as a missionary doctor to heal the sick and promote the Gospel of redemption—peace with God and humanity—had found acceptance, even encouragement, from the authorities. But all of that could change. The militarists had established themselves firmly in Tokyo. It seemed just a question of how far they would go. For his part, Arch would hold on as long as he could.

The morning after that Sunday evening shared with Ned Adams, when Arch went to the mission hospital rather early, the air seemed unusually tense. Tension had come to be a familiar companion. He walked up the stairs and down the gleaming corridor to his office. This was his work: the three-story, fireproof hospital, the result of the best years of his life poured into a dedicated medical effort in Taegu. He noted approvingly that the terrazzo floor of the corridor shone, and reflected the lights and soft colors of the sun parlor at its far end.

But in the office, both his secretary and Elder Pak, the hospital's veteran evangelistic worker, were waiting for him. Mr. Sihm, the secretary, glanced furtively at the door to make sure it was closed and then burst out excitedly:

"Doctor, have you heard the news? The Japanese, they've done it! They've attacked the United States—bombed the great fleet at Pearl Harbor!"

Elder Pak raised a hand and the younger man checked himself. One never knew who might be listening.

"Speak quietly," the elder's deep voice warned. He spoke with the benign solemnity that had lifted the heart and hopes of many a patient in the hospital; but that morning, for all the conscious dignity of his years, there was no hiding the excited gleam in his old eyes.

It was true. In the pre-dawn hours of what was Monday morning, December 8, in Korea, Japanese planes had roared in over the huge US naval base in Hawaii. No one knew the precise truth about the attack. The Japanese press and radio were blaring extravagant claims of having caught all American planes on the ground and having blasted all the ships in the harbor, the chief power of the US Navy. That would be as it would be. One fact was clear, and it was enough for the Koreans. Japan, in what they saw as the folly of her war-might, had taken on the United States of America.

A little later, Jessie reached her tiny downstairs office. She worked in the hospital as matron in charge of linen supplies and housekeeping. Her faithful co-worker, Mrs. Song, slipped in suddenly without announcement. Mrs. Song's round face was grayish, like old parchment.

"Did they tell you?" she whispered. "It's war."

On through the morning, Arch held determinedly to his deliberate routine. He could imagine very well what the news meant to his staff, as to any and all of the Korean people. For thirty-one of the thirty-two years of his service in Korea, the country had been called Chosen (Cho-SEHN), Japan, an annex of the Japanese Empire; but rebellion was always smoldering just below the surface.

He knew to walk cautiously. He saw to it that the occasional Japanese patient, usually a petty official of some kind, was treated courteously, and he cultivated polite relations with local empire officials. Now would come the test—now that Ned Adams' remark had proved to be prophetic. Those Japanese aircraft carriers must have been taking up their positions far out on the Pacific toward Hawaii even as Ned was speaking. Of course Washington would declare war. He and Jessie, as well as Ned, were now—or would soon be—"enemy aliens." The thing was not to let slip any comment, any noticeable reaction at all.

It felt strange, this new identity. Walking home up the sloping path that evening, in the already gathering dusk, Arch let his mind dwell on that, as he hadn't let it do all day while he kept everything carefully calm and routine on the outside, and inside as well. How many days and years had he walked up this path past the poplar trees to the front steps? Those were the trees, where he had a pole stretched between them for the children's swing and where Archie made a platform look-out, with Don's timid help, when the tops of one trunk and main branches were sawed off even. How long ago did that have to have been, with his and Jessie's three now through college—Elsie out and working, Archie in medical school, and Don in seminary? Well, he and Jessie were still here, and she would be home ahead of him with a warm supper waiting. Could it—would it still go on?

That would have to be as it would be. He wasn't going to doubt the Providence that had brought him here. God's way had been quite clear, and God's hand was strong, stronger than anything that could be thrown across his own path. He had trusted to follow God's way from his early beginning. Whatever test might come now, he would keep on following.

The evening was calm—almost tranquil. Jessie had arranged for a simple dinner, as he knew she would.

"Arch, what do you think of the news?" she asked as they sat at table.

"It gives us a lot to think about, but not too hastily."

Do you ever do anything hastily? Jessie thought; but that's a strong point with you. You think long and carefully before you leap, and I've been learning to act the same way.

They discussed their prospects calmly and then went to bed. There wasn't much to discuss yet—just conjecture, which Arch shied away from. Jessie knew well that it wasn't his way to play games of what-if. They would wait and see, while they kept strong their trust in what the Lord might have for them, out of the vast things that would be happening.

The following morning, Kang Si, the cook, arrived with a message. The "outside man" who looked after the house and grounds and did shopping had been taken to jail and would not be coming to work any more. A short while later, there was a quick, nervous tapping at the back door. It was Ned Adams' man, to say that in the night the police had come for Ned and taken him away. What did they say? Why would they do that? He knew nothing more to tell.

"Jessie, the thing to do is to act like nothing unusual is happening," Arch said.

"But what about poor Ned?"

"There's nothing we can do for him, and maybe we'll be next. See if you can find a small bag for each of us and put in just the most necessary things. We'll keep them near the front door, in case the police come and we don't have much time."

That was a frightening thing that kept on being frightening each time Jessie saw the bags there at the door, but a week passed and the police didn't come. After that first swaggering announcement of Japan's overwhelming triumph at Pearl Harbor, there was nothing—only an eerie silence.

Arch took a further step of preparation. It was absolutely important to make as sure as possible that the hospital remain in the hands of the Korean Church, and for that, all formalities must be exactly fulfilled.

On Tuesday morning—by now it was December 16—he and Jessie held a meeting of the Taegu station. With Ned in jail, they two were the station. Station meetings always began with a devotional part, so Jessie, as secretary, took out her *Daily Light*, a small book of selections, Bible verses for each day. As it happened, she opened to September 4, not the current date, and read aloud, a little tremulously:

> Sit still, my daughter.—Take heed, and be quiet, fear not, neither be fainthearted.—Be still, and know that I am God.—The loftiness

of man shall be bowed down, and the haughtiness of men shall be made low, and the Lord alone shall be exalted in that day.

With Arch presiding, the station voted to approve what he was about to do. Then he and Jessie went down to the hospital for a pre-arranged board meeting. The four representatives of the Korean Church's Kyung Pook Presbytery were there, and the two of them, representing Taegu Station of the Korea Mission of the Presbyterian Church in the USA. A Japanese detective and a uniformed policeman stood just outside the office door as the hospital board met.

Arch stood up and spoke distinctly. He was quite willing for his words, carefully chosen in Korean, to be understood by the men on the other side of the door. An era was coming to an end for him, maybe an end to the work of his best years, and he wanted to do it in the way he'd planned. He offered his resignation as superintendent of the hospital, and when it was accepted, he proposed the name of Dr. Whong, a staff member who had studied in Japan and knew the Japanese language and ways. The board approved. Then he and Jessie, as the last missionary members, resigned from the board, and that also was approved.

When they left the meeting, a higher-ranking police official was waiting in the reception hall below. He crackled out a few terse sentences to Arch in Japanese, which Mr. Pak, the treasurer, translated into Korean.

"Your resignation as Superintendent has been accepted. Now your presence here at the hospital is no longer necessary. You and your wife will remain inside the enclosure of your house in the future."

The era had really come to a close.

# 2

# Roots in Ontario and Nebraska

IN THE MONTHS OF internment there would be time for thought—much time for Jessie and for Arch, unaccustomed as he was to such a season of quiet and reflection. At least they were not in jail, nor behind barbed wire. Their fence was the tile-topped mud wall around the back of the compound, and the road along the front that linked together the now-vacant houses. They had room enough—only, isolation.

One could think back and remember. It was in Arch's belief—and the impress of his own personality—to look back with thankfulness to God over all the way by which he had come. He wasn't much used to philosophical reflection, but had no question that God's compassion, God's wise and sufficient providence, had marked each turning of the road, all the way back to the worn, white-clapboard farmhouse in Ontario that had been the Fletcher family homestead.

We once stood looking at that house, Arch—Dad—with my brother and me. It was a rare, sort of sentimental pilgrimage that just the three of us had a chance to make, leaving our families at Chautauqua, the lovely conference center in western New York, and crossing into Canada. The house was there, much as Dad told us that he remembered it. Around one corner from the front door was the four-paned window of a small, downstairs bedroom. That was where his mother went through her labor and he was born, the fourth of her five sons, after whom came the baby girl that completed her family.

We stood a good while looking at the house and the five elms that sheltered it—trees that were set out too close together and had grown tall, their branches interlocking, forming a single mass. There was no one around, but one could imagine that earlier time when the trees stood separately, when there was the noise and bustle of all those boys learning farm work, growing, close to the rich Ontario soil.

One could hear also the hushed voices, see the black, unfamiliar clothes, and sense the desolation of that fourth child, just seven years old.

They had let him go into the small, downstairs bedroom to see his mother, so white against the pillows, so weak when she touched his hand but couldn't hold him, and he laid his head against her; then the desolation when they all came back from the cemetery, from the deep hole in the ground and the room with its four-paned window was so empty—the yard and the trees, all of it so empty.

Their dad did all that he could, although his sister, their Aunt Beck, took Olive, the little girl, to be with her. But the shadow was still over them. Their dad's cough kept getting worse and sometimes there were flecks of blood, although he tried to hide them. Arch was older and knew these things. He was twelve when there was another long, sad walk behind the plodding, black-draped hearse all the way to the cemetery. His dad, too, was gone.

Jim, the eldest of them, took over. Jim was already engaged. He brought his bride home to try to be a mother to the whole family, but the shadow stayed over them. In only a short time, Jim began with the cough. He left the farm and went all the way to Nebraska, where they said the climate was warmer and dry, but it didn't help. Jim came home to Ontario to die.

Arch was about sixteen or seventeen when Tom, now the eldest, called a family council. If they stayed on the farm, they all must pitch in more. They knew well enough that farm work was hard. It was also uncertain and probably couldn't bring in enough for all of them to have a life, as they grew older. Arch, looking solemn, asked Tom what he had in mind, although he could guess it well enough, and they all agreed. Not that they wanted to. It was going to be hard; but they must sell the farm and move off the land. Each would have his part, equal shares all around, including Olive, surprisingly grown up and almost a young lady.

Arch had guessed also what older brother Tom probably intended. Tom had listened with close attention when Jim returned from Nebraska and told about the broad, open land, the promise and opportunities for enterprising people. That was Tom. He was good with figures and enterprising enough. It was no surprise, then, that Tom took his share and was off to Nebraska.

Gordon, next in line, had a similar but different idea. He would use his share to go to Toronto, as soon as he could qualify, to study medicine and learn to be a family doctor. Arch was surprised, because something like that had been in his own mind, although he had kept it to himself. As it turned out, with the necessary passage of years, all three of the younger brothers went into medicine, and their sister married a doctor. Gordon graduated from the University of Toronto, set up a practice in Orchard, Nebraska.

Arch's choice was the medical school of the University of Illinois in Chicago, not a long distance from the farm in southern Ontario.

∽ ∽ ∽

In a treasured photograph, a long, straight road of northeastern Nebraska stretches away under the light of a summer evening. Down the road, a buggy has stopped, its horse standing with drooped head. But nearer there has just been action. A man in black suit and derby hat—recognizable as Arch Fletcher, wanting to look like a young doctor, but still with something of the farm boy about him—strikes a pose, aiming a shotgun into the undergrowth near the road. Just visible, below the aim, are the head and tail of a speckled Irish Setter, moving through the undergrowth.

It is a July evening in 1906. Arch, finishing his three-year course in Chicago the year before, has been gaining experience in rural medicine by assisting in Gordon's Orchard practice. The horse and buggy are from a livery stable, as is the driver, who presumably is taking the picture. House calls to distant farmhouses mean long hours trotting home, for which a young doctor can slip his bird dog and gun into the buggy.

A minute or so before this photograph there had been a whirr of wings just up ahead, a flight of quail into the underbrush, and Arch had caught the driver's arm, almost simultaneously dropping to the road, he and Maizie, the setter. Here was a good shot, a chance for a couple of quail that would make for tasty eating when he brought them home to Gordon's Myra, in her kitchen. After the shot, this time, he celebrated by posing for the photograph. Such happy moments should be kept and remembered.

They were part of the two good years Arch had in Orchard assisting Gordon, years that were also good because of Clyde. Clyde was the Presbyterian pastor's older daughter, a college girl, majoring in music but home for vacations. Arch could find opportunity to be where she was, and Clyde seemed to be glad for that. As their friendship grew, there were evening rides into the countryside. Brother Tom, doing modestly well in business, had a clean, new buggy and kept a fine team of driving horses. Arch could borrow them for a leisurely ride and a long, pleasant talk with Clyde.

It was in one such talk that he told her what he had not shared with anyone else: that while still in medical school, he had begun to think about being a missionary doctor. That wasn't exactly in his family's tradition. His father had always been respectful, but not often in church of a Sunday midday. His mother was more devout, but the duties of her busy household left her little time for meditation. He did remember, though, one time when just he was with her and she took out a well-thumbed Bible.

"Archie dear," she said, "it tells here how, when Jesus had risen from the dead, he told his disciples to go into all the world and preach the gospel to all nations. That's how even our hard Scottish people in their northern land were finally turned to the loving Savior. Think of that, my laddie—how different we would have been without that light."

She must have said more; he didn't remember. And anyway, telling Clyde about it, he felt the mist rising to his eyes and a sudden tightening in his throat. He would not risk trying to say more. Clyde put her gloved hand on his arm—the first time she had ever touched him—and gave him a wonderful smile.

"I know," she said. "It is the Lord. I've sometimes felt the same, that I need to say I'll go. We have so much, and there are people out there, crowds and crowds of them, who have so little light, so little hope."

Arch let the horses go unusually far that evening, and they talked a long time. It was almost dark when they got back. They'd told each other that maybe they could go together—there might be a place that God had for both of them—Clyde with her music and he with medicine. It could be a wonderfully effective way to present the Gospel.

∾ ∾ ∾

There was just one more time for them, alone like that. Arch was not sure that Clyde's parents were approving of her seeing him that much. Then she was off to Omaha for further music study, and he, too, decided that he needed some different experience. If he were to find himself in the future assigned to a mission post where he must do it all, he'd need to have much more practice in major surgery than his schooling and his assisting in Orchard had afforded him. He wrote to the Samaritan Hospital in Sioux City, Iowa, the major city nearest to Orchard, and was promised a place on the staff. He would make the move in the fall.

Arch contrived one more time to share with Clyde. It wasn't as intimate. His two brothers and some friends were going hunting on Thanksgiving weekend, and the group was to include, this time, a few adventurous women. They would make camp several miles north of Orchard, where there was a chain of little lakes. At this season, migrating ducks and geese made a stop-over on the lakes. Morning and evening hunters could position themselves in the sedge and reeds, waiting and hoping for the chance of a good shot.

Arch talked Clyde into joining the hunters, and their adventure is recorded in a group photograph. There he is at one end in his hunting jacket, striking a relaxed pose, slouch felt hat cocked to one side, a shotgun, properly broken down, cradled in his left arm. And Clyde is there a little distance away, dressed in the full, hampering skirt that decorum required, but with a sly, triumphant smile. She had managed it, in spite of her parents' misgivings.

That fall they had exchanged a few letters from their new locations, she in Omaha and he in Sioux City. She was thrilled with her situation and experiences, and wanted him to come to Omaha after Christmas to spend a few days with her there. Her teacher had a friend with a large house where he could rent a guest room. The rent and other costs of an extended date were something Arch had to ponder, although he did have a resource. While still in medical school, and thinking about missionary service, he had told himself that at a mission post there would certainly be people with defective vision, but no possibility of finding corrective care.

So he squeezed in some study on the side, learning the basics of optometry. As it turned out, the field for using his extra training was not some distant country but the farming families around Orchard. They were glad to pay modestly for his services and save themselves the trips into the city for eye examinations.

Arch replied to Clyde's invitation. Yes, he would greatly enjoy visiting her in Omaha, in her new setting, and a few days of the week after Christmas would work out very well. He would just return to Orchard for the first part of the week and then proceed to Omaha. Of course, the fact was that he needed to arrange first for eye visits with some families in the Orchard area. That way he could provide some money and not be ashamed, whatever plans for entertainment Clyde might propose.

She caught him by surprise. A rather long letter came back from her, almost by return mail. It was no doubt appropriate in his judgment, she wrote, that he return to Orchard to see his brothers before coming to see her. She had made plans and advance arrangements for delightful activities that they could share in Christmas week in Omaha, but these apparently were secondary. She must understand that the relationship with his brothers was of first importance. Why, then, should he cut short his Orchard vacation days just to visit her? She would not wish to cause him to make such a concession. Rather, she would proceed with filling out her plans without a need for including him.

Arch sat for several long minutes staring at the letter, written in Clyde's graceful, feminine hand. Outside, it was cold already. The weakening December sunlight was not enough to warm his small room; he had lit a fire in the small, pot-bellied stove that his landlady supplied, set in one corner. There was no sound; the fire had burned down to coals. Then his chair creaked. Arch stood up, went over to the stove, lifted its round lid and dropped in Clyde's letter. That, as it seemed, would be that.

# 3

# "To Any Available Post"

Arch did not find it easy to discard outworn relationships, any more than it was easy for him to form new ones. He realized that to some people he probably seemed aloof. Growing up among all those brothers with their strong, sometimes aggressive personalities, he had developed a way of keeping thoughts to himself. He would listen to his own inner voice.

So with Clyde, he had enjoyed her companionship and had basked in the warmth of her feminine presence. He had even entered into that romantic notion of sharing with her a mission post in some exotic country, her music blending with his medicine—an Albert Schweitzer type of thing. But at the same time, his inner voice was telling him that likely she was not a life partner for him—she, the college girl with her artistic bent. His education, more scant, was practical and single-minded. While enjoying chances to be with her, he would do best to follow his own lead. With that, he accepted the break in their relationship over the Christmas visit to Omaha, and pushed ahead with work in Samaritan Hospital. The spring slipped away as he followed his lead.

Then on June 2, 1907, he posted a letter to Rev. E. W. Halsey, Secretary, Presbyterian Board of Foreign Missions, 156 Fifth Ave., New York, New York. The letter was brief, but it carried great weight for him:

Dear Sir,

This is to inquire about possibilities for service as a missionary doctor. I have completed medical studies, two years assisting in general practice, and am currently on a hospital surgical staff. Although with an interest in tropical medicine, I am prepared to go willingly to any available post and look forward to your reply.

Yours very sincerely,

Archibald G. Fletcher

The letter to the Rev. Dr. Halsey brought a quick response, a cordial but noncommittal welcome and a sheaf of forms to be filled out: personal history, along with reasons for and hopes in volunteering for missionary service, a health form to be completed by an examining physician, and a half dozen reference forms to be mailed in directly by people who knew him well. There were also three questions for him to respond to, affirming his stance on the broad, fundamental doctrines of the Presbyterian Church, plus this necessary and guarded query:

> Have you any opinion at variance with these doctrines, or any view of church government, which would prevent your cordial co-operation with the missionaries of the Presbyterian Church?

Using the hours that he could find, Arch responded firmly and positively on the board's forms. For recommendations, he turned to two physicians who could vouch for him well, two prominent lay people, and two uncles. One of these last was there in Sioux City, an elder in the Second Presbyterian Church. Arch would later refer to him as "one of the most saintly men I've ever known."

The completed forms went back to New York. Arch calculated what should be a reasonable time for his six references also to have responded, sending in their assessments of him as a prospective medical missionary, and the brazen Mid-Western summer slipped away. With the summer gone although its heat lingered, he wrote again to New York to inquire tactfully when the board might be acting on his application.

This time a reply came from a different secretary, Stanley White. White seemed to assume that the board had approved Arch's application. He wrote regarding a need for a doctor in the station of Chungju, Korea, asking if Arch would be willing and ready to consider this opportunity; while it appeared from his letter that the board was also communicating with another medical candidate. In November, Arch wrote back characteristically to Dr. White:

> In offering myself as a worker for the foreign field, I wish to do so with the fewest possible restrictions and trust that God will lead and direct me to the place and work for which I am best suited. In view of the fact that you have already communicated with another physician and for the additional reason of my experience here, both professional and religious, being so profitable and beneficial to my future missionary career, would it not seem that the Lord wants me to continue here for some months? However, if you should fail to secure a doctor for Chungju and

your heart is burdened with the need and you select me as best prepared to meet it, I shall gladly go.

Arch was clear on his long-term commitment—one that would hold far into the future—but he was finding in Sioux City a fresh and stimulating rhythm. There was the hospital work, with a chance to share in, or perform solo, one to four operations a day. And for patient care, the pattern at Samaritan was one that he responded to—each doctor was teamed with a particular nurse. While Arch kept the relationship scrupulously professional, he found an emotional satisfaction in it.

There was, for instance, a case of typhoid fever that he and his nurse cared for. Not much could be done, except to press fluid intake on the patient. It was thought that solid food might risk a rupture of the dangerously weakened intestines. Every few hours, Arch would stop by, where his nurse was watching their patient's struggle in the grip of the fever—until late one night, when she met him at the patient's door and a tear was starting down her cheek. Nothing needed to be said; they had lost their patient.

The "religious" part of the Sioux City experience that Arch was finding "profitable and beneficial" meant his participation at Second Presbyterian Church, where he had the entrée provided by his uncle. Bob Ecklin, the church's young pastor, was his own age and soon became a close friend.

Arch's religious convictions were bound up with treasured memories of his mother, but they lacked clear formulation. The Bible was a holy book about which he had only shapeless ideas. Pastor Bob could understand that, and set out to do something about it. Bringing together with Arch three others from the church's youth group, he got each of them to commit to a couple of hours once a week for a Bible study. They'd start at the level of Sunday School beginners, but he would push them along as fast as they were willing to go.

Arch relished that and responded wholeheartedly. He also found other times to join Bob in social gatherings and a few long, personal talks, walking out of Sioux City as far as some open fields, now harvested down to brown and yellow stubble. On one of those walks he told Bob about Clyde and about dropping her letter into the stove—a kind of confidence that came as a relief, while it wasn't natural for him to share.

After the turn of the year, Arch wrote to Dr. White; most of these officers of the mission board, as ministers, had after their name, "DD", for honorary Doctor of Divinity. He wrote to report on his progress, professional and religious. In the hospital he was gaining excellent experience, with one or more major surgeries every day. Religiously, he was profiting greatly from his pastor's Bible classes, and Sunday services and young people's meetings were inspiring. He found the opportunities for personal work with patients challenging—not surprisingly, "personal work," in that conservatively Christian vocabulary, meant testifying to one's personal convictions about the Gospel. The personal part—bringing up in conversation what seemed to him such a private matter—could not come easily, although he knew that evangelical Christianity expected it, and that, as a missionary, this would be at the heart of his mission. The risen Jesus had said, in the familiar King James version, "Go ye therefore, and teach all nations, . . . " (Matt. 28:19).

Dr. White wrote back about a vacancy, this time on Hainan Island in China. Answering, Arch held to his commitment. Dr. White knew his qualifications and limitations, and the characteristics of the place they needed to fill.

> When the board decides to appoint me, be it to Hainan Island or elsewhere, in so far as it is possible for me to discern at this time, you can depend upon me to go.

This brought a letter in early March from Dr. White stating that on March 2, 1908, the board had appointed Archibald G. Fletcher, MD, as a candidate for assignment. There was no specific post as yet, and that was all right with him. He was in no hurry to leave Sioux City, but the appointment was now definite and the future assured.

From the time he was in his last year of medical school, Arch had grown his black whiskers into a neatly trimmed mustache and short, pointed beard that set off his thick, wavy black hair. Now he wanted a sign—something to declare his new persona—a missionary doctor under appointment by his board. He decided to shave clean his upper lip and chin. Bob Ecklin had pointed out to them, as his Bible study group made its way through the book of Acts of the Apostles, that brief, intriguing mention in chapter 18, verse 18; how Paul, the great first missionary, made a stop at Cenchreae and "shore his head, for he had a vow." Arch, for his part, would dramatize his vow of missionary service by shaving, not his head, but all his facial hair.

Of course, the change was immediately noticed, and that gave him an opportunity to share his news at the hospital and also at church. The church officers, led by their young pastor and encouraged by Arch's Uncle Jim, voted unanimously to pledge support for him. Pastor Bob wrote to the board in New York that the Second Presbyterian Church would contribute six hundred dollars toward the support of A. G. Fletcher, MD, for the year beginning not earlier than October first. That would give the church officers some time to rally enthusiasm. Six hundred dollars was a considerable sum in 1908; it would go far toward a year of missionary support.

The wheels in New York seemed to turn slowly. Arch heard again from Dr. Halsey, on whose suggestion he had letters from two missionary physicians and a conversation with the wife of a third, all of them working in Africa.

Finally, in October, prompted by a letter from Arch enclosing one from his supporting church, Stanley White replied, stating that "just at present the only request we have for the immediate appointment of a physician is in Korea under the Korea Propaganda." The Korea Propaganda was a promotional effort launched by some fervent supporters of the Korea mission, based on the extraordinary way in which opportunity was opening up in that country early in the twentieth century. Arch, still focused on tropical medicine, wrote back that if climatic conditions in Korea were similar to those of China and Japan he would be very willing to go there, and they should feel free to present his name to the Korea Committee.

It was on December 29, just as the year 1908 was slipping away, that specific news came from Dr. White:

> I send you word to notify you that at the meeting of our board on December 21st you were assigned as one under appointment to the Korea mission. Dr. Brown has probably written you to this effect as the Secretary for Korea, and your future correspondence should be with him. He will tell you about the time of sailing and also about the question of outfit and other matters that concern your trip. I rejoice to welcome you as one of those who is to formally represent our board on the Foreign Field.

Arch wrote promptly to Dr. Brown, asking for information about the station in Korea to which he was appointed and about outfit, both medical and personal, that he would need. As for a sailing date, he wrote that he could be ready on very short notice, but could profitably use the next six months at the hospital in Sioux City. "The decision should be reached, in my mind, upon the urgency of the need in Korea."

Dr. Brown wrote back, expressing a very cordial welcome. As to appointment to a particular station in Korea, he said nothing. Arch was to learn how jealously the Korea mission kept such assignments in its own control. Nor, apparently, was the need that urgent. The board would be holding, in New York in early June, a conference for outgoing new missionaries—all expenses paid. Arch should plan on that; and since it was important for him to be in Korea by August 20 for the annual mission meeting, this gave him a window for a sailing date.

The New York conference was an exciting, stimulating experience. Arch had set out to pursue his missionary goal as a solitary quest. It was not until the June morning when he stepped off the Michigan Central train at 7:30 a.m., filled time until he could take a cab downtown, and crossed the threshold of the big doors at 156 Fifth Avenue, that his initiation began.

There were these men he had corresponded with, including the particularly warm handgrip from Dr. Brown. And there were young people like himself, a whole group of them, making up the 1909 class of mission appointees. They would spend several days getting to know each other, going to classes together, listening to secretaries, board members, and a few veteran missionaries, before they were commissioned in a solemn, memorable, joyful service of worship.

Yes, Arch felt, this was what he had been drawn toward, all the way back there in medical school. This surely was what God meant for him—this new family. He thought of how his brothers had regarded his choice, treating him with a kind of bemused indulgence. He returned, as happened only rarely, to the memory of his mother, opening her Bible in her lap. He felt sure that this was right; he was where he needed to be.

The surprise that came out of the conference—to the amusement of some of the recruits for other mission fields—was that Arch would be sailing for Korea in the company of seven other appointees, all of them women. As the only male, he would of course be expected to look after certain practical matters, such as the transfer, loading, and stowing of luggage—sixteen large and forty-two smaller pieces, as it turned out, to be counted and recounted. The ladies ranged in age from twenty to about forty. He, about to turn twenty-seven in mid-August, was to shepherd them all.

∞ ∞ ∞

There were the usual tensions and anxious moments of a sailing from San Francisco. Arch, with his hands full, had little time for nostalgia, and no family members could be there to see him off. Yet the long, largely subtropical Pacific crossing, including a stopover in Hawaii, afforded a peaceful, welcome transition for reflection and a sort of spiritual preparation. Then they were arriving in Japan.

Arch had gotten to know his charges, particularly the younger ones. He had taken notice of Edith, one of the youngest, who was spending increasing time, during the long, languid evenings, with a young, single businessman. In Kobe, the group was to board a small coastal ship to cruise through the Inland Sea to Shimonoseki, where they'd meet the ferry that would carry them across to Korea. Edith's new friend would be staying in Kobe. He knew Kobe well, all the interesting sights, and would show her some of them in the several hours they had, before the coastal steamer was due to depart.

The several hours passed. Arch's party was on board, they and their luggage—but no Edith. He went to speak to the captain, who only shrugged, nodding to an officer, who pulled the cord for a shrill blast on the ship's horn. Dockhands began loosing and casting off lines, and freeing the gangway to be hauled aboard. The remaining six of Arch's group surrounded him on deck. He was saying that he would have to get off and find Edith, then follow them as soon as possible. They had their passage to Pusan, Korea, and should go on as planned.

No! No! How could they do that? They needed him to be with them. That's what Dr. Brown in New York had said. If Edith foolishly got herself lost, she was with her shipboard friend. Let him look after her and set her on her way.

The ship's horn gave another shrill hoot. Arch started for the gangway, still in a whorl of indecision. The captain, watching all this from the bridge only a few feet above, gave a shout and pointed. Around a corner of the dock shed came a rickshaw, then another and another, the porters at a full run. In the first was Edith, shrieking and waving; in the second, her Kobe friend and escort; and in the third, her trunk, which they fortunately had had the presence of mind to pick up at the customs house.

Gloria, who had seized Arch's arm, gave a glad cry. In a matter of seconds, Edith and her trunk were on board, the gangway was hoisted in, and quickly widening water was showing between the dock and the ship's side.

Gloria, as Arch knew, had been doing some serious rethinking. During the Pacific crossing, he had observed that she was another of his charges who seemed to be discovering an intimate rapport with a male passenger, this one an American on his way to Harbin, in Manchuria, to take up a business post. Arch knew that Gloria was already engaged. She was going out to be married in Korea to a missionary she had met when he was on furlough in the United States. What Arch didn't know was that Gloria, an RN, had gotten to know John Hemphill, the missionary, when he was flat on his back in a hospital, recovering from a lingering bout of hepatitis.

Perhaps it was that Gloria, as a nurse, felt a bond of professional confidence with Arch, or perhaps, as their ship neared Japan, with Korea just beyond, she had an almost desperate need of someone to confide in and counsel with. On the last day at sea she had sought out Arch and had told him that she had misgivings about her marriage prospect and about becoming a missionary wife in Korea. He tried to reassure her, while counseling that she keep her mind and her heart open, trusting in God's leading. This was a strange, different role for him—to act as spiritual counselor. He was only beginning to feel his own way in concerns of the spirit, and was wishing that Bob Ecklin were there. In fact, he said to Gloria, "I believe my pastor friend Bob would say to you, 'Wait on the Lord; he will make known to you the way that you should take.'"

In Kobe, Arch had a further message for Gloria. There was a telegram from John Hemphill saying that he would be coming down to Pusan to meet her, to take her to Pyongyang for the annual mission meeting. But Gloria had reached her decision. When Arch showed her the telegram, she asked him to wait there while she found and brought her shipboard friend.

When they came back, she said, "George and I are going to be married. I'll be going with him to Harbin; he says we'll take the same train in Pusan as all of you, only that I won't get off in Pyongyang, but go on north with him."

What was Arch to do? Congratulate them, of course, and wish them joy; but also say frankly to Gloria that it would be up to her to tell John about her decision, when he met her in Pusan. She would need to do it as kindly and carefully as she could; this was bound to be very hard for John.

And it was hard for John, when he had to appear in Pyongyang, where everyone was expecting to welcome his bride, and to acknowledge that there was no bride for him—she had gone on to Harbin to marry another man. The great sympathy of John's colleagues might have been boundless, except that he showed himself to be resilient. Within a matter of months after the annual meeting, he discovered and married a fellow missionary who had been there all along and he hadn't had eyes to see her.

Then, for Arch's party, came the transfer in Shimonoseki from the coastal steamer to a somewhat larger ship for crossing the Japan Strait to Pusan, loading and reloading luggage; then, in Pusan, going through customs and getting them all aboard the train for Pyongyang. This whole sequence, what Arch remembered of it, was something of a blur. It was only on the train, when they were settled in their sleeping car and the conductor had been through to check their tickets, that he could settle himself at a window and watch the countryside move past.

This was Korea! Rice fields filled the view, rising in long, gradual steps up the wide valleys. There were villages, clusters of mud-walled, thatch-roofed houses, above which hovered wisps of smoke tinted by sunlight of the long, late-summer evening. And there were farmers still in the fields, and in the mud-walled enclosure of a house near the tracks, as the train slowed, laboring up a long rise, there were children and chickens and a woman bent over, fanning the embers in an open, clay fireplace. All the adults were dressed in white; only the children wore some bits of color, the smallest wearing nothing at all from the waist down. Korea. Arch drank it in. These would be his people; this, his home now, wherever he might find himself assigned.

# 4

# The Beginning of Protestant Mission

KOREA! THAT WAS A Korea far different from either North or South Korea as they are now. To understand something of Korea as it was then, early in the twentieth century, one needs to go back even a little further, to the late decades of the nineteenth century.

Over its history, the Kingdom of Korea had to resist domination by foreign powers. A glance at a map is enough to see how this would have been. The Korean peninsula thrusts down from the bulging coastline of Asia into the warm waters of the Japan Sea. It seems like an appendage of China, and Korea for centuries felt itself under the shadow, both political and cultural, of that Celestial Empire. Across narrow straits lies the crescent of islands that is Japan. For Koreans, the warlike Japanese were barbarians. They had swarmed up the Peninsula in 1592 under Hideyoshi and again in 1596, but had been driven back to their islands.

There was also the threat from the north, as ominous as the icy winds that sometimes swept down off the Gobi Desert. In the seventeenth century, the terrible Manchus, before whom even the Celestial Emperor himself was impotent and who brought to an end the mighty Ming Dynasty, marched on Seoul. The warning flashed by bonfires from peak to peak of the "fire mountains" scarcely seemed to reach the capital city more swiftly than the Manchu warriors themselves on their forced marches. Korea groveled abjectly before the northern barbarians, and they took whatever spoils they chose.

All Korea wanted was to be left alone, but always the foreigners were trying to thrust in, and always they brought destruction of old treasures and of old ways which had been good for the ancestors and should be good for their less happy children. Yet by the late nineteenth century, it was no longer possible for a whole nation in the heart of the Orient to live like a hermit. Japan had opened its doors to the West. The island people on whom Korea had looked for centuries with mingled fear and condescension had started on the social revolution that would carry them, in less than a century, into the first rank of modern industrial powers.

There were young Koreans who had been in Japan and had seen these things. Back in Korea, they were pressing vociferously for reform. The opposition of the conservative aristocratic families had to lead, within a few short years, to internecine violence and bloodshed that would bring an end to Korean independence. Japan, China and Russia, the inevitable trio, were crowding in on Korea, and close above them other, more distant powers seemed also to be circling.

In such an atmosphere, in May 1882, Commodore Robert W. Schufeldt of the US Navy could count himself lucky that his overture to the Korean government was kindly received. Schufeldt was wise enough to proceed cautiously and with full regard for courtly protocol. He secured an exchange of emissaries with the Korean Court from a respectful distance before proceeding on his frigate to the port of Chemulpo. There he waited until three Korean emissaries, who had gone to court on his behalf, came to meet him, and he had set up a tent on shore. Then Schufeldt peacefully planted before the tent the flag of the United States of America, to the tune of Yankee Doodle, and inside the tent he signed a treaty of friendship between the United States and Korea.

There would be other American tents set up in Korea seventy years later, and American blood shed on Korean soil, demonstrating, in a very different time and situation, the respect for freedom and national integrity that this late nineteenth century document affirmed. All honor to Commodore Schufeldt, the first emissary to conclude a treaty between any of the Western powers and the Kingdom of Korea!

∾ ∾ ∾

It was three months later that year, in August 1882, on an opposite round of the globe, that Archibald Grey Fletcher was born.

∾ ∾ ∾

In September 1884, H. N. Allen, MD, a Presbyterian missionary surgeon, reached Korea—just one generation ahead of Arch. Allen was resolved to be cautious. He got himself into the country by being named physician to the American Legation and, once in Seoul, he began with dignified restraint to establish contact with the Korean court.

Dr. Allen had been in Seoul only a few months when the seething political situation boiled over. Leaders of both factions—the Reformists, who favored Japan, and the Conservatives, who favored China—were assembled at a state banquet when Min Young-ik, who belonged to the aristocratic Min family and had recently been sent as an envoy to the United States and treated with great honor, was called out of the room. An assassin set on him in the courtyard and wounded him horribly with a sword. Immediately Seoul was thrown into confusion.

The Reformists, whether they had been responsible for this barbarous attack or not, decided that they must seize the moment or be liquidated one by one. Rushing to the palace, they surrounded the king, a young and vacillating man, whom they forced to send messages summoning his ministers. As these arrived, they were cut down in cold blood.

The triumph was brief. The king had been made to send to the Japanese minister, asking for a guard, and about four hundred men were dispatched to garrison the palace grounds. But this lent international proportions to the incident, giving an excuse to the strong detachment of three thousand Chinese soldiers stationed in the city to march on the palace. The grounds were wide in extent. After a brief resistance, the Reformists and Japanese decided that defense of the palace was hopeless and forced their way through the attackers to escape to the port of Chemulpo and to Japan.

This bloody affair, the failure of the Kapsin Coup, December 1884, put the Chinese for the moment on top of the heap of political intrigue in Seoul, but it also favored Dr. Allen. He was sent for to treat Min Young-ik, the wounded nobleman, and gained entrance to the palace. In the turmoil, many foreigners were leaving Seoul. Dr. Allen wrote to the Presbyterian board in New York on December 9 of that year, 1884, with the sort of slightly grandiose gallantry that was characteristic of him:

> We couldn't leave if we would and wouldn't if we could. I came to do just this kind of work and I can't leave all these wounded people. If I am not here when my successor comes he will find everything in the safe. We shall live in the Legation with the old flag flying, work hard for the people and trust the kind Father who sent us to care for us.

In the months that followed, Japan held on as best it could, although for the time China was definitely in the ascendancy. Russia also formally entered the confused picture. Dr. Allen recorded how, in September 1885, the Russian minister and his suite arrived in Seoul, and the gates of the city were let open for his entrance, a favor never shown before to a foreigner. China was stringing a telegraph line between Peking (now Beijing) and Seoul, which the Japanese disputed in view of sole telegraph rights that Korea had given them in 1883 for the laying of an undersea cable to unite

Tokyo with the southern port of Pusan and so with Seoul. The neighboring powers were circling over prostrate Korea, and their strident screaming was growing loud.

Through it all, Dr. Allen pursued the advantage of his new relationship with the royal family. Writing to the mission board in New York, he described the triumph of being called to attend the king's mother, his admission to the women's quarters of the Summer Residence, where he was sure that no other male foreigner had entered before. The elderly lady was screened by curtains—even her arm and wrist were completely bandaged, except for the small part where he was to feel the pulse. By 1886, when he had been in Korea only two years, Dr. Allen had been twice honored by the Korean government, given the Third and later the Second Degree of Nobility by personal decree of the king.

Early in the previous year, 1885, word had reached Dr. Allen that a reinforcement was on his way. The strong personality of the missionary surgeon was to be joined by another who was entirely his equal. The Rev. Horace G. Underwood reached Japan in January, but had to wait until the end of March for a boat to Korea. The delay didn't disconcert the brilliant, impulsive young Underwood, who used his time to teach English, study Korean, and get himself involved with some of the young Korean political refugees who had escaped to Japan after the massacre of the previous December.

On April 5, he arrived in Seoul. Dr. Allen, writing to the board in New York the following day, remarked that Underwood seemed to be business-like and that he hoped to have him act as treasurer. Allen was deep in medical work. On his initiative, and after his treatment of Min Young-ik, as well as Queen Min and other ladies in the palace, a government hospital, Che-jungwon, was set up in the repaired house of a wealthy gentleman, one of the victims of the Kapsin Coup, and with furnishings provided by the king. Soon Dr. Allen was performing four to six operations daily, as well as seeing seventy outpatients a day in the dispensary.

Underwood, for his part, was more than business-like. The zeal with which he set to studying the Korean language earned for him in a few short months the reputation of being the best Korean scholar in Seoul. With half a year in the country, he was hard at work on a Korean-English dictionary. As for Allen, he was too busy to study the language, although confident that he would "get a working knowledge" from hearing it spoken.

In October of that year (1885), the Korea Mission of the Presbyterian Church, USA, was organized. It had three members. J. W. Heron, MD, had arrived to second the work of Dr. Allen and he was elected secretary, with Allen as chairman and Underwood, of course, as treasurer. H. G. Underwood was a vigorous and aggressive missionary. Dr. Allen wrote of him with his usual candor in September, a month before the mission was organized, that Underwood seemed to have "gotten over his freshness," was a real Christian with already a fair command of the language, and "bade fair to become the strong man of the mission."

There was more than one strong man in the mission, although they were only three in all. Underwood's theory of Christian mission was simple and straightforward. He was in Korea to preach the Gospel, and his restive spirit chafed under the restrictions that caution imposed in a Korea that was only beginning to open its doors to the West. By the end of August 1885, Underwood wrote that he had two or three attending "a sort of Sunday School" and had been asked by several others to teach them Christianity. By the end of the year, he was joining with Dr. Allen in the visionary project of founding a university. It was Underwood who made and sent an order for apparatus, and this while the political situation in Korea was a powder keg. In January 1886, he wrote to New York suggesting that one way to begin might be to establish an orphanage, where, unlike in the government hospital, there could be Christian teaching. Many homeless and destitute children could be taken in, clothed, fed, and trained. Then, on January 31, ten months after his arrival in Korea, Underwood notified New York that his Korean-English dictionary was ready for printing; financing it was the problem.

On July 9, 1886, he wrote jubilantly of the first Korean applicant for baptism. The letter told how this man first heard of Christianity by reading what a Chinese writer said against Christians, and later sought out the missionaries to find any books or to see anything that would "give him light." Brought to Underwood, he attended a communion service, observed it and afterward asked to be baptized. A few others were studying the Gospels, and they in turn were telling others. Many out in the country, reported Underwood, were anxious to study Christianity.

Dr. Allen's philosophy of Christian mission was different. He subscribed to the theory of "influence", the so-called theory of "Christian civilization." Early in 1886, when a government permit was granted to open the orphanage, Dr. Allen wrote to New York that in his opinion it was "better to instruct a government in these institutions of modern civilization, as an orphanage, and secure their objective, than to carry on a feeble proselyting concern. Christianity," he thought, "always goes with the missionary, even if he is serving an institution where, if not prescribed, it is taught with more or less secrecy."

This was the fundamental point on which Allen and Underwood differed. Both were strong and able men, and the difference quickly deepened into a decided rift, in which Dr. Heron sided with Mr. Underwood. The conflict became so acute that by September 1886 both Underwood and Heron wrote to the Presbyterian board in New York to offer their resignations and to request recommendations to the Methodist board, as the Methodists had by this time initiated a work in Seoul.

The work of the infant Presbyterian mission in Korea seemed to be sliding toward dissolution. Dr. Allen wrote in the following month that George C. Foulk, US minister resident, thought that "mission work proper is about to wind up." According to Dr. Allen, the Methodists had no position and no means of obtaining one, and Heron and Underwood were cutting themselves off.

It was December before the Presbyterians in Korea received an answer from their board. Underwood and Heron were chagrined that the board did not seem to take seriously either their resignations nor the reason that they gave for offering them. As for Dr. Allen, he was grateful to the board for "your confidence in me and your candid and brotherly way of writing," but declared that he had decided on the happy solution of giving everything to the other side and pulling out.

Against this background, Minister Resident Foulk himself wrote to the Presbyterian board. As a great admirer of Dr. Allen, he described Allen as brave, energetic, skillful, broad in his views, and thoroughly unselfish, the only missionary in Korea who was a true pioneer. The differences between Dr. Allen on one side and Mr. Underwood and Dr. Heron on the other, as shrewdly analyzed by Foulk, were in methods of work. Allen aimed at influencing the official class, the king and the nobles, to incline them toward Christianity. The other two tended to direct their work toward the common people, and Foulk observed that "Korean people of the lower order hate the nobles and the officials." His personal idea had been that the representative of the US government should join hands with the missionary and do all that he could to make the work of the missionary effective, while receiving the latter's help in establishing among the people the highest regard for the Christian civilization of America; but Foulk lamented that his idea had been a failure:

> I am sorry beyond expression. In Korea, Japan and China the native, the missionary, and the foreign official stand in fair prospect of keeping up unwholesome quarrels directly in the face of the gentle Savior.

The initiatives of Christian missions in Korea were taking place at a time of intense rivalry between Japan and China for influence in Korea. From 1885 to 1894 China dominated Korean politics, and indeed the Chinese encouraged the US and other Western nations to come to Korea to check the power of Japan. At this time, a French diplomatic mission arrived in Seoul and spent some months there. The mission's primary objective: to press for a decree of religious liberty on the part of the Korean government that would permit Roman Catholics in Korea to come out into the open. Underwood wrote that there were some ten French priests in the country living in disguise.

In the spring of 1887, Dr. Allen wrote to New York that the Japanese were laying out a settlement in Korea and added, "I think you will be perfectly safe in launching out. If Underwood remains, grant him all the appropriations asked."

That fall Dr. Allen left Korea to return to the United States, having been appointed foreign secretary to the Korean embassy in Washington, DC. The king of Korea had decided to send a diplomatic mission to Washington to establish the Korean legation, partly in the hope of securing a loan of three million dollars to organize the exploitation of gold mines in his country. Dr. Allen was the American he knew best and trusted most, and the king urged him to accompany the mission to Washington. On September 27 Allen left Seoul, and that same month H. G. Underwood, after a year of negotiating with the board, withdrew his resignation. Soon after, he was off on a trip through the north of Korea on which a number of converts were visited.

The first Protestant Christian in Korea had been baptized in Seoul on June 18, 1886. By the end of 1887, although the official attitude of the Korean government toward Christianity had not changed, the Cheongdong Chapel in Seoul was holding regular services in Korean under Underwood's leadership, and there were twenty-five baptized Presbyterians in Korea.

Underwood wrote in December urging that the work in Korea be publicized to the church in the United States. He thought it wrong not to tell the church of the wonderful success with which efforts were meeting in Korea, a success "unparalleled in the history of missions." There can be little danger, he urged: Korean officials do not read church periodicals; anyway, the facts about Christian baptism in Korea have been known for almost a year, and nothing has been done. With twenty-five baptized Protestant Christians in all Korea at the time, Underwood's expression seems visionary: "a success that is unparalleled in the history of missions." He pleaded for reinforcements to extend the work:

Do you want us to take a backward move? This is what we will have to do. . . . I cannot keep on doing all the work that falls to me. I will work at times until my head racks with pain and get so distracted that I cannot think. Thank God, I have a strong frame. . . . I close now; when are the men coming?

In the spring of 1888, in one of Underwood's voluminous letters, was a significant paragraph on the "plan" of Dr. John Livingston Nevius of China. The Nevius Plan would play a significant role in Korea in the years ahead in the development of some of the strongest and fastest-growing Protestant churches in the world.

The essence of the plan was that groups of adherents must be self-supporting. Mission funds and support should not be used to supply, or help to supply, a place of worship nor leadership for new congregations; but should provide intensive biblical and doctrinal instruction for church leaders every year.

Dr. Allen was still in the United States when a new Presbyterian recruit, Lillian Horton, MD, arrived in Korea on March 27, 1888. In the previous year, after a single woman missionary who was sent out had become engaged in Korea, H. G. Underwood had written to the board, suggesting the assignment of ladies who would be unlikely to marry. This suggestion came to nothing, as he complained facetiously when he wrote again later in the year. In October 1888, he himself had become engaged to Dr. Horton; they were to be married in the spring.

Late in 1889, Dr. Allen returned to Korea to a changed situation in the capital and elsewhere. For a time he tried to settle in the seaport of Chemulpo (Incheon), and after that there was talk of his being sent to open a new medical project in Pyongyang. In the summer of 1890, a cable from the State Department offered him the secretaryship of the US legation and he accepted, resigning later that year from the mission.

It is curious that during the time that Allen was absent from Korea, a rift developed between Underwood and Heron. Dr. Heron, given now much of the official responsibility and recognition on the part of the Korean government that had been Dr. Allen's, began to share the inhibitions that Allen had felt toward the open proclamation of the Christian Gospel for which Underwood was so strong. But on July 26, 1890, just five days after the cable arrived appointing Dr. Allen secretary of the US legation, Dr. Heron died of dysentery. His body was buried on a little hill overlooking the Han River about four miles outside the city of Seoul, in a cemetery for foreigners provided by the government. Then, ten months later, it was the Underwoods' turn. In May 1891, H.G. left Korea to take Mrs. Underwood home to the

United States, so crippled by rheumatism that Allen wrote no one expected to see her return to Korea.

Dr. Allen remained in Korea for fifteen years after his resignation from the mission, serving as secretary of the US Legation, later as chargé d'affaires, and finally as minister resident and consul general. Throughout this period, he never lost his interest in the Presbyterian work, as attested by frequent letters to the board in New York with opinions and advice on this and that.

By 1892, two years after his resignation, it was becoming plain that the Presbyterian Church was in Korea to stay. The work had been successfully extended to several outstations, and quite a number of new missionaries had arrived. Dr. Allen was able to comment favorably on their personality and promise, although with his usual pungency he remarked regarding some that "Underwood must have used bright colors in painting Korea as a Mission Field. The new missioners are full of enthusiasm and ideas that may change."

In the United States, Mrs. Underwood was somewhat improved, and the medical opinion was that she would do as well in Korea as elsewhere. So, in February 1893, a year and a half after leaving Korea, her husband could write enthusiastically from shipboard on their way to London. The voyage had been rough and hard on Mrs. Underwood, but baby Horace Horton had stood the trip well: "He is strong and will, I hope, make a good missionary." Later that year, the Underwoods were back in Seoul. During their absence, the Presbyterian mission in Korea had flourished, and soon H. G. Underwood, who now had a doctor's degree, found himself in conflict with the mission on various points; but Allen's early appraisal still held true. He was a strong man, while not the only such man, or woman, of the Korea mission.

Eighteen ninety-four was a turbulent year. In May, in the northern city of Pyongyang, a serious action against Protestant Christians occurred. Several men associated with the two Protestant missionaries there were thrown in prison and tortured, the charge against them: selling their houses to foreigners (missionaries), which was illegal according to the treaty articles. At the root of this action, however, seems to have been some of the official corruption that was widespread. In time, restitution was made and the responsible officials were punished.

More serious for its political consequences was the Tonghak Uprising in 1894, in southwestern Korea. The government unwisely appealed to China for help. China immediately sent troops to stem the rioting, but the Japanese objected that the treaty of 1885, by which neither China nor Japan was to send troops into the country, had been violated. Japan declared war on China. Japan, already well on its way toward Western modernization, poured into Korea 60,000 soldiers armed with repeating rifles, 2,500 cavalry, and many pieces of artillery. As the war spread, the Chinese began to suffer defeats both on land and sea.

Dr. Allen, who was still in Seoul, wrote in September predicting that the Japanese would win and that, "should they redeem their promises to improve the conditions of Korea, all will benefit. Korea," he opined, "has reached the last verge. . . . official corruption, tyranny and incapacity. . . . China has had centuries to show what she could do for Korea, but things have gone from bad to worse. She has treated Korea as a vassal."

The Sino-Japanese War ended after Japan's troops, displaying an energy and skill that startled many observers, had marched up the length of the Korean Peninsula and across the Yalu River. It was neither the first nor last time that an army would make this march in one direction or the other, leaving behind Mars's wake of pillage and misery. Japan was now definitely in the ascendancy. By the Treaty of Shimonoseki, China ceded to Japan southern Manchuria and Formosa (Taiwan), and renounced all interest in Korea.

At this time, the central government of the Kingdom of Korea and the royal household itself were divided. One party was that of the Tae-won-gun (Prince of the Great House), the young king's father—who himself had ruled as regent during the minority of his son, and since then had maneuvered continually for power. The other was that of the strong-willed Queen, who came from the influential Min family. The queen's party opposed some of the radical reforms that the Japanese were anxious to push through.

Japan sent to Korea a new minister bent on a rapid and thoroughly pro-Japanese solution to the Korea situation. He made contact with the Tae-won-gun, and the stage began to darken. There is no doubt that the aristocratic old ex-regent would have only one plan to propose regarding the queen. It can't be known whether he egged on the Japanese minister nor to what extent the minister himself was directly responsible for what followed. The action was the final tragedy, in which the light of Korea's independence guttered out.

The scene is the palace at Seoul; the time, early dawn of October 8, 1895. A group of Japanese officials and some Koreans enter from the direction of the Tae-won-gun's residence down by the river, forcing their way through the gates to the palace grounds. Reaching the building occupied by their majesties, the Japanese form in military order around it, guarding all approaches. Others of the group rush into the building, kill several guards and, finally locating the queen, butcher her ruthlessly. Her body is carried out, wrapped in cloth soaked with kerosene, and burned at the edge of a pine grove near the pond before the royal quarters.

Who actually struck the blows? The broken king, who was made a virtual prisoner in his own palace by the Japanese, sent a message via James S. Gale of the Presbyterian mission to the American Generals Dye and Legendie, quartered near by. As Gale reported in a letter written ten days later:

> I saw the King at the time and was greeted by him. Shall never forget the sad expression on his face. Hope died for him within the palace when the Queen was killed.
>
> That night, as I sat with the two U.S. Generals in the building next to that of His Majesty, a Korean attendant came in to ask me to tell the Generals that the King saw the murderers strike the Queen and knew them to be Japanese and knew their names, as he had had audience with them.
>
> I said, "Ask His Majesty to write their names in Chinese and I will give them to the Generals." He returned with the names, the first of which reads in Japanese OKAMOTO, the fellow who confessed to have murdered the Queen.
>
> The King's message ended thus, "Tell the Generals that if they will avenge the death of the Queen and rid me of these Japanese I'll cut off my hair and weave sandals of it for them." It was the most imploring message that the Korean language was able to convey for him.

Early in 1896, the king and crown prince, by a clever ruse, slipped away from the palace grounds and were taken to the Russian legation, where they sought refuge. From there the king proceeded to re-organize his government, and Japan's dominance in Korea was checked for the time. For a full year, the king remained at the Russian legation, while a new palace was being built for him in the foreign quarter, flanked by three foreign legations.

With great pomp, he had himself declared Emperor of Taehan, and under this name Korea sought for itself a place on an equal footing with China and Japan. An Independence Arch was erected outside the Gate of Seoul, on the site where a gate symbolic of Chinese suzerainty had stood. There might seem to have been a chance for an independent nation; but the hour was late and the contending historic forces were strong.

Russia, under Tsar Nicholas II, was busy extending its influence in the Far East, including consolidating control of Port Arthur and pressing toward completion of the Trans-Siberian Railway to unite Moscow with Vladivostok. Located on the Liaodong Peninsula on the southern edge of Manchuria and thrusting into the Yellow Sea right opposite northern Korea, Port Arthur was vital to Russia as a year-round base for its Pacific Fleet. Vladivostok iced over in winter.

What inevitably ensued, given the imperial ambitions of both Russia and Japan at this point in history, was the Russo-Japanese War of 1904–05. After decisive, although costly, Japanese victories on sea and land, the war was brought to a close by the Treaty of Portsmouth, mediated by US President Theodore Roosevelt and negotiated and signed, intriguingly, in Portsmouth, New Hampshire. For his accomplishment, Roosevelt was awarded the Nobel Peace Prize, while adroitly balancing Russian and Japanese power in the Orient. At the time, supremacy of either one could have been a threat to the growth of American interests in the area.

On the Korean Peninsula, however, with both Chinese and Russian influence effectively eliminated, Japan could pursue its designs. In the same year, 1905, a Japan-Korea treaty was enforced by which the latter became the protectorate of Japan. Two years later, a second treaty gave Japan the administration of Korea's internal affairs. The process was completed by a third pact, in 1910, also called the Japan-Korea Annexation Treaty, in which Korea ceased to be a separate country, now formally incorporated into the Japanese Empire.

# 5

# Bewildering Assignments

> Mr. Chairman, have you noticed a particular, happy coincidence in our celebration of the Silver Anniversary of Presbyterian mission in Korea?

THAT WAS DR. BROWN speaking, Arthur J. Brown, Korea secretary of the Presbyterian Board of Foreign Missions, who had come all the way from New York, with Mrs. Brown, for this occasion. It was August 1909, and the Korea mission was gathered in Pyongyang for its annual meeting. There had been spirited discussions among its several dozen members, as generally there were, but on this morning all discussion was put aside.

Just a couple of hours earlier, young Dr. Archibald Fletcher and his group of six women recruits had stepped off the night train, been delivered to the homes where they were to be lodged for the meeting, and allowed scant time to freshen up and have a quick breakfast. Now they were gathered again, to be ushered into the mission meeting for presentation to their future colleagues.

They had to face the problem for John Hemphill that Gloria, his intended bride, was not in the group but on her way to Harbin with her new fiancé. That embarrassing development had been handled very quietly and diplomatically. The word had been circulated to all, so that no one might raise any question or comment that would discomfit him. For the rest, the presentation seemed a bit formal to Arch, which suited him well enough as he waited his turn at the end of the line.

Each of the just-arrived ladies was introduced by Dr. Brown, with data on her home town, places of study and preparation, experience, if any, and then a friendly anecdote or humorous touch to ease the formality of the proceeding.

When at last Dr. Brown came to the one male recruit, he allowed himself a few extra flourishes. After all, Arch was also the one non-US citizen, with his Ontario birthplace and Canadian passport.

The introductions were finished and James Adams, who was presiding, had responded with a warm and rather full speech of welcome, when Dr. Brown chimed in with his question about a "particular, happy coincidence." It brought an immediate response, but not from the chair. Before Dr. Adams could speak, Horace Underwood, who was on the front row, raised his hand, and simultaneously stood up and turned to talk.

> I'll point it out, as one who worked with him almost from the beginning. The groundbreaker we are honoring, my esteemed one-time colleague H. N. Allen, gained entrance to Korea as a missionary surgeon. Now here is another missionary surgeon, A. G. Fletcher, exactly a quarter-century later. Allen and I worked well together, even when we didn't quite agree. I'll look forward, Dr. Fletcher, to working with you.

Arch blushed with pleasure at the recognition, particularly coming from the mission's second, and surviving, pioneer. He would remember it well, after Dr. Underwood died just seven years later.

On that August morning in Pyongyang, the mission was convened in a lecture hall of the Boys' Academy. It was hot, the wide-open windows straining for a breath of air, but due order had to be observed. Refreshments had been prepared and there would be a recess for socializing and getting acquainted with the new mission members, but first, and most importantly, there must be mission action by which they were formally received.

Then, and of greater consequence, came the assignments. These had been pondered by the executive committee, and were proposed one by one and voted on by the mission. If there seemed to be surprisingly little discussion it was because, in most instances, the arguing, the pleas and counter-pleas, had taken place in the months, and sometimes years, before the recruits arrived. Priorities had been agreed on, however reluctantly, for this or that mission station and its projects. Now there were faces—living people—for whom the assignments could be read off.

Arch's turn was last. He was not just the only man, but the only medical recruit, on the list. He had kept very much in mind Dr. Brown's caution to him that the New York board could only suggest where he might be placed. The Korea Mission zealously reserved that prerogative; it would decide.

There was also the language question. New missionaries were generally expected to devote their first year mainly to language study. The written form of the Korean language, Hangul, devised by scholars in the fifteenth century as ordered by the enlightened King Sejong, is strictly phonetic and can be learned in a matter of hours, but mastering the spoken language, particularly for Westerners, is something quite different. For all its recruits, the mission had set a modest, but firm, standard—its first-year language test.

Arch soon discovered that medical recruits were not given an equal chance for language study. Their skills could be put to use with only a rudimentary language ability that they seemed to be expected to pick up on the side. They were too immediately useful to fill gaps where a doctor was more or less urgently needed.

The annual meeting assigned A. G. Fletcher to Wonju—although he never got there. He was sent, for a while, to Chairyung to substitute for a doctor who was going on vacation; then he was returned to Seoul, from where he was to commute to Wonju. But an emergency call took him to Taegu to attend a missionary who was dying, and he stayed on there for a month and a half of surgery. In these various transfers, he had only such language study as he could squeeze in beside his medical duties.

Meanwhile, some ongoing negotiations between the Methodist and Presbyterian missions were concluded, and Wonju turned out to be in territory designated for Methodist endeavor. Arch's original assignment was canceled.

His new assignment was to Andong, a town some fifty miles northeast of Taegu, to share in the opening of a new station. He was up there in February 1910, in the mild winter of southern Korea, looking at houses that could be bought and adapted as a base for preaching and medical work, when a telegram was delivered to him in the middle of the night. It was from the chairman of the mission executive committee, instructing Arch to take the next train he could get and head north to substitute for a doctor in Kanggei.

Kanggei (Kang-GAY) was all the way north, located on a branch of the Yalu River, not many miles from the border with Manchuria. It was not on the railroad, as Arch found out, but ninety miles away—ninety miles across rugged terrain in the brutal winter of northern Korea. Travel was by ox-drawn sled, making some thirty miles in ten hours on a very good day. Luggage and all sorts of goods were piled on the sled, with passengers riding on top or clinging to the sides. The road zig-zagged, laboring up mountain passes. Arch joined his personal helper and the driver to push at the steepest part; then a pause at the crest, as the ox heaved, making a cloud of frozen breath.

At one descent, Arch surveyed with misgiving the angle and sharp turns. He watched the driver take an axe from the sled and cut some long vines, which he bound around the sled's runners as far back as he could.

Then, with a nod to his passengers, he coaxed the ox toward the descent. At first the vines worked well, braking the runners so that the ox even had to pull a little on the down-slope. Then came that long, steep decline Arch had noted from the crest. The sled lurched forward and the vines shredded, trailing behind. The ox stiffened his legs, holding back as best he could. The driver shouted encouragement, but the loaded sled pushed hard.

Now the ox was all the way down, sliding on his haunches, trying to dig his hooves into the hard-packed snow. Abruptly, he gave up, got his feet under him and went into a clumsy gallop, the sled careening behind him and the riders jumping clear, until, at the turn, it swerved and rolled into a snow bank. Luckily, the bank held. Sled and ox stopped still. The three men were able to catch up and with some effort right the sled. Arch and his helper, their frosty breath clouding their eyes, began to reload, while the driver extricated his ox.

Two hours later, as they topped a low rise, Arch saw with huge relief the smoke of cooking fires of a village. There would be warmth, a hot broth of some kind and steaming rice, and he could bed down on a quilt spread on the smooth, warm floor of an inn guest-room, heated by a flu that passed underneath from the cooking fire. He was being given a strenuous initiation into the winter northland of his new country; but as a farm boy in Ontario he had learned to rough it, and here he felt that he could make this his own. A stray thought crossed his mind:

> Suppose that romantic notion had come true—that idea about mission together that he and Clyde shared far back, on a spring night in Orchard, Nebraska. How might she have fitted into this kind of setting?

In Kanggei, when they finally reached the town about noon of the fourth day, Arch's own challenge was to fit into a medical work that was already established. It was the kind of practice that one physician, working alone, with only the assistance of a couple of helpers to whom he had been able to give the most rudimentary training, could expect to carry on. The physician must also be druggist, dispensing carefully from a small store of basic medications that had come, mostly, from the United States, brought by missionaries returning from furlough. Some drugs were beginning to be available from Japan, although they were hard to get. And Arch, still new to all of this, was also coping with the frustration of being unable to communicate more than the most basic instructions to his helpers and his patients, talking more with gestures than with words.

Even so, as he would tell himself at the end of a particularly long and trying day, he was glad to be there. He was glad to use such means as he had, and to feel certain that in time he would have more to work with, doing this work in this fascinating country, among its people to whom God had called him.

When the doctor whom Arch was replacing returned, spring had come across the mountains and steep valleys. The roads were muddy, but the ninety-mile trek to the railroad could be made by horse-drawn jitney coach. Arch had heard of a different way back to the railroad, a somewhat risky mode of travel—by small boat on a spring-swollen river. He went down to the riverfront, managing enough Korean to bargain for a sampan barely ten feet long and to hire two boatmen to guide it. The plan was to let the current carry them northward to where this branch joined the Yalu River, then flow with the Yalu south and west until it reached the Korea Bay and the railroad at Sinuiju (Sin-we-JOO).

It was a daring plan, but the adventure appealed to him. As the river, swollen by melting snows, swept the tiny sampan through narrow gorges at a vertiginous speed, possibly Arch should have considered that it might be hard for the board in New York to find quickly a replacement physician recruit to send to Korea; but he was used to the outdoors. He was just twenty-seven, full of enthusiasm to explore and know better this new country that he wanted to claim as his. The days and the night lodgings along the twisting Yalu and the final emergence to the harbor and broad sea were a thrilling interlude, a bright square in the patchwork experience that the mission had given him so far in his first year in Korea.

The train from Sinuiju got him to Pyongyang in time for an intensive three-week language course. At the end of it, he took successfully the first-year test, in spite of having had less than a year in the country and only sporadic opportunities to work at language with a private teacher. Arch was glad, but not satisfied.

He proceeded south to Taegu, then to Andong, where he joined the evangelistic couple assigned, as he was, to open a new station there. They spent weeks in a careful search and then in negotiations, locating and purchasing several well-built houses of moderate size and enclosing them with a wall to give them form and also reasonable security, as a base for medical and preaching activity. But in late summer, at the annual mission meeting, Arch was moved again, this time to Taegu.

Dr. W. O. Johnson had initiated a medical service in Taegu, the major city in a large and populous province of southern Korea, some nine years earlier, and carried it forward, with frequent interruptions, as he struggled with faltering health. This year he decided to give it up and asked the mission to change him from medical to evangelistic work.

Sitting near the back in a general session of the annual meeting, which was held in Seoul that year, Arch listened with surprise to this kind of reassignment. He knew something of Dr. Johnson's health problems—principally malaria—but hadn't thought such a change could be made, that a doctor should hang up his white coat to turn to preaching and church work.

Then Arch was hearing his own name, and a couple of people were turning to smile at him. A. G. Fletcher would be reassigned, now, to the ongoing medical program in Taegu. Dr. Johnson's new function would be recognized, although for the immediate future he would be asked to move to Andong to help with the medical phase of the new station, until a replacement could be sent.

So, that fall of 1910, Arch settled himself to survey the medical work in Taegu and plan his share in it. With characteristic candor, plus the brash confidence of his young years, he wrote to Dr. Brown, the Korea secretary, in New York. First, he recalled the pleasure of sharing with him and Mrs. Brown the annual meeting and Silver Anniversary celebration of the previous year; then, to the business at hand. "Taegu's medical work," he wrote, "when all things are considered, spells almost a failure."

In a rather long letter, he proceeded to spell out the failure. The hospital building, erected in 1903, had fallen into ruins. All available funds were being used to repair it, with the result that "never a penny was available for a dispensary" (an outpatient building) and the low, cramped basement of the hospital had to be used for this purpose. Mud and water flowed in. Students, whom the doctor was trying to train, quickly forgot what they had heard about cleanliness and antiseptic methods. Arch wrote:

> Taegu, the third city in size in the country, with a territory of almost unlimited extent and over a million population to care for, should have, and I say it in faith, believing, the largest medical work in Korea. I further believe all it needs to bring this about is a hospital, which it has; a dispensary, which it has not; a nurse, which it has not; and a doctor, which it has only so far as one who has had but one year of interrupted language study can be called so.

Perhaps a little more than this would be needed over the years, but the earnest young doctor had mapped his program. He added, with the same candor:

# Bewildering Assignments

> The above remarks do not in any way reflect on Dr. Johnson, for no one knows of a missionary more faithful than he; but sad to say, he has been most of the time a cripple because of ill health.

The letter ended with a reference to the "Morphine Evil." As a part of the preparation for annexation, the Japanese had peddled morphine in Korea, using it to undermine any groups who might resist their domination. Horrible cases were met with, and Arch reported that Japanese druggists were not only selling morphine to "anyone large enough to carry the price in money" but also teaching the use of a hypodermic syringe, so that if the victim were nauseated by taking it by mouth he could still be trapped by the needle. In his fervent, slightly stilted and self-conscious style, Arch wrote:

> I know not what, if any, steps you could take to influence the Japanese Government, but something ought to be done.

What was done with Arch was that the mission moved him again, although temporarily, to Andong. Dr. Johnson's mother and sister were coming out to Korea for a visit, and the mission felt that he should be in Taegu, where he would have an adequate house in which to receive them. From February 1911 until that summer, Arch was back working in Andong, but on loan.

∽ ∽ ∽

This turned out to be a challenging and valuable experience. Medical work had not really begun in Andong, although the new station included the house set aside for it that Arch had helped to locate and purchase. In his "Personal Report," submitted to the mission in June 1911, he told how the work was initiated. With his Scottish reserve, he could never bring himself, at this time or later, to use the first person singular, but always held to an editorial "we," even when he was quite alone. Thus:

> The beginning of medical work in Andong is intensely interesting, equally for the physician and the patient. After placing a half dozen boards against one wall of the room in such order that our few medicines could be put thereon, and after making a small table and stool for use of mixing and dispensing same, we placed a long box affair against the other wall, which answered for those who had to take either a recumbent or sitting posture during examination. Thus equipped, we opened the doors to patient number one. No sooner in than sitting flat on the floor.

"Please take a high seat." Immediately he gets up entirely on the box, sitting upon his feet as usual.

"What is your name?"

"There's some round-shaped thing inside, and it travels here and there and everywhere."

"Wait a little! What is your name?"

"Name Kwan. They say if it ever stops at the stomach it means death."

"Where do you live?"

"This sickness started six years, four months and twenty-three days ago."

"Listen! Where do you live?"

"Yei An. The dog meat, it did not go down, and he almost died."

"Is it you or somebody else who is ill?"

"Both of us. I started after my early morning rice."

"What is your age?"

"I was born in the year of the dragon."

"Are you a Christian?"

"I have eaten all the best kind of Korean medicine."

At last we have got the facts necessary for our record book and proceed to try to find out what the trouble is, but he has already told all he ever heard from others and all he had thought himself, and now his mind is relieved, and he is amazed at the physician's glasses and shoes, and at the great number of bottles, and says it is a sight worth seeing.

"Have you brought the price of the medicine?"

"Please give me drinking medicine, for I have tried the eating varieties."

"Have you the price?"

"No. I came first to inquire what my disease was."

"Please return with the money, and we will give you your medicine."

During the first month we averaged about ten such experiences each afternoon. Now our methods are very familiar to those who live in the city, and many others, so that before the new patients reach us they have been coached on how to act, and we see twice as many with one half the trouble.

It was during these months in Andong, as he was beginning to get a grip on the language and was launching out on his own in medical work, that young Arch got some idea of the enormity of the task facing his profession in southern Korea. Under the stoic surface of the people's lives, he saw opening up all around him appalling gulfs of disease and human misery. His report of 1911 contained a moving paragraph on leprosy and the first proposal of a way to make at least a small beginning on attacking this problem. Leprosy was a concern that would come to loom large for him, yielding some of his most satisfying achievements.

There was a paragraph on tuberculosis and a proposal regarding that, too; and there was a section on "Other Diseases", among them malaria. Arch wrote:

> Last year we learned by experience something of the aches, extreme exhaustion and, above all, the intense, almost unbearable headache of malaria. Now we are only too willing to get up in the middle of the night or any other time, if called to a case of chills and fever.

He had, in fact, been very ill in Andong with what was probably a form of malaria; although out of the illness came one of those anecdotes that circulated for years in the family of the Korea mission and was told delightedly to each newcomer. It seems that when news of Arch's illness reached Seoul, a missionary doctor and nurse were sent to do what they could for him. It would take them three days to reach Andong, so they sent ahead a reassuring telegram which was supposed to read, DOCTOR COMING WITH NURSE; but the Japanese operator slipped on one letter. Arch got the wire, DOCTOR COMING WITH HURSE.

The final section of Arch's 1911 report on medical work in Andong was on the "Evangelistic Phase." He was enthusiastic. The infant church in Andong was loyally supporting the medical work. The house adapted as a small hospital included a "guest room," where several of the church members came daily, with Bibles, hymnbooks, and Gospel tracts, to meet the patients.

At any hour during the whole afternoon one will hear either heart-to-heart, earnest personal preaching or a volume of song and praise ascending from this room.

It was the sort of simple, fervent, personal witness to their faith that seemed to come naturally to many Korean converts, and to which Arch—although the spontaneous outward expression was far less easy and natural for him—was pledging his life. There, at the beginning of his career, in that 1911 Personal Report, is the outline of a life's passion and work: Leprosy, Tuberculosis, "Other Diseases," and, above all, "Evangelism." It is all there.

# 6

# Taegu Station

ONE THOUSAND EIGHT HUNDRED seventy-five patient visits—an impressive number in just four months in the new but rather primitive, one-doctor facility in Andong. That was Arch's accomplishment in the spring of 1911, a testimony to the urgent need for that facility. But he was only on loan. At the annual meeting that summer, he was assigned definitively to Taegu. There would be no more sudden shifts. From then on, for thirty years, the mission's annual meetings would pass like milestones, but his assignment would not change.

Back in Taegu, he went to work eagerly. He had the hospital building to work with, cramped and limited as it was, and the welcome word came from New York that there was money for a dispensary, or outpatient department. Plans were drawn and work begun on a one-story brick structure just below the hospital. Arch wanted a second floor, reasoning that the Taegu medical program was sure to be expanding rapidly; but the mission executive committee wouldn't back his request. Who could imagine a two-story dispensary in a small station like Taegu?

No matter—there was much that needed doing. The Japanese government, following up on annexation, was expanding its efforts in Korea. It established a hospital in Taegu, staffing it with doctors educated in Japan. The sort of quaint medical pioneering Arch had experienced in Andong was well in the past in Taegu. The mission hospital must offer professional quality, as well as compassionate care.

To start with, until he could rely on trained assistants, Arch would see every patient himself. That was a large order, since the patient census kept growing, but he knew that the prevailing opinion in the city was in his favor. The American doctor was seen as more able and better prepared than the Japanese physicians.

By mid-1912, Arch was hitting his stride. He had been in Korea for three years. The language and customs were becoming familiar. In spite of having little time to study Korean, he had passed the second and third-year language tests. The small hospital kept busy, every bed occupied, with as many squeezed in as possible, while he trained assistants to help in the operating room and with nursing duties. The dispensary building was nearing completion and would be occupied in the fall.

∽ ∽ ∽

"Welcome, Arch. Glad you could come over. There, take Kang's chair."

"Does that make me secretary of this meeting?"

"No, no meeting—just a friendly consultation."

"Good. That's what your note said. Any consultation is fine, as long as it's not medical."

"Oh, I thought that's what you physicians specialize in doing."

After a few more humorous remarks, the two friends get to the subject in hand. On this warm Saturday afternoon in September 1912, Arch has walked from the house where he is living to the study door of the Bruens' home.

Henry (Harry) Bruen is about ten years older than he. Harry had a hand in the early development of Taegu Station. When he arrived in Taegu, young and single, in October 1899, the mission had already acquired a property for a permanent location. It was a bare, stony hill to the south, outside the city wall. The city elders were willing to sell it because it reputedly was a haunt of evil spirits—quite suitable, some thought, that the "foreign devils" should live there, along with the long-time residents. Taking possession, the missionaries set slips of trees on the hill, so that by the time of my youth a quarter-century later, it had become a refuge of green, with the expanding city beginning to grow around it. It was on a lower slope of this hill that Harry, in that winter of his arrival, worked alongside a carpenter to help Woodbridge Johnson, MD, prepare and open the first rustic clinic.

Now, thirteen years later, in his cluttered and comfortable study, Harry pursues the subject that is on his mind:

"You know that Herb Blair is leaving on furlough in a couple of weeks. You might not know that he has responsibility for contact with eight churches in and near the city, along with all else he has been carrying. These are important churches, but what with taking on Herb's other work I have as much as I can do. I was talking about it with James Adams, and he suggested that I consult with you."

Arch has been wondering what Harry might bring up. In the years since his arrival, Harry had married, and Martha Bruen had borne him two daughters. Arch has developed a hearty regard for the whole family, who received him warmly as co-worker and friend. And now Harry is mentioning

James Adams, founder of the Boys' Academy and respected senior member of Taegu Station. Arch glimpses what they might have in mind, although it seems too improbable. These men are seminary trained, but he is not. He says nothing, waiting to hear, as Harry lets a moment pass and then goes on:

"Our idea, to put it simply, is that you might lend a hand with these churches. We know, Arch, that you're very busy with the medical work and we're tremendously impressed with what you're doing. Woodbridge did what he could, but now it's really starting to move. You're a human dynamo, and that's your main job. We respect that."

Harry pauses, although he expects that his friend Arch, cautious as he is, will have no comment yet.

"So, we think you could make an admirable contribution, just helping a little on the side with these churches. You know about the Nevius Plan and how it operates, that we let the church grow spontaneously, whatever way the Korean Christians want it to grow. It's up to them; you would only need to encourage as their leaders lead, and it's just these eight that we're talking about."

That is a compelling way to put it. Arch likes a challenge and can probably be counted on to respond, as both James Adams and Harry have calculated. After a brief silence his voice sounds in the small room:

"All right. It could be a good thing to know something about the churches from the inside. Tell me about them, which ones they are and where."

Harry reaches for some papers on his desk. He knows his colleague's inclination toward order and method, and is prepared for that. Over the next hour or so, Arch comes to know about each of the eight churches he is asked to help with—its situation, history, and possibilities.

As that year moved along, through fall and winter and the following spring, up to summer, Arch was frequently at church gatherings, or in earnest conversation with church leaders on a Saturday or Sunday afternoon. It broadened his vocabulary and use of the language, and it broadened in the churches their awareness of this fervent young doctor who kept encouraging each forward step. They naturally found his Western name long and too difficult to pronounce. As with other missionaries' names, they used—more or less—a sound from it to give him a Korean name. From Fletcher came Pyul—which was pleasant because it was a word meaning "choice" or "special." He became Pyul Ee-saw, the last two syllables signifying his title as "doctor."

By late spring, when he was drawing up his annual Personal Report for 1912-13, he could summarize regarding "his churches" that average contributions among members had nearly tripled. They were now paying the support of two pastoral assistants, and half that of a third, in place of one the year before, and of two "Bible women" in place of one. During the year they had completed construction of three tile-roofed church buildings, one of them two-story, and had added many members, for not a few of whom the hospital was chiefly responsible.

∾ ∾ ∾

"Arch, you're doing a great job, helping in the city churches. I hear about it all the time."

The Taegu Station is gathered—all seven members—in the Bruens' living room for dessert and coffee/tea, an informal meeting. James Adams makes the comment as a lead-in. After a couple of appreciative remarks by others, he goes on:

"I was wondering if anyone has said anything to you about the book room. It's in a rather precarious situation, and that makes it hard for churches to get hymnbooks, tracts, and such when they need them."

"Why precarious?" Martha Switzer asks. She is an organizer of Bible classes and other forms of outreach to women.

"It's because prices keep fluctuating, and the government keeps putting out new regulations," James explains.

Arch responds, "Yes, I'd heard about it and dropped by to have a look. It's dilapidated, sure enough—in rather bad shape."

"And bad financial shape," James adds. "Of course it's the churches' business, but it needs to be run like a business."

This is Arch's opening. He takes it up, but in a slow and cautious way. "I agree, and have a thought about that—maybe it might work, maybe not."

James is pleased: "What is your thought, Arch? You seem to have good ones."

Arch sits a little straighter, as all eyes turn to him.

"We could suggest that the church make it a stock company, a common enterprise—sell shares in the Bookroom, modest shares, priced so that churches, organizations, and individual believers all can buy them. That way the Bookroom raises capital for its operation and the churches and church people get involved in supporting it, because it belongs to them."

He has proposed the idea simply. It's talked back and forth. In the end, the station agrees to pass it on to the Presbytery for the church leaders to consider, and delegates Arch to move it along.

He moves it—carefully. He had remarked to Harry Bruen that he was not trained in church work, but he understands very well some things about people. Among the churches, he plants the idea of a bookroom company and advances it in small, patient steps. In time, the church leaders take it up on their own. Shares are sold, even among the smallest, most widely scattered congregations. The hospital staff gets involved, too. By late spring the Bookroom has its own small building well stocked with Christian literature and an efficient service, largely of volunteers who keep the literature circulating.

Is Arch driving himself too hard? Week-day mornings begin with a hospital round—what can be managed with a staff in training—then attention, in the dispensary, to the lengthening queue of out-patients. Afternoons are for surgery. As the days lengthen and surgical cases increase, the afternoon can stretch into evening. Arch is young, single, and full of zeal. It's in his nature to be intense, even while his exterior shows a controlled, disciplined calm, and because he lives alone, not much distracts him from his dominant purposes. He has not enjoyed a broad education and has never been a reader, and his situation offers little else for leisure-time attention. His tendency is to stay focused on projects that he has in hand, and to take on more projects.

That is all right. He doesn't need leisure. He is deeply into his medical work, while quite ready to help in any other way with his forthright, practical approach.

# 7

# The Scourge of Leprosy

JESSIE RODGERS RECALLED MEETING Arch Fletcher in late September of 1912. It was on the evening of her arrival in Seoul. She was one of the young women recruits whom the mission board was sending out, in response to its Korea Propaganda. Arch had been staying at the home where she was to be lodged for a few days; in fact, it was she who dislodged him. When she walked into the living room, he stood up, dressed in a grey suit that set off his wavy black hair. They talked for a few minutes, and she remembered later how he leaned against the door in a casual way. She had known his name, like the names of the others there in Korea, from poring over the list in the board's *Yearbook of Prayer for Missions*, but she would not meet him again for another year.

Miss Rodgers was from Philadelphia. Her father was a railroader, a quiet, self-disciplined man who worked all his life in the offices of the Pennsylvania Railroad. He had little formal schooling, but over years of diligent reading made himself a well-educated man, and he instilled in his daughter his chief virtues: love of God and kindly concern for others.

Jessie's education accorded with the ideas of the time. She attended the prestigious girls' high school in Philadelphia, which gave her a grounding on which she could build by reading and experience along her lines of interest and service. In her adult years, Jessie conveyed always the impression of a thoughtful, cultured person. By the time she volunteered for foreign service in behalf of the church, her father had settled the family in friendly, suburban Ridley Park, just outside the city. It was a long way from Ridley Park to Korea, but Robert Rodgers did not oppose his daughter's decision. He had watched the growth of her faith and her eagerness to give herself for it.

The Korea mission assigned Jessie Rodgers to Andong, while deciding that she should have a year in the north, in Pyongyang, to study the language and to observe mission work in a large station, before being sent down to be mostly on her own. Because Taegu was the rail point nearest to

Andong, during that year she exchanged several letters with Dr. Fletcher of Taegu Station about arrangements for sending to Andong the furniture and other goods that she had brought to Korea. One can imagine what Arch Fletcher's letters were like, written in his formal Scots style, about as wordy as telegrams.

At last, after the annual mission meeting in 1913, Miss Rodgers was going to her permanent station. In Taegu, Dr. Fletcher kindly helped her, as he had promised to do. In fact, she had a picture taken when she was in her sedan chair, ready to start out for Andong. It was still so in Korea, at that time, that the only way for a lady to make such a journey over unimproved footpaths was by sedan chair. Behind the chair, in the picture, is a little pack pony that already seems to stagger under the burden of her steamer truck, loaded on one side, and her folding "country" table, chair and other accoutrements for rural itineration, piled up on the other side. In the background stands the helpful Dr. Fletcher.

Jessie's trip to Andong in the early autumn was full of color and expectancy. Hour after hour, the four chair bearers, two in front and two behind between the poles supporting her chair, swung along rhythmically over narrow paths, crossing level fields, ascending gradually narrowing valleys where the terraced rice paddies climbed like steps, reaching at last the tops of the low passes to pause and rest and gaze out over a fresh autumn panorama before beginning the descent to another valley floor.

Jessie delighted in the panoramic beauty and the thought that this was now her scene, as she was making herself a part of it. All around spread the ripeness and warm golden beauty of autumn under the afternoon sun— white-clad harvesters in the fields, a farmer and his ox starting the winter plowing, the bright-plumaged glimpse of a cock pheasant flying down to glean in a distant field, the lingering honking of a V of wild geese far off in the gentle sky, and crimson red peppers drying on the new straw thatch of a farmhouse. At evening, there would be the curling smoke of cooking fires, as they approached a village.

At last, in the courtyard of a little inn, the weary bearers could set down the chair, as a wonderful aroma of steaming rice reached Jessie's nostrils. She had some uneasy feelings, riding in the sedan chair, not because she was alone, a young woman with these four men. It didn't occur to her to feel anxious about that. The unease came from watching the backs of the men in front of her, to see the sweat beginning to soak through the course fabric of their short jackets. It was the idea of her weight being carried by these other people over sometimes-rough terrain that bothered her, up and down, hour after hour. They passed places where the road was being built, and she thought how much she wished that it were finished and she could move along on the wheels of a vehicle and not on human shoulders and hands.

∽ ∽ ∽

In Taegu, Arch felt a reassuring rhythm in his work. The brick dispensary was finished, giving him an adequate facility for examining patients and for systematic training of a few selected assistants. He had also been able to make some improvements in the hospital building, particularly the first-floor operating room, still essentially rustic but with a more adequate arrangement for surgical wash-up and for sterilizing instruments in a small autoclave. Starting early each morning, after a brief breakfast and a brisk walk along the compound road and then past the hospital to the dispensary, Arch put in a long day, quite often returning in the evening to check on a surgical patient in the hospital. The work was long and it was tiring, but he was doing what he wanted to do, and was finding glad fulfillment in it.

There was one problem that troubled him—more troubling because there was little that could be done about it. Back in 1911, while he was still working in Andong, he had written in his Personal Report for the year:

> The physician of southern Korea soon realizes that India is not the only country which has its "open sore," for on every side, and in all stages, are to be seen, as someone has designated them, these "butt ends of human beings."

In southern Korea, as in India, the warm climate, combined with the poverty and unsanitary conditions in which the poorer people lived, bred the dread disease—leprosy. In that report, young Arch had a plan to propose. The chaulmoogra oil treatment had been discovered in India, and variations of it were being used with fair success in many cases. Arch ventured that "every hospital in southern Korea should have its lepers' wards, where those in the beginnings of the disease could be placed under wholesome surroundings and given medicine, until it is thoroughly demonstrated whether or not they can be helped." Then the hopeless cases might be sent to a central asylum.

It was a quixotic solution. True, the Korea mission had set up a Committee on Leper Work in 1904, and a few years later, with help from a British organization, the Mission to Lepers in India and the East, began to develop a small asylum for victims of the disease in the southern port of Pusan. But in Taegu, the meager, crowded hospital hardly offered space for "lepers' wards," where patients could be isolated and treated for months on end.

There were some cases that drew, forcibly, Arch's attention. In his first winter in Taegu, two boys were brought to the dispensary, which was still functioning in the basement of the hospital building. They were lepers and their feet were horribly burned. Their story, as he heard it while supervising the cleaning and bandaging of their wounds, was a common one, as his assistant assured him. The boys had lost most of their toes to leprosy, which had also deadened feeling in the rest of their feet. Homeless, they had found open flues that passed under the sealed floors of houses, where the family slept. The boys had thrust themselves, feet first, into the flues to gain some warmth, as they often did, but their deadened feet hadn't felt the heat from a fire stoked high, causing hideous burns before they knew what was happening.

Arch talked with the boys, as he was beginning to be able to do. They seemed bright and responsive. They, of course, had no family; their families had shunned them from the time they showed signs of leprosy. The family they now had was a small group of fellow victims that held together and shared whatever they could beg. Who were they, and how many? They were six, some older, some younger, all from the same village district. Arch told them to try to keep the dressings on their feet clean and dry, and with sudden decision, he told them to come back on the next market day, five days later.

Arch took counsel with Moon Han-chik, his principal assistant. He knew that there was little chance that his assignment, the Taegu medical work, could be stretched to include anything for leprosy, nor that the Korea mission or the board in New York could be asked for funds for such a project; but he had to do something. He went into his own pocket, made inquiries quietly through Moon, and in a matter of days had bought a small house, just a single room with an open kitchen. There he would lodge the boys, their group of six.

I once saw an old photo of them—a plain, mud-plastered wall and the lower edge of a straw thatch roof, and in front of it the group, three men and three boys, faces damaged by the disease, wearing serious expressions for the photographer. Arch had no means for an expensive, protracted chaulmoogra oil treatment of uncertain effect for these advanced cases. He *could* see to it that they had shelter and enough food for what was left to them of life.

∽ ∽ ∽

It was in the following summer, 1913, that Arch heard that Wellesley C. Bailey, founder of the Mission to Lepers in India and the East, would be coming to Korea with Mrs. Bailey, while on a tour of mission projects. Arch immediately invited them to Taegu, and that was how, on a market day in late September, word having spread, a crowd of lepers gathered at the wide dispensary steps looking out across the market square.

The marketplace—a broad, open square—spread out just below the new dispensary. The earth of the square had been packed by millions of feet on thousands of market days. It would lie open and empty for four days, a thin layer of dust swirling and eddying in the hot wind of the dry season; but every fifth day the marketplace came alive. People poured in from every direction, choking it with color and noise and a richly compounded odor of fish, all kinds of wares, and of humanity. That was an opportunity for begging—lepers, specially the advanced cases with their stumps of hands and feet, would move in as close as they could, holding out the broken shell of a gourd for scraps of food or whatever might be tossed to them.

All through the morning they waited, on that September day, and into the afternoon. The market was ending, and the vendors were packing up their unsold wares, when at last the Baileys appeared with Arch. Aging and nearing retirement, Bailey stood and looked into the ruined, pleading faces of the large crowd below him. It was as if he were again a young Irish teacher of forty years earlier, gone out to India to have the mission of his life laid on him by the sight of India's lepers. He said a few words, which Arch translated. Bailey's heart obstructed his throat.

"We must do something more," he said to the doctor. "Take in twenty of them; we'll see somehow that you are able to take care of them."

Arch could not stop at that. The Baileys stayed a couple of days. Almost immediately they found themselves growing fond of this young doctor. The three of them sat and talked late into one night, and the next evening they shared their dream with other members of the Taegu station.

There would be a leper hospital in Taegu—not just an asylum for hopeless cases, but a *hospital*, where a hundred patients could be housed and treated, and some of them, at least, restored to the comforting daily traffic of society. Arch had his estimates: to buy property and erect the basic buildings would take about five thousand dollars. (A dollar could be made to go far then in Korea.) They all discussed the plan and, because it was the weekly prayer-meeting night, they knelt down and prayed:

"Lord God, give the money! Let hope shine into outcast lives—Jesus Christ, who said, 'Because I live, you, too, will live'!"

The Baileys left Korea and went back to London. Several months later, a letter came from them. On their return, they had discovered that during the same week when they visited Taegu a British donor had sent to the Mission to Lepers a gift of five thousand dollars. No one could argue with so clear an answer to prayer! The money was for the Taegu Leper Hospital; they were enclosing a draft for two thousand dollars and would reserve the balance also for that project!

∞ ∞ ∞

"Come in, Arch. It's good to see you—good to have a chance for uninterrupted conversation."

Harry Bruen is again opening his study door and greeting his neighbor with a warm handshake. This time it is in January 1914; the air is crisp and Harry has fire in a small stove opposite his desk.

"I have to say again how happy and impressed we are by the remarkable reports we continue to hear from the eight churches you were helping with."

"As for me, I'm happy that Herb is back and looking after them. I now have an appreciation for what that kind of work means."

Responding to Harry's gesture, Arch is turning the secretary's chair and seating himself as he speaks.

"But, I'm here to consult you about something else. We all know that the term of service between furloughs is seven years. Do the mission and the board make exceptions to that pattern?"

"Yes, it's been done—usually for health reasons. What do you have in mind?"

Over the next half hour, Arch shares his thinking. The medical work is taking shape. He can see his way ahead. But he can also see that if it is to be developed adequately, he will need to be training assistants, and for that he will himself need some further training, particularly in tropical diseases directly applicable to conditions in southern Korea. The best source he knows of for such training is in London, the British having much more experience than Americans with tropical medicine; and he knows of an intensive three-month course there, starting on May 1. If he were granted a proportionate furlough beginning in the spring, his almost five years in Korea might entitle him to eight months and some days, rather than the twelve months after seven years—in fact, if it began on April 1, it would be eight months and twenty-three days.

He gives the precise figure with a whimsical shrug, and Harry laughs, but the general proposition calls for serious discussion. For any of them, and especially for people in their first term of service, when four or five years had passed, that seven-year-furlough goal could seem tantalizingly near, yet far away. Should Arch really ask for special consideration? Does the Taegu medical work in some way depend on it?

Harry probes with kindly and insistent questions. What he is probing for is to guess what his young colleague's mind and spirit might be experiencing. He has measured Arch's intensity and almost obsessive dedication. Is there a risk of burn-out? Maybe this kind of break is what is needed to save him for a longer career.

In the end, Harry says, "All right, let's go for it. Put it before the mission executive committee and at the same time write to Dr. Brown. I'll write to him, too, and ask for a cable in reply. Of course, we'll get Taegu station to concur."

Harry was chairman of the station that year. As the petition went on up the line it moved fast, much faster than such requests usually moved. Possibly the reports coming from the Taegu medical work were drawing particular attention, disposing a favorable response to what Arch Fletcher might be asking. Within two months he had an affirmative answer—and could confirm the advance arrangements he had already been making.

This was the spring of 1914. News coverage was not what it would be a century later, but there was enough for Arch to be aware of extreme tensions in Europe. He must get to London by the first of May at the latest. On April 4, he took the train northbound, as he had in his first winter in Korea. He rode all the way to the Yalu River, but this time stayed on as the train continued northward. Much of Manchuria went by in the night. By morning he found himself in another world from the populous, domestic landscape of Korea. From the railroad track, broad grasslands swept away clear to an undulating horizon. Occasionally there was a herd of wild horses—small, shaggy, tough-looking animals. Even the people of the rare villages looked more compact, more hairy, and somehow more alien than the now-familiar Koreans.

At last they arrived at Manchuli. Here were some weathered wooden houses, as well as mud-walled huts, clustering together on this edge of the Siberian loneliness. There must be forests not too far on ahead, Arch thought, realizing how startling it was for him to see wooden houses again; he had become so accustomed to plastered mud, thatch, and tile. Manchuli was where one changed to the Trans-Siberian line. With a thrill, he saw his train waiting as they pulled in. There it stood, gleaming, its engine chuffing lazily. The engine looked big and powerful, and the train had been washed from end to end, and every brass fitting shone. It seemed already, just in its appearance, to be a link between the Orient and Europe.

Arch got settled in his compartment. More and more, he had a curious feeling that he was in Europe. In climbing the three steep, iron-treaded steps to the train car's platform, he had climbed out of the East, out of the world of his first term of service, which had started as so exotic and grown familiar, and back into the Western world, which was familiar and yet now foreign. Feeling a little heady, he sat down in the sleeping compartment.

A fellow passenger came in, a florid man with a bushy, reddish moustache who bowed and spoke to him in German. He understood little German, and the man's Western appearance and ways intensified the confused feelings in him. He seemed to be on the *S. S. Korea* again in Kobe harbor on that morning nearly five years ago, when he had wakened to the rattling of chains and a sudden shout of a voice in Japanese just outside the porthole. Now he was trying to back through that doorway, out of the East and into the West once more.

It would be a while until departure time. With personal effects arranged, Arch climbed down to the station platform, and so back to the Orient—fascinating to cross back and forth from one hemisphere to the other by three short, iron steps. He wandered around and looked at the town, which was rather quickly seen. It must have rained heavily in the night. The streets, rutted and muddy, ran off from between the houses to become dim trails, like the wakes of ships, getting lost toward the grassy horizon. It reminded him a bit of the American Mid-West, although he was here in the heartland of a remote continent.

The engine finally blew a couple of warning blasts and, when everyone had been gathered on board, the gleaming train began to move. For eight days and nights, rolling most of the time, it would travel six thousand miles—the distance across the United States, from sea to sea, and back again. Angling northwest over the steppes of eastern Siberia, they came at length to forests—dense with evergreens interspersed with silver-white birches—then to beautiful, lonely Lake Baikal. Hour after hour, they rode where they could glimpse shining water between the trees—Baikal, the largest fresh-water reservoir in the world.

Later there were, again, broad, open stretches while the train rattled across a part of the Russian steppes. Settlements were few, and the towns looked poor and primitive, until finally they picked up a second locomotive to climb laboriously through the Ural Mountains. After that, one began definitely to be in Europe. There were cities, factories, and then, for a day, Moscow—raw and gusty in spring of 1914.

Although interested in what he saw, Arch's mind kept pressing on to London and the School of Tropical Medicine. Very possibly, he would enjoy many of the experiences of life more if he *weren't* always pressing on in mind toward something else. Further, the effort of the last months in Taegu had left him nervous and tense. He couldn't relax. Endlessly, he walked the corridor that ran down one side of the Trans-Siberian sleeping car, next to the windows. At length the train pulled into Warsaw, looking drab and sooty, streaked by the water and stale tea they had poured out its windows during the long trek. Leaving his carriage, Arch continued to pace his way tensely through Europe.

Even the three months in London, which he had so carefully planned for, didn't seem successful. The specialists in tropical medicine that he listened to seemed to be discussing and emphasizing things he had already become familiar with, examining his patients in Korea. Some of the technical terms they used were different, and some of those difficult. There were too many words, too much talk. He found himself dragging through each day, trying to make his mind absorb what it didn't feel ready or able to absorb. He had been determined to have these three months of study in London. Now he was glad when they were over and he was boarding the British S. S. *Arabic* for New York.

Over him hung an air of general turbulence. Arch's private tensions merged into the huge conflict gathering in thick darkness over Europe and the Near East. Shortly before the *Arabic* sailed, word spread that Germany had declared war on Russia, and two days later, on France. The captain, as he followed through on his departure date, August 4, got the news that spread quickly through his ship: Britain had declared war on Germany.

The *Arabic*'s rather slow Atlantic crossing was uneventful until, late in the voyage, the captain announced that they would be changing course, to land in Boston. No explanation was given; but from the aft deck, the passengers could make out the shape of a German gunboat that shadowed them into Boston Harbor.

Although he had left Ontario quite far behind, Arch was a British subject. Arrived in Boston, he began gleaning eagerly such shreds of news as he could find of the growing conflagration in Europe. The journey across northern Asia and through Europe, the few months in England, and the sea voyage ending with the silhouette of that German gunboat—all had been bringing him back from Korea, situating him in the West again. This was once more his world, and he could feel the fever of it. The day after disembarking in Boston, he wrote to Dr. White at the board in New York:

> If the war is to continue any length of time, I would consider it my duty to volunteer and cross the Atlantic with the Canadian troops. . . . What would your opinion be in regard to my volunteering?

Whatever Dr. White's opinion may have been, the war did continue, but Arch did not volunteer. He stayed with the earlier volunteering he had done, when he first wrote to the New York board seven years earlier.

Traveling west now to Nebraska, he was grateful to be in the town of Orchard again, in Gordon and Myra's white frame house, even in the same upstairs bedroom that he had occupied when he was just out of medical school, assisting in Gordon's practice. It was all familiar. Sometimes he felt like he belonged here, but mostly that feeling was gone. When he leaned out the window to try to get a breath of air in the persisting heat of September, the broad, familiar fields of Nebraska were there, but in his mind were the dry rice paddies of Korea.

He even found Korean words coming to his mind occasionally in conversation. His life was overlaid irretrievably with that whole additional complex that no one here would share or understand.

As fall came on, Arch had opportunities to visit churches and church groups in that section of the country, talking about the mission in Korea, promoting interest and helping to raise funds. He was expected to make such visits, and he did.

At first Arch felt awkward doing so. He had no training in that kind of speaking; but his good friend Bob Ecklin, who was still pastor of Second Presbyterian Church in Sioux City, coaxed him to let flow out some of the Korea scene that now so filled his thought and feeling. People didn't want to hear formal speeches, just a sharing of what was happening in Korea, what had been happening to him in his work and life there. Arch found, to his surprise, that he was effective when he spoke that way.

Unfortunately, he found also that some of his ailments came back. Was it a lingering effect of the malaria that he had battled in Andong four years ago? Possibly so. Whatever it was, it drained his strength, forcing him to cancel some commitments and even to stay in bed, as his brother Gordon prescribed. Both he and Gordon knew well the shadow of the tuberculosis that killed their father and their brother Jim. After some days, though, Arch turned a corner and began a slow recuperation. Gordon's Myra, a generous, frugal, frontier-type of housewife, saw to it that he ate well, as his appetite returned.

There were some happy interludes—as at Christmas, when the family got together. Arch's younger brother, Dave, now worked with Gordon in a joint medical practice—a close arrangement that they held to, even though it quite often brought their distinct personalities into sharp conflict. In the long winter, there was also an occasional sleigh ride. Brother Tom had kept his horses, even though beside them in the barn he proudly stabled his 1914 Dodge Touring car, one of the first automobiles in the northeastern corner of Nebraska. It was pleasant for Arch to fit again into the small-town social life of Orchard; but as his strength returned, so did the people and scenes of far-away Taegu—sometimes closer and more present in thought than what was actually around him.

The date for the end of his almost-nine-month furlough was approaching, but from New York, Dr. White made known his own concern for Arch's health: he should stay in the United States and take the time and whatever measures were necessary to make sure he was in robust health before returning to Korea. That was kind and generous, but Arch felt happy and relieved when a date could be set, passage secured, and he held in his hand the actual ticket.

The packing and departure from Orchard was done with more eagerness than nostalgia. Then came the transition of the long voyage across the Pacific. Arch's thoughts were far beyond the prow of the ship, and among them—a bit hazily remembered, and perhaps to his own surprise—was the face of Jessie Rodgers. How might it be with her? How would she be doing by now, carrying out her assignment in Andong?

8

# A Brief and Furtive Courtship

JESSIE HAD THOUGHT ABOUT Arch Fletcher quite often since that September day in 1913, when he stood and watched as the bearers lifted the chair poles to their shoulders and began to carry her from the Taegu compound, heading toward Andong. Once settled there, she had listened with private satisfaction when remarks were made about his four-month stay in the winter and spring of 1911—how effectively he had initiated a medical work when the new Andong Station was getting established. And she had found herself sharing, for her own reasons, the general regret that young Dr. Fletcher had been returned to Taegu, where he continued until his early furlough. She would be glad, she thought, if their paths should cross again when he got back.

On that September day, in 1913, Arch had felt no particular emotion about sending Miss Rodgers off to Andong, unless it was that, for no logical reason, it left him feeling a little lonelier than before. The thought of her traveling alone did cross his mind a time or two in the next three days, but he dismissed it when a note came to him a week or so later, written in her neat, round hand. She thanked him cordially for all his helpfulness; he had been most kind. Arch read the note, smiled and nodded his satisfaction, although there was no one in the room to nod to. Then he put the note in a desk drawer and soon forgot that it was there.

More than a year later he began to remember and to think about Jessie Rodgers. It was when he was lying ill and then gradually recuperating in Gordon and Myra's house in Orchard. And so it was with him later on shipboard, returning to Korea; although he could have no inkling of what Martha Switzer was unintentionally setting up for him.

Miss Switzer of Taegu station was a disciplined, capable person. She ran her Bible Institute for Women with utter dedication. Of course, she had to have help and had to fall back, rather often, on the married women of the station for teaching. But experience had taught her that this was uncertain help. In her view, the married women, with their pregnancies, their children's ailments and their husbands' demands, were at best only "broken reeds," as she used to say.

She was pleased, then, when the mission authorities she had to persuade granted her request that young Jessie Rodgers be sent down from Andong for a month to teach in the big spring Women's Bible Institute. She invited Jessie to come a few weeks early and prepare her material in Taegu; and that is how Miss Rodgers happened to be right there when Dr. Fletcher got back from his furlough. Meeting him, Jessie noted right away that he was looking heavier and more robust than she remembered him. His clothes fitted him well, and he seemed fresh and eager to get back to work.

The hospital had been closed for a year, having no doctor to keep it running. Recently, queues of seventy or eighty patients had been forming daily outside the door of the dispensary, as word got around that the doctor was returning. On the morning of May 1, Arch personally drew the door open and bowed smilingly to the patients at the head of the line. He had regathered a number of his former helpers. All day they worked at the queue of patients, which grew at the rear as fast as it was reduced at the front. Arch exulted; it was good to be back on the job.

It was May in Taegu. On the mission compound, the trees were green, their leaves large and delicate. Roses were blooming and strawberries ripening. Arch was finding the work at the hospital intense. The wards were filling up, and at the dispensary, some days as many as a hundred outpatients were examined and treated—but unexpectedly, providentially, Jessie was there.

At the end of a long day, when the velvet dark of a spring evening wrapped the trees, when the city's noises grew drowsy and a faint fragrance of honeysuckle hung on the air, an hour or two for a discreet meeting could be found.

The courtship was brief—so brief, and discreet, that the other members of the station never suspected what was happening. Arch was almost thirty-three and Jessie was thirty-one. Both had made firm choices before and had stuck by them, and both had known the maturing effect of lonely experiences. Now they knew quite sufficiently, in their different ways, that God had brought them together.

On May 18, scarcely a month after Arch returned, they were secretly engaged. Jessie confided the news to Martha Switzer and Harriet Pollard, the "girls" with whom she was staying. Beyond that, the couple planned to keep the secret for a while, then announce the engagement, maybe in the summer, and be married in September.

It was the next evening that Arch called Miss Switzer's home over the compound telephone system. Might he speak to Miss Rodgers? The other two nodded knowingly while she went to the phone. He had a difficult case—a woman with complications, who had been in labor for two days. Could Jessie come down to the hospital and lend a hand?

Light from the hospital windows shone out whitely into the warm evening. Inside the corridor, as Jessie headed toward the women's ward, the air was close with an odor of ether and antiseptic. She was no nurse; but, she told herself, if she was going to marry a doctor she would need to get used to this. Just then the door of the operating room opened and Arch came out. She thought he looked strained behind his mask; but his eyes smiled at her and he squeezed her hand, as he led the way into the ward.

Jessie watched him check the bed quickly to see that the rubber sheet was in place. Then he disappeared, and in a few moments came back with a small bundle. He put the new-born infant in her arms:

"Here, can you take care of this?"

"What do I do?"

"Clean up the baby, dear. Get some cotton and oil, and boil some water. We ought to have a nurse; but we don't."

Some time later, they brought in the patient. She was a small woman, and young, although the pain and weariness on her face were ageless. Arch helped to lift her and lay her gently in the bed, and she opened her eyes and looked up at him.

"Thank you; thank you," she murmured.

The faint words were spoken in the respectful, melodious "high talk" of the Korean language. They held relief and wonder, Jessie thought—the wonder of an Eastern woman at this Western man whose skilled hands could be so patient and gentle. That night, her long ordeal over, the little woman died; but in the morning her family came and, with deep gratitude, took home the small bundle. She had given birth to a baby boy.

It was only a few days later that concern spread through the station with the word that Dr. Fletcher was ill. He had not been able to go down early to the hospital, as he usually did. Martha Switzer took care that Jessie got the news, but in a studiedly casual manner, and not until the first Bible Institute class was over. What she didn't anticipate was that Jessie should slip away a moment later, taking advantage of the break between classes.

In fact, Jessie was surprised at herself as she hurried along the compound, her skirt swishing the grass at the edges of the packed earth pathway. What if someone should notice her, or, worse yet, encounter her and ask where she was going? Fortunately no one did, and at last she approached the low, brick outpatient building of the hospital. She wasn't sure just what she intended to do when she got there, even though the experience of the other night had given her confidence.

Her shadow fell across the doorway of the outpatient waiting room. There she hesitated. A few patients looked up, but none who would recognize her. Jessie looked in uncertainly, pausing for an endless moment with one foot on the doorsill.

What to do next? The door to the consulting room opened abruptly, and in that moment she glimpsed Arch, sitting perched on a high stool, peering into the ear of a patient. So, he was all right, and at work as usual. As quickly as she had come, Jessie turned away, feeling suddenly ashamed of her anxiety. How had it seemed so urgent that she find out somehow if Arch were at the hospital or not?

Jessie made it back to the institute unobserved. But at noon, as they were sitting finishing lunch, the phone jangled. Martha Switzer went out in the hall to answer, discreetly closing the door, yet her muffled voice could be heard in several exclamations of surprise and concern. Jessie tried desperately to tell herself it might be something entirely different.

When Martha came back into the room, her grave composure was enough to confirm every fear. It had been Martha Bruen calling. Arch Fletcher, she reported, went home ill from the hospital, so ill that he scarcely made it to his bed, and Kim Chu-ho, his male house-helper, had to call Harry Bruen to go and undress him. He had no idea what he had contracted, or if he did have an idea, he wouldn't say. "You know Arch; he just isn't very talkative." Yes, Jessie knew him—better, she felt, than any of them.

What could—should—she do? She had to see him, had to get to him; but he had not wanted their engagement announced. He disliked any kind of public stir. Would he be annoyed if she tried to see him, and how could it be done within the bounds of propriety? With immense thankfulness, Jessie discovered that Martha Switzer understood her dilemma.

"Why don't you send a note over to him, dear? Ask him if he wants to see you, even if doing so lets people know your secret."

The note went and came. Yes, he wanted to see her. Could she come at once? So, the die was cast. She walked over to the MacFarlands' home, where he was living. As resolutely as she could manage, she told Mrs. Mac-Farland that, as his fiancée, it was her right to see Dr. Fletcher. This was a serious business. Why did Mrs. MacFarland have to stare, and then laugh outright and pat her arm so affectionately? Still, she herself was amazed by the swiftness with which the new role had been thrust on her, as she was led toward Arch's room and quickly left alone there at his bedside.

Arch was very sick—no doubt about that—and with their doctor sick, the others felt helpless as lay people. On the judgment of Dr. Adams, as senior station member, a telegram had been dispatched to Severance Hospital

## A Brief and Furtive Courtship

in Seoul. By evening there was a reply. Dr. Mills would be coming down—a two-hundred-mile trip—on the night train.

Meanwhile, Jessie did what she could, as did Kim Chu-ho. Of course, with the evening she had to go home. Kim had his home, too, but he wouldn't leave. When the others had all gone to bed, he stole out of the doctor's room, spread his mat, and lay down just outside the door.

In the morning, Dr. Mills was there. He found the symptoms puzzling and decided that the patient should be taken to Seoul that night, where there was a larger and better-equipped hospital. Jessie, having had the courage to make public the engagement, was determined now to go along. The Women's Institute was almost over, but not quite. She resolved to ask Martha Switzer to arrange for one of the women of the station to take over her notes for a review and final examination.

"It seems that you were right, Martha," Jessie told her, "about married women being 'broken reeds.' Look at me; I guess I'm cracking already." Married women—it was exciting to adjust her mind to such a role!

That night she got a different sort of introduction to it. Harry Bruen had made all of the arrangements for Arch to be taken to the train. They were simple enough—just the provision of four bearers to carry an improvised stretcher, which was nothing more than an army cot with the legs folded under. But kindly Harry had forgotten about Jessie. When the stretcher bearers appeared, about an hour before midnight, and he and Kim Chu-ho were seeing to the final details, he was terribly chagrined when it suddenly came to him that there was no way for Jessie to ride to the station. Too late, now, to send for a rickshaw—and where could one be found at that hour? Jessie would have to walk. Nothing for her to do but to behave like a proper Korean wife—even though not a wife yet—and to follow modestly on foot behind the stretcher of her husband.

In Seoul, Arch's fever ran high for five days. The doctors were baffled; no diagnosis seemed to fit. It was in the fifth night that abruptly it broke and his temperature dropped to normal. When Jessie went in to see him, he lay propped up, pale and thin, against the pillow.

"Well, dear," he smiled, his smile trembling a little, "the end of a horrible night, but the beginning of a 'perfect day.'" He had brought back a phonograph record from furlough, and the song on it had become a kind of theme song of their brief courtship: "When You Come to the End of a Perfect Day."

The day was not so perfect yet; but while Arch convalesced, they planned. In those days, the mission had a kind of family organization. Some of the senior missionaries, who had earned their right through decades of service in a land that venerated age, did not hesitate to give counsel to their younger colleagues. James Adams wrote to Arch and Jessie from Taegu. They would understand that according to Korean custom, it was scarcely commendable that Jessie should be there with Arch when they were merely engaged. Furthermore, long engagements were not usual in this society. Hence as soon as Arch were a bit mended, might it not be better if they should proceed to be married?

If they needed further encouragement, the Adams were planning a summer vacation in Japan at beautiful Karizawa. They would be delighted to have the young couple make the trip with them to a perfect honeymoon spot.

Jessie and Arch took up the marriage suggestion; certainly the national custom should be respected. On June 19, they were married by the Rev. Dr. Horace G. Underwood, himself. The groom was thin and rather shaky. He had been out of bed less than a week, and the well-fitting clothes he had brought back from furlough looked a size or two too large. What was worse—as an after-effect of the fever, one eye was beginning to bother him. He couldn't say that he felt up to a honeymoon in Japan. Instead, he put a patch over his eye to nurse the iritis that was developing and took his bride back to Taegu.

It was the beginning of Taegu's sultry, humid summer. As a convalescent patient, Arch could hardly reopen the hospital. After a month in Taegu, he and Jessie went back to Seoul to be married again, and then on to remote, lovely Sorai Beach, on the northwest coast, for a real honeymoon.

A second marriage was deemed necessary because His Majesty's consul in Korea was out of Seoul at the time of the first one, and Arch was a British subject. So in June, although the requisite forms had been filled out at the consulate and due record made, no civil ceremony could be held before the religious one. Dr. Underwood had questioned, at first, this "certain irregularity," but had proceeded to pronounce them man and wife.

Others questioned more audibly the newly-weds' interpretation that they were really wed. Was it as legal as it should be? All were more comfortable when, after a month of conjugal happiness, the couple retook their marriage vows according to the form of His Britannic Majesty's government.

From Seoul, they went by train to Chemulpo, at the mouth of the Han River. There they put up for a day. The little coastal steamer that was to carry them northwest, along the coast, to Sorai Beach was due, but of course it was not there. No matter. They found a Japanese inn and a room with a view. The room had been freshly redone—soft, fragrant rice-straw *tatami* covered the floor—finely-wrought lattice windows opened at the back on a delightful little garden, complete with a dwarf pine and a lotus pond, all in miniature. At the front spread a verandah, with a view of the whole harbor.

They were really beginning to enjoy one another. The first, rather awkward days of their marriage were behind them. Both had been single for quite a number of years—long enough to make adjustment to married life an undertaking.

Arch had commented once, in his matter-of-fact way, during their month in Taegu, "You know, each of us has lived alone for a good while, and we might better not expect to change one another very much." That had left Jessie wondering what sort of changes he might have in mind.

By now, though, the strangeness was banished. They enjoyed to the full the small tub of steaming rice, the fish and cold bamboo sprouts and other salty side dishes served them for dinner—then sitting on flat cushions on the verandah, holding hands while they watched the flickering lanterns on fishing boats taking positions for the night's work, out in the bay. Let the steamer come when it wanted to—they felt they didn't really care.

They had two nights at the inn. Then, on the third morning, the boat was there, anchored in the harbor and surrounded by sampans. They hurried to get down to the port to find space on a sampan that would ferry them out, although the haste seemed useless: the creaky gangway still hung high on the ship's side three hours later. Baskets and rope bags of fish kept being hauled out of the hold, to be dragged across the deck and dropped into waiting sampans.

All the way up the coast, the little steamer must have been taking on fish at every stop, to be disgorged for the Seoul market. Everything glistened and smelled of fish. Accommodations, when they got on board, were the simplest. Arch felt proud and relieved that, by luck and the judicious placing of a few coins, he was able to get Jessie one of the half-dozen berths in the ship's single cabin above deck. He would sleep out on the boards, unless foul weather herded all the passengers together in the dank, cramped space below the deck. Happily, it turned out to be a good voyage—one of the best.

∞ ∞ ∞

Sorai Beach had a fascinating history. The nearby village of Sorai had actually been the isolated and unlikely cradle of Protestant Christianity for all Korea. The story ran like this: Suh Sang-yun, a young merchant from this village, went to Manchuria in the later nineteenth century, when Korea was still the "Hermit Kingdom," resisting with bitter suspicion all foreign ideas. In Manchuria, Suh fell under the teaching of Scottish missionary John Ross. He was baptized a Christian and returned to organize, clandestinely, a first group of Protestant Christians in Korea. Later, three members of this group, hearing that foreign Christians had arrived in Seoul, went to seek them out.

They found the Rev. Horace G. Underwood, who was trying to make his first convert. He baptized the three from Sorai—it was 1887—and that fall made the long overland trip to their village, where he baptized seven more. It was an entering wedge. Conversion to any foreign religion had been held to be a capital offense in Korea, but the old isolationism was breaking down.

In 1894, the Rev. William J. McKenzie, a Canadian Presbyterian, linked his name with Sorai village by going to live there, resolved to dress, eat, and live as a Korean. McKenzie died the following year, but he shepherded the village congregation long enough to inspire and direct the erection of a church building. The building was dedicated by Underwood in a memorial service, ten days after McKenzie's death.

Visiting Sorai Church, it was Underwood who walked across a few fields and up to the crest of a sandy dune, to see, curving away from his feet, a three-or-four-mile crescent of dazzling white sand shelving out gently into sheltered blue water, surely one of the most beautiful beaches of the world. Underwood examined and tramped over a jutting headland with a level, grassy top, which shielded one end of the beach, and that is what he bought for the future Sorai Beach Association.

The headland ended in a point thrusting out into the bay. On the highest part of that point there was an overgrown mound with a fire-pit still visible. There, in the days of an earlier Korean kingdom, lookouts were posted, and at evening, a low fire was kept burning. If the sails of marauding junks were sighted, kindling could be heaped on the fire to flash a signal to a hilltop further inland. From there, the signal would leap from fire to fire across the mountains a hundred miles to the capital of the kingdom.

Taegu station was the first group to support Underwood and begin to boost the Sorai Beach Association. Three families—including the Bruens—bought lots and, by that summer of 1915, had built a variety of cottages. Over the next few years, many more cottages would be built all along the high bluff fronting the bay, the site that Underwood, with his rare vision and his private financial resources, had picked out and purchased in order to set up a Sorai Beach Association. The odd assortment of cottages these missionaries built came to express the rich variety of personalities among them.

"Now, Jess," Martha Bruen had urged, when it was evident that Jessie and Arch couldn't go to Karizawa for a honeymoon, "you two just come on down to Sorai any time. We have an extra room there, you know." They had all of three rooms, in total, set in a row with a connecting porch, and, at one end, a tent that housed the cooking facilities.

No one minded primitive accommodations, at least not while the sun shone and the nights were full of stars. When an infrequent storm rushed in off the Yellow Sea, driving thundering breakers and near-horizontal sheets of rain before it, the occupants battened down the wooden shutters of the cottage as best they could and cowered in the half-dark interior among drips and puddles of rain water, waiting for the storm to pass.

The Bruens' cottage was not far from the Underwoods' and the old signal mound. Jessie and Arch sometimes climbed the mound or else went out to the far end of "the Point." One evening they spread a rug on the grass, to sit and watch the incredible glory of the sunset.

Out on the water the homeward-bending sails of a fishing junk, dyed in ox blood to a rusty brown, caught the light and flamed deep crimson. The whole bay, with its ring of offshore islands under that vivid sky, began to burn with gold and almost seemed to smoke like a censer, pouring upward into the glory of the heavens an offering of praise. Jessie began to sing softly. She did not have a trained voice, but she loved to sing, and hear sung, some of the classic hymns of the church.

"Day is dying in the west;

heaven is touching earth with rest;

wait and worship, while the night

sets her evening lamps alight

through all the sky.

Holy, holy, holy, Lord God of Hosts!

Heaven and earth are full of thee!

Heaven and earth are praising thee,

O Lord most high!"

Arch joined in, where he could, with the bass part. His arm squeezed her a little tighter, as Jessie leaned against him. Watching, they fell silent while the intensity of light began to drain away.

No words were needed, nor any movement, until at length the fires in the sky were damped. The junk had rounded the promontory, making its harbor. The bay was filling with shadows, leaving only a soft pink on a high cloud to the east. Slowly they got up, and Arch folded the rug. He still said nothing—he had never learned words for such a moment. As for Jessie, she felt so full of the beauty she wouldn't trust herself to speak.

# 9

# Would God Ever Bring Them Back?

Arch felt that he was really squared away. The honeymoon at Sorai Beach, while the arrangement had been a bit provisional, had provided a restful and refreshing interlude. There were many thanks due the Bruens for use of the third room of their cottage, with particular thanks because, for the final ten days, he and Jessie had the cottage to themselves. Martha Bruen, who had plainly taken a special liking to Jessie, insisted that although she, Harry and the girls needed to return to Taegu, Jessie and Arch should take a little more time by themselves, with space to relax and enjoy one another. The Bruen girls, who occupied the middle room, were daughters Nan and Harriet, aged eight and four, playful and imaginative children who seemed as thoughtful and generous as their parents. Now a married man, Arch was taking more notice of children, deciding that the Bruen model would be a good one to emulate.

Those last ten days at Sorai Beach were a delight. Then it was time to close up. Jessie spread on the table the notes Martha Bruen had given her—instructions on how to leave the cottage as tight and secure as could be managed, until the next summer.

"Arch, did you find the hammer and nails? Martha says here to nail down the shutters, but be careful of splitting. Is there no way of locking them?"

"None that I can see. Nails are a bit primitive, but effective."

Jessie heard the hammering for a while at the far end and then it stopped. She let a little time go by before calling.

"All finished, dear?"

She knew he wasn't, but that his mind was probably already back in Taegu, planning what to do first when he got there. She was getting to know him, maybe as well or better than he knew himself. She poured a cup of coffee to take to him.

"Here, you can rest a while and think."

"That's right. I guess I was thinking about getting back—about Taegu."

"And it's all right. I can see that thinking ahead is a specialty of yours."

"Well, maybe so; but let's get finished here." He was putting down the coffee cup and reaching for the hammer. "What comes after the shutters are done?"

With affectionate teamwork, they finished closing up the cottage, then returned south to take their place in Taegu Station, warmly welcomed now as The Fletchers.

By the first of October, Arch had re-gathered and strengthened his staff. For the first time, he had a professional associate, Dr. Chay, who had trained in Japan. Korean doctors were graduating there now, although it was not easy to find one who would work for the salary that a mission hospital could offer. Arch was willing to keep looking until he found an associate who would share his vision of the hospital as an evangelizing force committed to spiritual, not just physical, healing.

He and Jessie even had the prospect of a house of their own. The mission, at its annual meeting, had put high on its property list a request for six thousand yen (about three thousand dollars) for a house for the physician and his family in Taegu. It might be a good while before the board in New York could answer the request, but with the mission giving it high priority, there was hope. Meanwhile the new couple used a borrowed house that a family had vacated to go on furlough.

For the first time, also, Arch would have a professional nurse on his staff. Elizabeth Bekins, RN, was on the way, appointed to Taegu and due to arrive in mid-December.

"You know, dear," Arch said, "Miss Bekins will need a place to live, and we have extra space—."

It was logical; Jessie would admit that—like many of Arch's suggestions, not easy to adjust to, but logical. She prepared the extra room, five-month bride that she was, and Miss Bekins moved in with them. Another thing—Jessie was already pregnant. To her relief, she discovered that Elizabeth Bekins was thoughtful and diplomatic, actually a considerable source of comfort and reassurance right up through that first baby's birth.

As for Arch, he seemed unaware of any potential difficulties. The hospital work was humming, and he was immersed in it. All morning, every day, he and Dr. Chay were kept busy without a break, attending the still-growing queues of outpatients. As the reputation of the hospital spread, they poured in from the crowded city and the surrounding valley, and even from distant villages across the mountains.

In the afternoon, Arch would scrub up and put on his gloves and surgical gown and mask, to operate on a rich variety of cases, using everything he had ever learned and improvising new techniques as new surgical problems confronted him. It was challenging and exhilarating; and always there was the goal, to urge home the Gospel, the healing of the spirit. To heal bodies, to relieve suffering was not enough, without the healing of the living Christ.

A young man arrived in an advanced stage of syphilis. The disease had ulcerated and completely destroyed the soft tissues of his leg and jaw, beginning to attack the bone. For eight years, local witch doctors had tried everything in their power to exorcise the evil spirits. The boy's father had sold everything, even his house, to pay those doctors, and had died in despair. At last, from somewhere, young Chun had heard of the hospital.

It was a bare story, quickly told. Arch knew most of it already by heart. The thing now was to work over the patient, which they did. Because he was young, he responded to their treatment. His suffering was checked, and as he improved, he began to discover a new world. Here were people who did not live in fear. There was no talk of demons. Rather, they seemed to possess an inner serenity, and they treated him with an affectionate concern he had never encountered and was at a loss to understand. Who were they and why did they act this way?

Chun's mind began to revive from the numb, self-centered stupor of pain. He began to observe intently what was said and done within eye-and-ear-shot of his bed. In particular, he observed Elder Pak, the hospital evangelist. For days he simply listened, his boyish features an impassive mask.

Warned in advance about this Jesus' Way, he would not be taken in. But finally curiosity overcame fear. He began to ask questions, began to grasp what would, to his fathers, have been incomprehensible: a religion built on mercy and on love. Before he left the hospital, Chun was baptized a Christian.

This kind of result, although it was certainly not possible in many cases, was worth Arch's best effort, and he and his staff kept pouring on the effort. Their hospital wasn't much to work with. The second floor consisted of just one large room, which was the men's ward, and two cubicles for private patients. On the first floor was a women's ward, smaller than the men's, an office, and a makeshift operating room. In the basement, Arch had improvised two private rooms for women patients.

A need felt with increasing insistence was for some place to hospitalize Japanese patients. Two or three dozen of them a month were coming to the outpatient department for treatment, in spite of the fact that their own government had established a hospital in Taegu. Arch was gratified, and he also saw a further opportunity to preach the Christian gospel. It was for everyone, without distinction.

But the Japanese patient couldn't lie down beside the Korean, the occupier with the occupied, in the same hospital ward. So Arch, with approval from New York, did some private soliciting among his brothers in Nebraska and a few friends, and got together a fund to build a row of low, Japanese-style rooms against the back wall of the hospital property. There he could receive Japanese patients, with their familiar straw *tatami* for hospital beds, and care for them with the help of a Japanese-speaking Korean doctor and Korean nurses.

∽ ∽ ∽

In all of this, Arch hadn't forgotten the leprosy work. With the two thousand dollars from the Mission to Lepers still on hand, received from the Baileys before his furlough, and the sketches he had made with them for basic buildings of a hundred-patient leper hospital, Arch set out to find a site. On repeated Saturday and Sunday afternoons through the fall and winter of 1915, he and Elder Pak tramped the countryside around the northern edge of the city, looking for some suitable land they might buy.

At last, one chilly afternoon, they saw the ideal location. Pak, in his traditional quilted winter clothing, was the first one there. Arch came up beside him, in black topcoat and felt hat. They stood under a gnarled pine, its trunk rimed with streaks of frost, and measured with their eyes the pleasant sweep of open ground before the next clump of woods and a small village off to the right. They were about two miles from the city and near one of the main roads. This would serve admirably if it could be bought, and if the vacillating Japanese authorities would agree.

Although the government sanitation officers wanted to appear progressive, it was hard for them to overcome their dread of contagion. They couldn't seem to make up their minds as to just what precautions must be taken if a leprosy facility were to be considered, let alone sanctioned.

Even so, by spring the site had been bought, and Arch was burning brick on it and making preparations for building. The first outing he took his wife and their new baby on was by rickshaw one Saturday late in May, to see what progress was being made.

∽ ∽ ∽

Jessie's pregnancy had been an absorbing, sometimes scary experience for her, but she had tried not to make too much of it. She was a missionary, and the wife of the doctor: when she felt sick and frightened and uncertain, she had kept her feelings determinedly to herself. Even on the night after May Day, when her pains started, she tried not to be much trouble, though she had to crawl on her hands and knees after midnight.

By early morning, the contractions were close enough that Miss Bekins was called. She and Arch made ready, and about eight o'clock the baby was there, a little girl born on a lovely fresh May morning when the air was redolent with the blooming of white and purple lilacs. As she and Arch had agreed, Jessie named her Elsie, after her own younger sister.

Of course Arch couldn't take off from work just because his first child was born, and probably he wouldn't have. He was down at the hospital as usual and only a little late, while Nurse Bekins washed up the baby and turned an improvised delivery room back into a bedroom.

At the hospital, the members of the staff, hearing about the birth, watched their doctor with furtive curiosity. What would a Westerner say or do? Actually, his Scottish reserve left Arch too acutely self-conscious to say or do anything at all that would show the pride and joy that was welling up in him at being a father. Not until Miss Bekins came down did the staff get the word: the new baby was a girl. Then the nurse's aides grinned and nudged each other. "Look at the Chief; he isn't really so foreign; he just thinks he's lost face because his child isn't a son!"

Elizabeth Bekins told Jessie about it all later, when she was bathing the baby. She didn't think it was so funny.

"Just look at her!" she said, propping the wobbly head against her wrist. "Just look at her, Jess, with those big, dark eyes and black ringlets. She's as pretty as a picture. Why couldn't he say something nice about her, and let them see how proud he is?"

When Arch came home at noon, he paid the sincerest compliment he knew. He went over to the bassinet and stood a long time looking down at the baby.

"You know, dear," he said, "she looks just like my grandmother."

Jessie laughed outright—which wasn't so good. It hurt to laugh. "But, Arch, how can this little mite look just like your grandmother?"

Still, to Arch she did, as he looked down at the black hair, moist and stuck close to her forehead, and the unmistakably prominent little nose.

～ ～ ～

All through the next fall and winter Arch and Dr. Chay kept up a blistering pace at the hospital. The medical work was expanding rapidly. Taegu station had begun to ask for a second missionary physician—without much likelihood, to be sure, of being given their request. When a report was made for 1916–17, the statistics were impressive for so small an institution: 17,047 treatments given in the outpatient department, 794 inpatients cared for, 280 operations.

Meanwhile, Arch's other dream was being realized. The three basic buildings of the Taegu Leper Hospital stood complete, and had been occupied as soon as finished. The design was exactly what Arch had sketched that night four years earlier, when he and the Baileys had sat and talked into the morning about such a project. There was a central building with an office, a treatment room, and a small chapel. The other two buildings were dormitories, one for men and the other for women. Each had ten units, set side by side in a continuous row, every unit a single room large enough to sleep five patients.

The rooms were built of brick, but in traditional style, each with a raised floor under which several flues passed from a cooking fire at the front to a chimney at the back. In winter, hot, smoky air could be directed through those flues to heat large, flat stones above them. The stones were covered by a layer of smooth, baked mud and then by the heavy, oiled paper that formed the floor. It was a frugal, ancient Eastern system of radiant heating, very practical in low rooms where everyone sits and also sleeps on the floor.

The patients of each unit would cook their own food, mostly a mixture of rice and barley, with a few vegetables and, rarely, a little meat. There were places for the women to wash the clothes, which they ironed in the traditional manner, squatting by large, flat stones on which they pounded the garments with a rhythmical beating of smooth wooden paddles. The women also mended clothes, and sewed new ones as needed, while the men worked in the fields, made roads, and helped to develop the little community.

Among the leper patients, there were no accommodations for married couples. They were all learning to be part of a new sort of family. They had been taken out of misery and despair. With the disease, everything in their former lives, whatever those had been, had died for them. Now they were discovering a new way.

As they began to learn and adjust to that way, the patients began also to learn of a God who cares, whose love leaves no one forgotten. At least some of them discovered that they, too, could praise God with each morning's ray of light, with each breath of life.

Nor did they need much theology. They were met by Jesus in the form of the doctor who became their father, in Elder Pak, and in the assistants who gave them treatments. In the Gospel, Jesus laid his hand on the leper from whom others recoiled. Such Gospel could be very real to them.

In September 1917, a great celebration was held. The Leper Hospital had been in full operation since early spring; now it was to be dedicated. Arch wanted to do this fittingly. He had in mind the donors whose gifts had made the institution possible. He also had in mind a critical opportunity for public relations. The still-hesitant Japanese authorities needed to be convinced; the vision of the Mission to Lepers needed to be confirmed; and there was a wonderful chance here to shout across the province that the God of Jesus Christ is concerned for all people.

Arch planned a mammoth celebration for that special September day. William M. Danner, secretary of what had come to be the American Committee of the Mission to Lepers, who was on a tour of leprosy work around the world, would be there, as also Dr. and Mrs. McKean of Siam (Thailand). McKean had pioneered the widely known leprosarium at Chieng Mai. Arch was further elated when Japanese officialdom responded positively to his invitation.

When the great day came and the official photograph was being taken, the honored guests lined up beneath crossed flags, before the entrance of the central building, while the photographer shifted the legs of his tripod around, and darted into and out of the black hood of his camera. There they were, the representatives of the Rising Sun. At this distance, seeing them in the handed-down photograph, they don't look impressive—men of small stature wearing unflattering military tunics, plain collars high around the neck and a straight row of brass buttons down the front. The flat-topped caps set exactly straight on the head add nothing to their stature, but several of them wear the decoration of the Imperial Cross. Proudly they pose at ease, each with left hand resting on the hilt of the cumbersome sword he has set up like a cane in front.

The Imperial Government, which they self-consciously represent, has at this point been ruling Chosen (the historic name the Japanese used for Korea) for seven years. The governor of the province is among these officials, as well as the chief of gendarmes, and the "physician in charge" from the government hospitals of Taegu, this last in white uniform, mustached and bespectacled, with white Panama hat.

After the photograph, all move to the rostrum, set up under a large tent. Underneath and beyond the canopy, seating mats are crammed with three thousand spectators. It is a superb September day, arching a stainless sky over the fields and hills. Warm and exultant, Arch perspires in his frock coat, striped trousers and black derby. A band strikes up and all on the platform stand at attention while the pupils of the Presbyterian Boys' and Girls' Academies of Taegu city lead the singing of the Japanese national anthem. Then the Christian Scriptures are read and prayer offered, before His Excellency, the governor, stands up to speak. Arch smiles whimsically to himself: it seems an odd mixture of Christian and non-Christian, Western and Eastern, the occupier with the occupied, all in one ceremony.

The governor is speaking, his remarks in Japanese translated by an interpreter into Korean. He has rehearsed briefly the achievements of his government in health and sanitation, in its few years in Chosen. He adds:

> Now that I have seen the hospital which is established here, it is with a glad heart that I express my thanks to the one in charge. There are a good many charitable works in the world, but caring for these lepers is the greatest, because leprosy is hated by all people.... One who is cared for in this hospital and thus taken out of his suffering and grief must not forget such kindness. There is an old saying that "A man who receives a favor and does not acknowledge it is only an animal." How then can one repay such kindness? Since this hospital is a charitable institution it is not to be paid by material things, but by you, out of a thankful heart, cleansing your body and ruling your mind so that you may exert a helpful influence for the welfare of this hospital and this country.

The governor is a valuable man, Arch notes to himself, a man who represents enlightened Japanese policy, the more liberal side of Imperial Rule.

When he has finished, William Danner speaks, and then Dr. McKean, the speeches being translated into both Japanese and Korean. Arch himself has no speech. He has planned it more fitting that Elder Pak should represent them in thanking the guests, since the two of them together had trudged the paths around Taegu looking for a site for the leprosarium. Pak relates in feeling words how the leprosy work began there in Taegu, and how it reached this point under the grace of the Almighty. He does it with an eloquent flourish, in his musical Korean, and when he finishes they all stand, while the Christians among them bow their heads for the benediction.

The formal ceremony is at an end. From across the hills comes a breath of cool breeze. It flutters the flags crossed above the entry to the central building—the round, red Rising Sun of Japan, crossed with a white flag bearing a red cross, both a Christian and a medical symbol.

That evening the members of Taegu station gather around a dinner table with Danner and his party as their guests. The talk is on the ceremony of the afternoon and on the contribution such a project can be making. Someone asks Dr. McKean about the impact of leprosy work in Siam.

"All of you already know—," McKean begins, and an eddy or two of small talk dies out. Attention is turned to the visitor, whose voice now reaches the end of the table.

"I don't need to be telling you how little the ordinary person understands, in general, the idea of a gift freely given. He is accustomed to look for an ulterior motive, even in the apparently philanthropic acts of his neighbors, and usually he finds one."

Several heads nod assent. Warming to his subject, McKean goes on, "Among the people we are trying to serve, one may feel he sees some material benefit that the Christian missionary receives for his work. Most of us Western missionaries live well, perhaps too well, in countries of extensive poverty. But when the observer sees people spending and being spent for the leavings of humanity, for the outcast leper, he has to admit a motive which he himself cannot explain."

McKean pauses a moment, but the silence is deep. He has touched near home. "Then, too," he goes on, trying to brighten his voice a little, "until we began our leprosy work in Siam, we had not fully carried out the Great Commission in Matthew 10:8. We had healed the sick, as Jesus told his disciples to do, and had literally raised the dead when malaria was carrying off its thousands. By the power of the Gospel, demons had been cast out.

"But we had made no attempt to cleanse the lepers. From the day that work was begun, I sincerely believe, God's blessing began to be poured out in a new and powerful way on our efforts in Siam."

Smiling, just a trifle self-conscious, the visitor pauses. He is a medical man, not a preacher, but no one in the group is eager to break the silence. They have heard again, each in his and her own way, the simple, biblical fervor that through the Great Century, since the early 1800s, has been thrusting Christian missionaries into every corner of the Earth.

With Arch already in bed, Jessie sat by the lamp in their bedroom that night and wrote on a piece of note paper:

> In the hush that followed Dr. McKean's words, so full of conviction, a great desire was born in our hearts to carry out more fully the Divine injunction, "Freely ye have received; freely give," a desire to share Christ himself with these poor, suffering ones of His.

She slipped the folded paper into her Bible, snuffed the light, and slipped in beside her husband.

∞ ∞ ∞

Arch kept accelerating his pace. They had not gone away to Sorai Beach in the summer. Jessie was expecting her second baby. This time she had company, since Susie Blair, down at the far end of the compound, was waiting for her fifth, after four girls. Meanwhile, the annual mission meeting was being held this year in Pyongyang early in July. Susie's child was almost due, but both husbands, Herb Blair and Arch, went off north to the meeting. One didn't miss an annual meeting if it could possibly be helped. Too much might hang on the votes that were cast there.

What Herb and Arch hadn't reckoned on was a sudden coming of the rains after weeks of panting drought. As the meeting got under way, rainwater began to sluice down the gutters and drainpipes. All over Korea, it was pouring down. Isolated in Taegu, with everyone else away at the meeting and going on vacation after that, Jessie and Susie watched the rain with uneasiness, and then alarm. Reports filtered in that the rivers were flooding. Houses were being swept away; fields, and then whole valleys, inundated. Wretched queues of refugees began streaming into the city.

Some three hundred fifty miles to the north, Herb and Arch had forgotten about the meeting. Their one idea, now, was to get back to their wives. They made it as far as Seoul before the trains stopped running altogether. The report was that outside the city, at the main bridge, the Han River was churning a scant two feet below the girders of the trestle. Telegraph lines were down. Herb could only pace restlessly from window to window, and blame himself for deciding to go to annual meeting at all.

They did make it back in time, on the very first train that crept out of Seoul and crawled cautiously over flooded embankments, like a blind insect feeling its way, all the way to Taegu. Susie's baby was born on a hot, muggy July 24—another girl. Jessie's program was to ease the boredom of her own waiting by walking and panting over to the Blairs' each morning to bathe the baby.

So it happened that, on the way home on August 2, her own pains began. They started strong. She was only halfway back when one caught her so hard she thought she was going to cry out. Desperately, she made for the nearest place to sit and sank down on the steps of the single women's house. Fortunately it was deserted, with everyone away for the summer. She closed her eyes until her head stopped reeling. There had been a silence in the hot, close air. Now, suddenly, a thousand crickets struck up their loud chorus. The contraction passed, and Jessie got up. She must hurry. Maybe she could make it home before the next one.

Jessie would give Arch his "justification" this time: she would bear him a son. The hospital staff congratulated him, and he was obviously delighted. He and Jessie named the baby Archibald Grey Fletcher Jr., and soon began to call him Archie, so as not to get confused.

Arch's workload kept increasing. Again in 1917, as the year before, Taegu Station called for a second missionary physician. They made the request more urgent, but the mission had no one it could spare. One problem was that while everyone praised the leprosy work and acknowledged its value, it had no place in a mission doctor's regular assignment.

Arch served under the Presbyterian mission—assigned to the Presbyterian Hospital, that is, the general hospital in Taegu. Leprosy work was a sideline, conducted with help from the non-denominational Mission to Lepers. It was, as another physician in the same situation wryly quipped, "the missionary doctor's golf."

Through the winter of 1917–18 and into early spring, Arch kept rising and going to the hospital earlier in the morning and getting home later at night. For a man with his obsession, there seemed to be no other way. There was another way, of course, which he wasn't wise enough to see, until a night in early March.

On the morning before that night, he and his associate personally dealt with nearly eighty outpatients in their consulting rooms. It was part of Arch's theory that he and the Korean MD who had succeeded Dr. Chay must do this work themselves. If they left even routine cases to their scantily trained assistants, the patients might begin to prefer the Japanese hospital. It was, after all, larger and better equipped. The only advantage the mission hospital could still hold was the amount and excellence of personal attention that was rendered. With more patients than he could care for, Arch was dreading to lose any of them, driven on by his compulsion to bring the Christian Gospel to all.

Home for a brief lunch that day, he went back to the hospital's meager operating room to stand over the table for six successive operations. He and Jessie were invited to the Erdmans' that evening for dinner. When it was already past time to leave for that event, Arch called from the hospital to say he couldn't possibly make it. An emergency case had just been brought in, and he was going back for his seventh operation. At last, about eight o'clock, he made it home, slumped exhausted at the table to eat a pickup supper, and fell into bed.

It was about 2:00 a.m. when Dr. Adams got himself awake. Someone was calling outside the bedroom window. He groped and stumbled his way to get the window open.

"Why, Jessie, is that you?"

"Please, Dr. Adams. Come quickly. Arch is sick. He needs help!"

Veteran James Adams shivered in the chill breath from the window. He had faced all kinds of emergencies. In the darkness, he tried to find a match—Oh, bother the light! Instead, he groped for his topcoat from the hall closet, found his shoes, and joined Jessie's huddled figure outside the front door. Arch had wakened her in the night, she said. He felt sick. When she had gotten a light and a basin, he had started to vomit, and had retched up a quart, she thought, of bright, red blood.

James Adams was no physician. He was relieved to find Arch resting somewhat easier, although deathly white by lamplight. With little idea of what the prognosis might be, he tried to calm and reassure Jessie and then went to knock up the compound gatekeeper and send him down to the telegraph office at that hour of the morning with an urgent message to Severance Hospital in Seoul.

This time it was Dr. Ludlow who was sent to Taegu to take charge of the patient. He had him moved to Seoul for more precise diagnosis. Weak and shaken, Arch was half-carried to a rickshaw, and so onto the train for the six-hour ride. At Severance Hospital an x-ray picture of the left lung confirmed the presumption: acute pulmonary tuberculosis.

Arch's medical work in Taegu was done for. Another doctor and his family were leaving Korea on furlough and, providentially, a small cabin could be secured for the Fletchers on the same boat, the Pacific Mail's *SS Columbia*. Jessie had two weeks to pack up in Taegu—with Arch looking on helplessly, under strict orders to make no exertion, and with Archie a babe in arms and two-year-old Elsie clinging to her skirts.

Somehow, what had to be done was finished. Jessie left their goods packed and stored in the attic of the house where they were living, and on April 1, 1918, the family left Taegu. Spring was coming to the valley, as they rattled away from the huddled roofs of the city and across the fields. Green shoots of rice were showing—new life beginning. Jessie looked at her husband, white and drawn, at little Elsie with her nose pressed excitedly against the train window, and at baby Archie in his basket.

Would God ever bring them back to this once-alien place, which had been their only home together?

# 10

# Laid on the Shelf

ARCH LAY FLAT ON his back on his cot. It was early, but already it was broad daylight. By turning his head he could look into the leafy upper branches of a maple just outside the screen. The sleeping porch was high above the ground at this end. Rich sunlight was already flooding through the leaves, and a squirrel was running along a slender branch. Haven't seen squirrels for quite a while, he thought—no squirrels in Korea.

Korea—it all seemed so remote and dreamlike. He didn't want to sleep, but it was early and he would still have to lie here for several hours. Then up—but just to pull on a robe and move to a cure-chair. He didn't feel ill—in fact, he felt rested and well—but this was the discipline. It was to be followed. In the late morning they would let him walk, but slowly, down to get his mail, if any, and to buy a paper. Still in robe and slippers, he would take a full half-hour and enjoy every minute of it. Then back to the cure-chair and the cot.

Lying there now, he calculated the days. It had been thirty-five—might be another three months, or four. But this was a wonderful place—God be thanked for that. Arriving on the West Coast, he and Jessie and the children had come across the country by train, stopping off in Nebraska to see Olive and brothers Tom, Gordon and Dave. Poor Jessie, it was her first meeting of them all, and not under very happy circumstances—more relief for her when they reached her parents' home in Ridley Park, just outside Philadelphia.

The first doctor he saw in the city had suggested that a single hemorrhage wasn't something to be too much staggered by. Take warning and be careful—not too much work, more rest, good diet. Arch hadn't been satisfied. He had fortunately—or providentially, rather—found Dr. Kaufmann, a specialist with a personal history of tuberculosis and a complete recovery. No half-way measures, said Kaufmann—thorough-going discipline, and an environment, at least at the beginning, where the discipline could be carried out. Did Dr. Fletcher know about Trudeau?

Arch had read with admiration the story of Dr. Trudeau's own battle for health in an isolated cabin in the Adirondacks and of the growth of a pioneer center he established there for study and treatment of tuberculosis. As soon as possible, Arch was booked to begin his cure at the Trudeau Sanatorium. It wouldn't be cheap and he had little money. The mission board had no policy of caring for the medical expenses of its missionaries, but he and Jessie had a small fund which family and friends had given them, to put a heating plant in the home being built for them in Taegu. If I don't get my health back we won't need the house, let alone the heating plant, he reasoned. So Dr. Kaufmann made the arrangements and Arch was received as a patient in this lovely, lonely spot in the Adirondacks.

He was emerging by now from his earlier fatigue and torpor. As his body gathered strength, his mind also rallied; but there was nothing to do. Even reading was sharply curtailed. There was little for an active man but to lie still and think.

What did you do wrong? Where were your mistakes? You were doing a work in Korea—now the Lord has put you on the shelf—you may never get back there again. Why?

His mind went over the years—his boyhood—his training and call—the early experiences in Korea—all the shifts and fumblings of his first two years of service. After that, the opening of a way ahead—the swift unfolding of the Taegu work, with every sign of promise—and then, abruptly, a blind turn in the road. How had he sinned? What was the fault? Why?

Arch was feeling sorry for himself, true; but the stern, Scottish conscience of his forebears came in to take up the dialogue.

Don't pretend that you have done everything you ought to have done. You failed your God; you fell short. Think of it now. Consider in what you fell short, and how you might do better—if God should give you another chance out there.

A son of the Scottish Reformation, Arch shared its deep, elegiac sense of the fleetingness of time, the insignificance of mortality—a sense which does not, however, lead to an attitude of futility in the face of death, but rather to a fervid will to act and be—yet always in a context of eternity. Arch wanted to heal, so that he could give himself to the relief of suffering—but in so doing, he had to reach deeper. He had to get to the soul, and to find there a final vindication of his call. He knew it could not be enough to heal bodies, to postpone by a few years or decades their ending in the grave. What one did must be translatable in terms that reached beyond mortality.

This was the spur to his thinking, on the screened porch in the Adirondacks. And because he was not primarily a philosophical person, it did not lead to a conclusion of philosophy, but of method. There must be a better way—a more effective way—of doing what he had set out to do at Taegu Hospital. The conclusion he arrived at was a simple plan, but one which would become the most distinctive contribution of his missionary life work.

Until that time, the Taegu medical work had followed the traditional pattern of a mission hospital. The hospital employed a chaplain, or "evangelist", to visit the men patients, and a "Bible woman" to visit the women, according to the strict segregation of sexes of the Orient. Quite frequently there were conversions to the Christian faith, but they were not often enough—Arch decided—nor were the results as lasting as they should be.

Korea was a country deeply rooted in its ancient animism. There were Buddhists—Buddhist shrines and some very old Buddhist monasteries—but Buddhism had never gained the hold in Korea that it achieved in neighboring China and Japan. Confucianism also—although it gave to the philosophically inclined a code of ethics—chiefly impressed the people with its customs and filial piety, and the veneration of one's ancestors. On a spiritual level, the emphasis was on fear. There were spirits everywhere—demons—and most of these were evil. The religious dimension of life, which permeated everything, consisted chiefly of an endless effort to placate the demons and to escape their malevolent influence.

In such a context, Christianity might be a refuge. A patient in the hospital, receiving relief from suffering in an environment of compassion and concern, might respond with eagerness. He might even be baptized. But old, familiar patterns of thought are not so easily changed. When he went back to his village, he would feel all the pressure of society—the stigma of being a renegade, a betrayer of the honorable way of his fathers. Then, out of the dark recesses of his own mind would come the leering demons, taunting and tormenting him for having fallen so easily into the beguiling snare of the foreign doctrine. Weren't they Koreans, he might protest—weren't those people in the hospital his own countrymen, who had taught it to him and whose lives had seemed to possess that strange luminosity which had so attracted and warmed him? Fool! Of course they were Koreans, traitors who had sold themselves to the foreign devils and who wanted him to barter away his soul as well.

So the dialogue might go on, and the demons might win. In the language of the Korean Church, "backsliders" were common. The church put up a safeguard by treating prospective members simply as "adherents" at first. When their sincerity had been demonstrated, they might then be enrolled as "catechumens." The catechumen stage would last at least a year, during which time they must learn to read, if illiterate, and must study the Bible, committing certain passages to memory. Also—and this was most important—they must supply evidence of having spoken to others about their faith and must try to win at least one other person to a like commitment to Jesus Christ. All this was preparation, after which the catechumen might be examined and admitted to full membership in the church.

What troubled Arch was the weakness of his hospital's witness and the lack of effective follow-up, once an ex-patient convert left its doors. The plan that came to him at Trudeau was only worked out fully years later. It is best seen, perhaps, at a point of full development—and in living experience, because the fact is that Arch did go back to Taegu.

It wasn't soon. He wrote Jessie from Trudeau in mid-September:

> They tell me I can leave in a couple of weeks. I know it's been hard for you, staying with your parents and having the children and now another on the way, but I've found a place where we can be together and by ourselves. The ladies of the Pennsylvania Medical Missionary Society have several cottages in Ventnor, at the New Jersey shore, and in October we can have the use of one, a new one, that has a bedroom with many windows for fresh air. Here, they think that would be ideal.

There was just a little more. Jessie read and re-read the letter and she closed her eyes and bowed her head: "Thanks and praise, O Lord God! Bless the Lord, O my soul!" This time, climbing the stairs to the third floor, she didn't feel so exhausted.

Arch left Trudeau in early October, just as the leaves were beginning to turn and there was a nip of frost in the air. He was able to move the family to Ventnor to have a home of their own, even if a loaned cottage home! The name of the cottage was Sunny Haven. When they entered the front door, Jessie looked up from watching the children. Across the living room was a fireplace of beach stones, and above it, carved in the wooden mantel, she read, "Around our restlessness His rest." Yes, she needed that; she was ready.

Nine hours a night Arch slept that winter in his corner bedroom with the windows thrown open to the icy Atlantic winds—except one January night, when he didn't sleep. A check of the Atlantic City Hospital downtown had confirmed his concern about the cost of a hospital delivery for the coming baby. He had delivered the other two children at home in Taegu. He and Jessie decided that he would do it again here. A letter to brother Gordon in Orchard was answered promptly by a parcel containing a complete obstetrical kit, even including a surgical gown and the latest drug in use—pituitrin.

On the night of January 6, 1919, lights burned late in the two-story frame cottage on Portland Avenue. Mrs. Hartzell, a missionary nurse on furlough from Siam, was there assisting, and Jessie's sister Elsie was on hand to do the nervous waiting in the hall that Arch himself was too busy to do. In the early morning of January 7 a second son was born.

They named him Donald, because they both liked it and it was a good Scottish name. When Arch went to the municipal building later in the morning to register the birth he saw a headline: PRESIDENT ROOSEVELT DIES. That was ex-President Theodore Roosevelt. Death and birth, Arch thought, the patterns of our life.

He and Jessie now had three children spanning less than three years, and they were both in their middle thirties. Jessie said it was quite enough family.

∾ ∾ ∾

From his family history and from his own brush with the disease, Arch had contracted a great interest in tuberculosis. In the spring he decided that he could try a little more exertion. He began commuting to Philadelphia, to study a half-day at the Phipps Institute of Tuberculosis, and in the summer, when he went back to Trudeau for a check-up, he stayed for a six-week course in diagnosis and treatment at the Saranac School.

By now the question had been up as to when or how he might return to Korea. In the spring he had written to New York, offering his opinion:

> ... It would be folly for me to return to Taegu and again undertake that work alone. There will be a deluge of patients. I had twenty-five on the staff; now they are all scattered. ... I earnestly desire to return, but cannot do so unless another missionary physician is to be associated with me from the first day. ...

Arch tried to stand his ground. As an alternative, he suggested that he might be sent to Severance Hospital and National College in Seoul. There was a lot of correspondence about the alternative. With his new interest, Arch wanted to see the setting up of a department at Severance for tuberculosis treatment and teaching. Tuberculosis was widespread in Korea, and on the increase. The correspondence brought in Dr. O. R. Avison, the president of Severance, who was interested in the project. Then it veered to the possibility of a department of leprosy, with backing from the Mission to Lepers.

Meanwhile another year passed, with the family living at Ventnor in a cottage made available by Mrs. George Doane, just across the corner from Sunny Haven. Arch was in Baltimore at Johns Hopkins, getting home only every other weekend. He was working in tuberculosis, soaking up inspiration from men like Dr. Baetcher, pioneer radiologist, whose hands had been burned by the little understood effects of radiation, his fingers painfully crippled. When Baetcher looked at a chest x-ray, his disciples swore that he could tell not only the condition of the lungs, but the whole life history of the patient.

In the end, it was decided abruptly that Arch would go back to Taegu. This was in the fall of 1920. His "health furlough" had grown to two-and-a-half years. He had been getting valuable specialization—but it was time to be back in harness, and more than time that Jessie and the children should have some stable home. Arch was given the promise of a second missionary doctor and a nurse, as soon as available. Miss Bekins had carried on for a year after he left Taegu and then had resigned and gone home to be married. For the rest, it would be up to him to gather as many of his former staff as he could locate and to take up where he and they had left off.

# 11

# A Hospital Preaching Society

Arch was off and running almost as soon as their train pulled into Taegu station, as Jessie knew he would be. Friends were there to meet them—Harry and Martha Bruen, along with several people who had been on the hospital staff. How glad Jessie was to see Martha, who had brought twelve-year-old Harriet with her to hug Elsie and Archie and to chase after and pick up little, curly-headed Don.

Arch was glad to see all of them, too. He was so glad to be back in Taegu. It was reassuring to find that the language, unused over such a long hiatus, seemed to come back rather well, as he and Harry formed a cluster with the hospital friends. Harry's Korean was excellent—a good model to follow. And Harry had a bit of news that Arch, being on the way, probably would not have heard. The mission executive committee had worked things out to assign Dr. R. K. Smith and family to Taegu. Arch was going to get his wish for a second missionary physician.

What Jessie wanted to see was the house—"the doctor's house"—that money had come through for and that was being finished, almost ready to be occupied, when they were suddenly, drastically pulled out of Taegu. When they had entered the compound and were coming up the hill, there it was, looking much as she and Arch had left it. Well, it had been she—Arch, with the alarm of his hemorrhage, had been totally set aside—inactivated. She'd had to do it all.

Harry was handing Arch the keys, making a jovial bit of ceremony, and they were going in. The house had been finished inside and used provisionally by a couple of families that were in transit, but had little feeling of having been lived in. Their furniture was there, hers and Arch's and a few pieces they had added after they were married—odd pieces, now in this and that room. Jessie remembered how she had planned to set it up, back when she, more than Arch, was eagerly anticipating having a house of their own after three years of living in borrowed houses.

It all came back forcefully, as she went from room to room, and specially as she climbed the attic stairs. For a moment that harried, panicked feeling swept over her again—seeing the boxes and trunks as she had closed them up, each one, with two-year-old Elsie dragging at her skirt. Elsie was there now, a lively, inquisitive four-and-a-half, finding all of this to be a joyful adventure. I'll be so grateful, Jessie thought, just to get settled—as soon and as completely as we can.

∽ ∽ ∽

In the midst of the pressures of re-opening the work, Arch kept faith with the promise he had made to himself at Trudeau, limiting his work hours and keeping a check on stress. After a month the Smiths moved to Taegu. Richard was congenial. He seemed anxious to be cooperative, even to a point of appearing diffident at times. And Arch had not had a missionary colleague—ever—to share a medical work with. He knew that he needed to recognize that. The Taegu work was his project, but he needed to share it—to listen—to accept different ideas—to make some changes, even. As the weeks and months of that year unfolded, he kept reminding himself of these things.

Fortunately, there were no serious clashes. No doubt Richard, on his side, was also talking to himself—counseling himself on how he ought to act, how to be part of a team when he was the add-on to form it. Then, after just a year, the mission moved the Smiths again—this time to Chairyung. Arch was back to being the only Western doctor at the Taegu hospital.

In that year, however, he had begun immediately to introduce the plan that had come to him as he lay on his cot in the Adirondacks. A first step was to sell it to his staff members and invite them to organize a Hospital Preaching Society. All of them were Christians—the hospital, with its Christian purpose, employed only Christian personnel.

Now the proposal was for them to take over responsibility for the hospital's Christian impact—all of them together. In the Preaching Society there was to be no distinction of professional caste. All would share equally and democratically, with voice and vote in its affairs, from the superintendent (Arch) down to the shoe-boy who tended the door. And in order to share, each one pledged his or her contribution. Their financial, as well as personal, investment in the Society would ensure that it would really be theirs. It would cost each one something, according to her or his means.

One could see, in the outline of this plan, Arch's positive experience with the Bookroom project, all of those years before, when he was a young, single missionary there in Taegu.

Also, he had in mind the Biblical story of King David, when David wanted to erect an altar and make sacrifice to God at the threshing-floor of Araunah the Jebusite. Araunah pressed the king to accept the site as a gift, and the oxen and threshing tools as well for the sacrifice; but David refused. He insisted that he first buy the land, the animals and all, at full price—for, he declared, "I will not offer burnt offerings to the Lord my God of that which costs me nothing" (2 Sam. 24:24).

Out of its budget, the Preaching Society began by paying a major share of the salaries of the hospital evangelist and the "Bible woman," or women's visitor. These two were now their own employees, their representatives. Responsibility for the preaching work no longer came to rest, ultimately, on the missionary doctor who was hospital superintendent. It rested on each one of them—each carried a share. Plans for the program were made together, in monthly meetings of the Society, when progress reports were heard and discussed.

At the same time, the whole program was kept entirely voluntary. No one was required to belong to the Society. When a new member joined the hospital staff, it was up to the others to infect him or her with their enthusiasm for what the Society was doing. That person could choose to come in or stay out.

Nor did the Society members believe in requiring patients to listen to their preaching. No religious services were held in the outpatient waiting room, for example, where patients would have to listen before they might have a chance to see one of the doctors. Even the evangelist and Bible woman were urged not to preach at the sick. They should all learn to show a sincere interest and concern for those who came to the hospital. The witness to Jesus Christ might then come spontaneously, in answer to the patient's own question.

By the early months of 1921 the plan was in operation. The Hospital Preaching Society was beginning to scan monthly reports. Over the next few years it improved on its methods and rapidly expanded its work, inspired by such experiences as that of Farmer Pai of Paltal. Pai's story illustrates the working of the plan. Arch checked on it, and later had it written up in full, colorful detail to promote the work of Taegu Hospital among friends in the United States. Here is the story, much as it was published at that time, an eloquent example of the Taegu Hospital Preaching Society plan at work.

The only son of a prosperous farmer, Pai somehow falls victim to the demons. For years they torment him, not letting him work, giving him no peace to eat or sleep, for the fire that keeps burning in his abdomen. The sorcerers try what they can to drive the demons out.

There, Pai crouches in his mountain village. A sorceress is beating a drum and chanting on and on monotonously. She has spread a low table with sacrificial food, hoping to entice the evil spirits, while an assistant rhythmically waves a sacred wand. But Pai, hunched over on a straw mat behind the table, head bowed in agony, feels no relief. The demons riot within him—ten years of torment—always this pain that will not let go of him.

The sorceress attempts the venerable art of acupuncture. Ceremoniously preparing a ten-inch needle, brown with rust, while Pai clenches his teeth against the ordeal, she plunges it several inches deep into the center of his pain, loudly adjuring the demons to follow the needle as she draws it out. No use—the stab of the inflamed punctures is only added to his suffering.

He tries a Buddhist temple in the hills, famed for its magic. For a whole month he lives there, paying to eat food that has been presented before the images, and drinking holy water. It does no good.

Inevitably the day comes when Pai's father says to him, "It is useless. We have sold all our land and the money has gone to pay sorceresses, doctors, priests. They have taken everything. The only inheritance I can leave you now is the inheritance of all men, to die."

Pai bows his head. He has no answer, no wish for anything any more but to die, as his father is saying. There is a long silence. The members of the family council, which has gathered, ponder each one his thoughts. When, after a suitable time, none of the older men has spoken, a cousin clears his throat.

"I have heard it said that in Taegu at the Dongsan Hospital . . ."

One of the older ones breaks in sharply. That is the place run by foreign devils. Others also chime in to cry down the suggestion. Go to the foreigner? That is all that is needed to complete their kinsman's catastrophe.

But Pai is desperate, and the futility of what he has suffered has shaken his belief in the honored traditions of his ancestors. The next day, ignoring all consequences from the family council, he persuades a friend to take him on his back and carry him the three miles to Taegu.

He has no money, but is not turned away. Instead, the people here put him under magic stronger and more mysterious than any he has ever known. He is given a tall glass of thick white liquid to drink. Then the x-ray throws Pai's demon into the spotlight—ulcer of the stomach. They lay him on a table with wheels and move him into a room with a bright light, where he is made to breathe heavy, sweet air from a bottle that drips. His senses begin to reel and he loses himself.

When he returns very slowly, not knowing how long afterward, he is in another place. He is still on a table covered with white, but it is soft and comfortable. Turning his head, he can see other such tables and other men lying on them. But his pain—it is gone! He tries to sit up. Ay! Something grabs at his stomach. Gingerly he puts a hand down there, but can feel nothing. They seem to have wrapped him round and round with cloth. Still, this soreness of his abdomen is nothing, compared to what the ten-year pain has been. Pai sinks back. There are a few people moving quietly about the room, most of them in white, like the sleeping-tables. It seems to his drowsy mind that there is kindness on their faces. They are a part of the strange, blissful peace that is invading him.

As Pai grows stronger, his curiosity quickens. His personality begins to move out from behind the cloud of suffering which has shut him away from friendly communication. He ventures to talk with the man nearest him, who was there when he first woke up. From this man he learns many things about the strange ways of the place where he is.

And then there is that venerable gentleman who stops to greet him and who comes back, passing through the room each day. Pak Tuk-il is the venerable one's name, Pai's neighbor tells him. Here he is called "the Elder." Pai would have risen, if he could, to bow low when the Elder first spoke to him. Although perhaps not as old as his own father, the Elder has a very full beard—a rare and respectable thing—and the beard is already white. Above it the man's eyes are deep and kind.

The Elder asks Pai if he would like to send some message to his home. He would, very much. He specially wants his father to know what wonderful things have happened to him, but he doesn't know how to write. The Elder smiles, and comes back a short while later with a scholar's ink and fine-tipped brush.

"Tell me what you would like to say," he invites. "I can write it for you."

The next time he comes, the Elder says, "You don't read. Let me read to you."

He takes out a large book and opens it. Truly, the Elder is a scholar. Pai listens with deep respect as the Elder reads words such as he has never heard:

> And he lifted up his eyes on his disciples, and said, "Blessed are you poor, for yours is the kingdom of God. Blessed are you that hunger now, for you shall be satisfied. Blessed are you that weep now, for you shall laugh" (Luke 6:20–21).

It is then that Pai asks his question—years later it still makes him smile to think how naïve it was: "Sir, are you of this religion that they call the Jesus Way?"

"Yes, son." The Elder goes on to interpret to Pai what he has read from the book.

What happens in a human spirit when a new light breaks through? It is a natural process—as natural as the birth of a child, as the first gasp of air and the first quavering cry—and as mysterious. But every birth is different. Farmer Pai has his. He opens his heart to the new faith. The Elder teaches him to read. He comes to possess his own copy of the Book and to be able, to his endless delight, to spell out its messages.

At length they send him away from Dongsan. He is reluctant to go, but the Elder has promised to visit. Receiving careful instruction as to how one gets to Paltal, the Elder says,

"I will be there soon, and I will stay a month in your village. No, son, I'll not stay with you—then some might say that we have won you to faith in Jesus just so that we might come and live with you and eat up your living."

Pai winces. His family has little left back in Paltal anyway, that he might offer to his honored friend.

"When I come," the Elder says, "you can help me find a place to stay, where I shall pay for the rice I eat."

It comes about, then, that Pai reappears in Paltal. It is true that he is well again. He has walked on his own feet up and over the mountain from Taegu. It is also true that he has fallen under the influence of the foreign doctrine; but he will not answer their derisive questions. He only says,

"Wait until the Elder comes. You can ask him."

The Elder does come, and with him a Bible woman, as they call the women's visitor. They live in homes of the villagers all month. He talks with the men; she, with the women. The Elder is an educated man, a man who easily understands the problems of the people of Paltal and who counsels them on the most practical matters—how better to raise their rice and to care for their infants. But most of all—early and late—he reads to them from the Book and explains its meaning in terms they understand.

More than a score of the village leaders come to profess the new faith. The Elder and the Bible woman leave at the end of their month, but later they come back, and regularly, to visit the village. For a month, Elder Pak and the Bible woman with whom he is teamed up are at the hospital, working with outpatients and in the wards. For a month they are in some village, living as they had lived in Paltal. The third month they spend traveling around to re-visit the Christian groups already established.

In time, the Christians of Paltal put together enough to buy an old house and transform it into a church. In the yard they set up poles and make a rustic, straw-thatched belfry. In the village there are no clocks—the bell is indispensable to regulate the life of the new church. Gradually, it comes to regulate the life of the village as well. Paltal becomes, in its majority, a

Christian village, with a new drive toward righteousness and progress. The demons lose their hold.

∽ ∽ ∽

This was Arch's plan in full operation. The Hospital Preaching Society added a second evangelist and Bible woman to its staff, and then a third. With three teams it could rotate them each month, keeping one always for visitation in the hospital itself, one living in some ex-patient's village, and one on the road, revisiting and building up the Christian groups already established.

The goal set for each such group was that it should provide its own place of worship, however modest, and should begin to contribute regularly toward the support of a "helper." Helpers were lay Christian workers, used extensively by the Korean Church, which lacked the money and the qualified candidates to provide a sufficient number of ordained ministers. When a village group reached the goal of having the services of a helper, the Hospital Preaching Society would transfer responsibility for that group to the regional authority of the Church—the Presbytery.

Even in its early months, before the Society's work was large enough to support a full complement of personnel, it began to show remarkable results, stirring up interest elsewhere. In 1922 Arch outlined the pattern in an article on hospital evangelism for the *Korea Mission Field*, the small magazine of Protestant missions in Korea. The article was picked up by Dr. Cochrane of the British Advisory Board on Medical Missions, an arm of the Conference of Missionary Societies, and sent to every mission hospital he had contact with throughout the world.

After two-and-a-half years of experience, Arch had a fuller report prepared and printed. The statistics were startling. In the thirty months, twenty-six new Christian groups had been established. Two of these had later died out, but twenty-four were active, and sixteen already had their own church buildings, entirely the result of their efforts.

Would the figures hold up? Could the Hospital Preaching Society's level of dedication and enthusiasm be maintained? Two years later, the *China Medical Journal* asked for and received a progress report from Taegu. The period covered was now four and one-half years. Fifty-two Christian groups had been established in the period of fifty-four months. Eight of the groups had disappeared, but there were still forty-four, of which twenty-nine now had church buildings, and eighteen had reached a level of sufficient strength to be transferred to the presbytery. A sketch map showed the location of the forty-four groups, some within a radius of twenty-five miles from Taegu, others fifty, seventy-five, and up to a hundred miles away.

Arch's report was direct, earnest, and candid. "We believe it is not sufficient," he wrote, "simply to sow the seed of the Gospel in the hearts of patients in the hospital and expect that in due time it will be harvested." The social pressures of a non-Christian environment were too great. There must be a type of follow-up that would afford the new convert the "fellowship, help and protection which only fellow Christians can give."

In his report, Arch analyzed the reasons for the loss of eight groups out of fifty-two. It was like losing eight patients—only to him this loss was more serious. Five of the eight groups, he noted, had been the work of a certain evangelist. He was a man of less preparation who showed marked ability as a preacher but was weak on organization. Of seventeen groups he had established, he had lost five, while one of the other hospital evangelists had lost just one out of eleven and the other, two out of twenty. The Hospital Preaching Society, with Arch's participation, had replaced the evangelist in question. The society, rightly in Arch's eyes, considered that inadequacy in this supremely important phase of the hospital's service should be dealt with as severely as inadequacy behind the drug counter or in the operating room.

## 12

# "The Doctor is Safe, and All of the Children"

IN THE SPRING OF 1922, Arch sat down to write his annual Personal Report, a duty every missionary had to fulfill. He decided to try to picture the medical need of his province, North Kyung Sang (of which Taegu was the capital); that is, medical need as it was in southern Korea almost a century ago. His province, as statistics revealed, was roughly equivalent both in area and population to the state of Massachusetts; so, imaginatively, Arch invited the reader of his report to form an idea of public health in North Kyung Sang by eliminating most services from Massachusetts.

All the larger hospitals should be removed, leaving only half a dozen of the small ones. After all, Massachusetts General had as many beds as all of the hospitals of North Kyung Sang together. Then all children's and maternity hospitals must be eliminated, as well as most dispensaries offering care to the poorer people. After that, the sewers of the cities should be filled in, and all institutions working for private or public health must close their doors. Harvard Medical College must disappear, and whatever scientific knowledge the state's two million people had on the cause and transmission of diseases must be erased.

The report went on:

> Now for sowing the diseases. Take this forlorn state and pack it full of tuberculosis. Leave no city without smallpox. Sprinkle broadcast hookworm and various other intestinal parasites. Scatter everywhere the countless more common diseases. Then, over all this stricken state spread the loathsome leprosy. And when this is done, summon just as many people as there are in Massachusetts, all of whom desire, as we, to be healthy and strong, and whose hearts, strangely enough, love and suffer and break, even as ours, and say, "Here is where you must live." That is North Kyung Sang Do.

Arch was stating the case in emotional terms. He'd returned from furlough not long before, and the memory of the clean, comfortable life in the United States, the care at Trudeau Sanatorium, and the superb medical facilities at Johns Hopkins was still fresh. In Taegu, working day after day in his consultation room, he thought, and wrote in his report, "How much of this needless suffering might be prevented if only the people were enlightened in regard to the cause and methods of communication of disease."

It was not only Korean nationals who died of disease in those earlier years of the Korea mission. The Western missionary, in spite of such precautions as he or she knew how to take, was often sick and sometimes fatally so. In 1921 the Mission History Committee recorded twenty-seven deaths in active service on its field. Up until that date there had also been sixty resignations, a surprisingly high figure, but this included at least nine whose health had broken and seven widows who had resigned after the death of their husbands.

Service in Korea was rugged, particularly for the "evangelistic" men, the ordained ministers whose work, as the pattern developed, consisted mainly of "itinerating." That involved taking long trips into the country, covering a wide circuit of churches and small groups scattered over the area that comprised that missionary's territory. Missionaries who were single women also made trips into the country, although not as frequently nor on such wide circuits.

Missionary families lived together in "stations," which served as their bases of operation. This "compound" pattern was adopted, at that time, not in any spirit of segregation or aloofness from the indigenous people, but primarily for reasons of health. Even so, by 1923, forty-five children of missionaries—a ratio of one out of six!—had died in Korea.

To go out and live among the people would seem like the best way to reach them. Arch had experience with that approach early in his service in Taegu, before he was married. The Salvation Army, which also worked in Korea, sent a dedicated young woman officer, a Swede named Kohler, to serve in the Taegu area. Although she spoke no Korean, she had an intense desire to learn the language quickly, and immersed herself in it.

Miss Kohler took a Korean helper and went to live in a Korean village. At first her progress was excellent, but after some weeks she began to lose her appetite and felt tired all the time. She wrote that she had been sick for a couple of days and was returning to Taegu until she felt well again.

A few days later, a wire went from Taegu to the Salvation Army headquarters in Seoul. Miss Kohler had arrived very ill. The diagnosis was typhus fever. An adjutant was dispatched from Seoul to help nurse her, and Arch had her moved to the house he was occupying, where he could watch her progress closely. Through days of raging fever, he and the adjutant waited tensely for the crisis. In her lucid moments, Miss Kohler was almost pathetically grateful for such care as the medical service in 1913 knew how to give her. At last, another telegram went to Seoul. The crisis was passed, but she was still very weak.

Then shortly afterward, the last wire: "Suddenly worse. Passed away at seven."

Typhus was one of the dreaded killers in Korea. Spread principally by the body louse, *Pediculus humanus corporis*, the infection entered the body through abrasions of the skin or through the bite punctures of the insect. Ten to fourteen days later, usually, would come the rapid onset of symptoms: vomiting, severe frontal headache, pain in the back and limbs, and a fever that might rage for two weeks. In the critical second week, the patient might sink into a coma, and death would come with the collapse of the circulatory system.

Arch and Jessie knew that long vigil again, years later, when in the 1930s their niece Olive, Tom's daughter, known to everyone as Toots, came to Korea from Nebraska for a summer and stayed to teach the year in a school for English-speaking children in Seoul. Somehow Toots picked up typhus, perhaps on a streetcar. Such public conveyances were a fair trading place for diseases, although by the 1930s cases of typhus were comparatively rare.

Toots had the best possible care in Seoul, but there were days and nights of fever, of lucid intervals followed by delirium, fitful dozing and lurid nightmares. Arch went up to Seoul to help take care of her for ten days, and then Jessie took over for the long convalescence. The entire family was tremendously relieved when Toots could finally return to her Nebraska home, fully recovered.

Typhoid fever was another constant peril, particularly to the itinerant missionary, in a country in which most of the supplies of water then available were contaminated. Arch had an encounter with typhoid fever in his first year in Korea. The new station of Andong was being opened up, and the town was more than two days' journey from Taegu by pack pony. The Rev. C. C. Sawtell of Taegu Station, together with the Rev. A. G. Welbon, went up to Andong in October 1909 to survey possible sites for the new station. After a few days in the town, they separated, heading into the districts to visit some small, scattered groups of Christians. Welbon, a veteran missionary, went to the west, and young Sawtell, just two years in the field, went north.

Ten days later, when they met again in Andong as agreed, Sawtell was running a fever. Welbon wanted to get a chair—the type carried by four bearers—to transport him back to Taegu. Sawtell refused the offer. He wouldn't, he said, put the mission to that expense. He could ride a pony.

Korean pack ponies were small, slightly built, and notoriously vicious. Twice, on that interminable two-and-a-half-day ride to Taegu, Sawtell fell off the pony, too weak to keep his balance. He nonetheless reached Taegu in better condition than might have been expected. Young Arch was called from Seoul to help attend him. The turn for the worse came some days later, and two days after that, Sawtell died. Welbon, his senior partner, survived him by nineteen years, only to die of the same disease in 1928.

∽ ∽ ∽

In parts of the world today, particularly in the tropics and subtropics, dysentery, both amoebic and bacillary, is still common. Anyone traveling abroad from temperate countries to warmer climates is cautioned about avoiding fresh leafy vegetables, raw strawberries and the like, and about drinking only boiled or bottled water. Minor inflammations from one or another of a host of intestinal parasites lead to the so-called "tourist complaint," variously and unscientifically named maladies; but real dysentery, whether due to a severe form of amoebiasis or to an infection by bacilli of the dysentery group, is not at all humorous.

In Korea, in the earlier days, dysentery, too, claimed its victims among the missionary force. The Roger Winns were a gifted young couple stationed in Andong, effective at putting their alto and tenor voices together in duets in English and Korean. In October 1922, word came to Taegu that Roger was down with dysentery.

The care of missionary colleagues took priority. Arch dropped his hospital program and went to Andong, following up with several trips to do what could be done in those days for bacillary dysentery. Given the inadequate laboratory facilities, even the diagnosis could not be completely established, although presumptive symptoms were clear. One or another of the sulfa compounds might have saved the case, but this was years before their discovery. On November 22, Roger Winn died. Representatives came from mission stations all over Korea to attend his funeral.

As a single woman in Andong, Jessie had been close to Catherine Winn. When Arch got home from the funeral, he suggested, after a few days, that she go up to Andong to spend a weekend with Catherine. Travel was easier and more rapid than when Jessie first went there, riding in a sedan chair some nine years earlier. There were automobiles in Korea by this time, and the Japanese had put some roads through. One could take a jitney.

That was an early-vintage Ford touring car in which the second seat had been moved forward, resulting in scant legroom, and a small third seat, with the shortest legroom of all, had been crowded in above the rear wheels. The jitney rattled along the dirt roads on its thin tires at what could seem an alarming speed. There was dust—and in the wet season, rain—only some of it kept out by flapping black canvas curtains with tiny, isinglass windows; but the modernization was tremendous compared to entire, tedious days in a sedan chair and the uncomfortable feeling of being carried on the shoulders of four of one's fellows.

This was the first time Jessie had left her three young children. She went off with some misgivings, but the visit seemed to help Catherine, and Jessie agreed to stay an extra day and arranged to take six-year-old Ruth, the youngest of Catherine's three, back to Taegu to play with Elsie, also six. Even so, it was a relief when the Ford jitney finally made it into Taegu and turned up a street that ran close by the foot of the small, abrupt hill on which the compound stood. Jessie leaned over and peered out of the side to glimpse her house.

Strange, she thought, that one could get so turned around, being away just a few days. The house wasn't at all where she expected it to be. Instead, there was an old, ruined building. Confused, she noticed the details: brick walls blackened, roof gone, upstairs windows just gaping holes through which she could see the tranquil evening sky. It was about five o'clock, and the December night would be falling soon.

In a flash of recognition, she saw that it *was* the house. The shape was the same, what there was left of a shape, and it stood on the same spot. Interminable moments later, while her mind raced in horror over the possibilities, the jitney honked its way around the corner and drew up in front of the hospital dispensary. Song Poo-een, the hospital Bible woman, had been watching for Jessie's arrival, conjecturing with loving concern what the shock would be. She came running to the jitney, almost before its wheels had stopped.

"Don't feel badly," she called, throwing away the formality of greeting that Korean etiquette would require. "Don't feel badly! The Doctor is safe, and all of the children!"

And so they all were. But not the house—*our* house. It was as good as gone.

Returning to Korea with his family in 1920, Arch had found that the heating plant he had arranged for, for the doctor's house, had been shipped to China. It took all the money he had for installation—money contributed by family and friends to replace the previous installation fund, which he and Jessie had used to pay for his recuperation at the Trudeau Sanatorium—to get the heating plant reshipped to Taegu, Chosen, Japan. No matter: with the drawings accompanying the plant, some basic pipe-cutting and threading tools, and help from valued friends like Kim Chu-ho, Arch made the time necessary to install the heating plant himself.

The flu pipe from the basement furnace was brought up through carefully insulated openings in all three floors and into the attic, where it made a turn and entered the chimney, joining the flu from the kitchen range. In this way, the large, exposed pipe could help to warm the downstairs and upstairs hallways as it passed through them. A problem, as it turned out, was that soot from the poor grade of soft coal available tended to accumulate in the elbow of pipe in the attic.

On this morning in early December, Arch had a new outside man, who would do the gardening in summer, feed and milk the cow, and tend the fires in winter. This workman knew well the common method of kindling a hearth with *soh-kahp*—pine brush brought in from the hills. The long, dry needles and resinous branches would take fire as if soaked in kerosene. So he applied the same method on a large scale to the foreigner's big furnace contraption.

With a whoosh and a roar the brush heaped in the firebox took hold. Flames shot up the flu pipe all the way to the attic, and the soot in the elbow-pipe took fire. Apparently it was more than the metal could stand. In a few moments flames were licking out, igniting clothing and whatever else stored in the attic that was combustible.

It was breakfast time and we were all at the table, except for Mother, who was in Andong. Dad had a visitor, as happened sometimes, and was discussing some matter of business while having his coffee. We three—Elsie, Archie and I—had come to breakfast in our slippers and had kicked them off under the table, according to our honored custom, when suddenly the *ah-mah*, who had begun work upstairs, came rushing down, literally speechless with fright. Her frantic, incoherent gesticulating sent Dad bounding upstairs, two at a time, with Archie, always the boldest, close on his heels. Elsie went half-way up, and I, not quite four, stayed on the main floor.

The flu pipe in the upstairs hall was red hot and glowing, and in the ceiling, where it went through to the attic, little tongues of flame were licking down around it, held back by its ring of insulation. The *ah-mah* had heard a noise and opened the attic door, to find the attic full of smoke and flames. Fortunately she slammed the door shut, holding back for a few minutes the rush of fire.

Then everything was happening at once. With rare presence of mind the *ah-mah* was rushing into closets, gathering out armloads of our clothes, everything she could jerk off the hooks. Our slippers forgotten, we three ran out onto the cold gravel of the yard, looking up to see flames belching from the attic windows. And because the house stood at the end of the compound, on a steep, stony rise, the alarm was spreading with no need of bell or siren. The structure burned like a torch, plainly visible to much of the city.

Students from the Presbyterian Boys' Academy a quarter of a mile away were the first ones there. They were gathering to go into classes when someone saw the smoke, and their teachers sent the older ones over. Without their help, not much would have been saved, because there was very little water up on the hill, only a slow trickle from faucets downstairs. The boys rushed in and threw trunks, dresser drawers, mattresses, everything they could, out the upstairs windows. Downstairs, they carried almost everything outside, even a ponderous upright piano, one of the old "self-players," which had been left with us by a family going on furlough and which we could hardly have replaced.

One of the most adventurous people helping in the rescue was the Rev. George Winn, a station colleague, although no relation to the late Roger Winn. George made innumerable trips, bringing things out, and was the last to leave the burning building.

"You know, it's a funny thing," he said later, "what it occurs to you to do. That last time in, I saw the curtains hanging between the dining room and the living room. I yanked down the wooden rod, pulled them off it, and then carefully put the rod back up in its sockets."

Moments later, the ponderous tile roof let go with a roar, and the second floor caved in. Nothing was seen of the curtain rod George had put back in its place.

The Japanese police were there, of course, and the firemen. There wasn't much the firemen could do without water, but the police ringed the place and there was no looting. Almost nothing saved from the flames was lost, in spite of the confused melee. The police, always having to arrest someone, locked up our outside man, who had lit the blaze in the furnace, although Dad was able to persuade them later to let him go free.

Most of this we heard afterward, in the recounting and discussion from all angles that so startling an event stirred up in our small community. We three—even Elsie and Archie, who were old enough to have taken in some of the event—didn't see much of the excitement for ourselves. Harriet Bruen next door, who was fifteen, thought it wouldn't be good for impressionable children to watch their home burn. She quickly corralled us and put us in a bedroom of their house, with the blinds drawn. Perhaps she was right. We had seen enough. For the rest of that winter, when we were in another house heated by stoves and the stove door in the bedroom had been left open a crack, letting a ruddy reflection of fire play on the ceiling, we would cry. Mother would have to close that small door to show us that nothing was burning.

Harry Bruen's study was heaped shoulder high with a welter of goods carried from the burning house or gathered from our yard, where they had been thrown from the upstairs windows. The sorting was a long, disheartening job.

Jessie had one treasure, the sterling-silver table service that her family had given her as a wedding present. It was stowed away in the top drawer of an upstairs closet where nobody knew to look for it, but it was the first thing she thought of when she began to take stock on the evening of the day after the fire. What would have happened to it? The drawers and the whole closet were gone. In fact the second floor, most of it, was gone. One could stand on what remained of the first floor and look up to the fireplace of the upstairs bedroom, where, by an odd freak, a fire was still laid and the wood unburned. But the silverware?

That same night two or three of the teen-agers of the station took flashlights and went to probe cautiously in the still-warm ashes directly under the spot where the second-floor closet had been. Sure enough, they uncovered the remains of the silver. The knives had been in cardboard boxes and there was nothing left of them but blackened steel blades. The handles had melted away to so many drops of silver, sunk somewhere in the ashes; but the forks and spoons and flat pieces were wrapped tightly in flannel bags. The flannel was charred and some of the outside pieces were pretty much gone, but those on the inside were in surprisingly good condition.

It was a while yet until the Fletcher family's furlough; but some five years later, in Philadelphia, Jessie took in for refinishing the silver pieces that had been saved. In World War II, they were the only such treasure that survived the breaking up of her and Arch's household. Lugged back to the United States in a suitcase, they somehow made it through the endless baggage inspections to which the "repatriates" were subjected.

## 13

## A Quiet World, and Small

THE TAEGU MEDICAL WORK had reached a stage of steady, uninterrupted growth. From late in 1920 to the spring of 1928, Arch filled out a full term of service, even going a few months beyond the statutory seven years. He had learned his lesson at Trudeau. Now he worked steadily and hard, but he knew his limits.

The biggest concern during this period was for more space. Keeping a steady rhythm, the medical work went on expanding. The quaint, red-brick hospital with its steep-gabled, tiled roof, not much larger than a private dwelling, already seemed like a relic of the past. And although Arch himself had planned the low dispensary building that stood just down the slope from it, this was not much better.

Modern medicine called for specialties and for departments. Arch had an idea of developing a staff of specialists, Korean nationals who might be given an opportunity for training abroad in the specialties they'd shown aptitude for. Personnel, he realized, was the key to a successful operation. He was always on the lookout for people who showed unusual ability and promise, ceaselessly measuring the capabilities and growth of his staff. Above all, he had to gauge the spiritual dimension, the capacity for dedication to the impelling spiritual purpose of this enterprise.

He would not rely on missionary personnel. There was not much choice and, in any case, missionaries were temporary. An institution, to be deep and lasting, must be built on the people of the country. An illustration of this was the experience of his young missionary associate, Spencer Hoyt, MD. Spencer arrived in Korea in 1922, but served in Taegu just five years before his wife's poor health forced his resignation. After that, with the work still expanding steadily, there would be no second missionary physician assigned to Taegu until after World War II, when Arch was no longer there.

He did have the able assistance of Claire Hedberg, RN. Coming to Taegu in December 1923, she took charge of nurses' training and service, giving efficient direction to this department for eleven years, until her marriage in

September of 1934. In terms of missionary personnel, she and Arch were alone for most of that time.

∾ ∾ ∾

As early as 1915 when he was just back from his first furlough, Arch had begun to dream of a modern, fireproof hospital and to sketch tentative plans for it. The board in New York didn't have much money for buildings at the time, but Arch went on sketching and planning. He also busied himself with working his own angles, getting out publicity and cultivating contacts where he could.

The first attempt proved abortive. Capitalizing on the sentiment in the United States toward the close of World War I, Arch prepared a little brochure called "Preparing for Peace," which described medical opportunities for investment in this remote corner of the world. It was sent only to a few friends; the mission board did not look kindly on individual missionaries who canvassed the churches for support of their private projects.

By the mid-1920s, with the same small hospital and dispensary buildings still doing duty in Taegu, Arch's effort began taking on a more formal organization. He had some friends in the United States who agreed to serve as a "home committee" for fund-raising. The goals were both a new outpatient building and the long-projected fireproof hospital.

The campaign proved serious enough that the New York officials began to be somewhat alarmed. There was an exchange of letters. Arch defended his intention. He was soliciting funds among private contacts and not from churches, so that money given would not interfere with the giving of the churches to regular causes of the board. Also, there was already an agreement by the board that some land held in Taegu should be sold and the proceeds applied toward the new hospital. With that much recognition, he argued that the solicitation of the balance needed should be legitimate in the eyes of the board.

The point was granted, and at the end of 1925 Arch was even emboldened to write to Dr. Brown suggesting that a line from him to certain influential persons would surely stimulate their interest in the Taegu hospital.

The campaign moved forward slowly. Promotion in person was the best prospect, after all. Arch saw that the money for the new hospital could not soon be in hand, and began to make plans for an all-out effort on his next furlough. But meanwhile, New York came through with funds for a new dispensary. Ten thousand dollars was granted—an amount that at that time was a beautiful sum.

Joyfully, Arch set to work with a Chinese contractor, Mr. Moh. In the fall of 1927, the walls went up on a long building, severely simple, with an unfinished half-story above the main floor and the possibility of a full basement being excavated below it. The lines of the roof were clean and neat; the material, a whitish asbestos slate, used also on our house when it was rebuilt after the fire, was a tremendous improvement over the heavy and clumsy baked tile.

Archie and I knew about the basement of the new dispensary. As the building was going up, we were old enough to be fascinated by the process; at least he was fascinated by it, and I, the kid brother following his lead, pretended to be equally so and equally knowing. One morning we even played hooky from school.

"School" was Mother teaching us at home with the Calvert School method from Baltimore, which still educates thousands of American children living in far-away places. There was a mid-morning recess, when the three of us went out in the yard to play until Mother rang a bell from an upstairs window to call us in.

On this particular morning, Archie and I didn't hear the bell. We had gone down to the dispensary to watch Mr. McMurtrie, an industrial missionary who had come down from Pyongyang, install the plumbing. He took white asbestos insulating jackets, cut them and fitted them on the hot water pipes, binding each one in place with shiny copper ribbons. It was lovely to watch, all so clean and new.

After a while, we took a kerosene lantern and clambered in under the floor in the half-basement, exploring the nooks and corners, where curly wood shavings were still piled high. Archie had the lantern and began to swing it, watching fantastic shadows dance on the wood shavings, on the floor beams that our heads were just touching, and into the distant corners. When we took up a rhythmic chant, he swung the lantern harder—until suddenly the handle slipped from his fingers.

There was an arc of light, a crash, then a darkness of hideous expectancy. The kerosene would be soaking through the shavings. We could almost hear them ignite with a roar. All the warnings we had heard flashed into our minds, exaggerating the danger; but nothing happened. A few moments passed and our eyes were more accustomed to the darkness. We groped for the lantern—found it, cooling, harmless, and still in one piece. Very quiet and subdued, we crept out of the basement, gave the lantern back to Mr. McMurtrie, and went home to school.

Our world was small in Taegu Station. In the early 1920s it had been larger. Then, there were several families in the station with children older than we—"big kids" whose grown-up games and apparently inexhaustible inventiveness kept us constantly in excited wonderment. There were such novel projects as a rummage sale organized by one of the older boys, at which I paid ten *sen* for an old earthenware ink jug with no stopper and lugged it proudly home.

For a time, the station even had a school. Parents with school-age children went together to support a teacher to come out from the "homeland" (in the expression of that era) and teach their children. Miss Lynette Maas was in Taegu to teach from 1918 to 1920; then, in our time, Miss Clara Gordon opened school in the fall of 1922.

Mother taught Elsie and Archie first grade at home that year. It was evident that six-year-old Elsie needed glasses, but there was no provision for that in Korea. In the spring, after teaching us children at home through the winter, Mother made the long trip with Elsie to Peking, China. There was a skilled oculist at the Peking Union Medical College, a product of Rockefeller philanthropy built in beautiful Chinese style, with sweeping roofs of burnished green tile.

Travel of that sort was an adventure, at best. On the way north to the Korea-Manchuria border, Jessie noticed signs in the railroad stations announcing a new regulation requiring a Japanese visa for return to Japanese territory. As soon as she arrived in Peking, she checked at the Japanese Consulate, and was assured that as a permanent resident in Chosen (Korea), no visa would be required of her.

That was the opinion in Peking. When she was on her way home ten days later, had passed the border at Antung and was rolling south into Korea, the Japanese inspector who came through the train had a different idea.

"You must get off the train," he said. "You have no visa—must go back—must get visa."

Jessie looked out the window in dismay at the northern Korean countryside flicking past. It was getting dark. "But I can't get off the train now with the little girl, and go back."

"You say you can't get off?" the Japanese official bristled. "I put you off."

Jessie saw she must take another tack—it wasn't wise to cross the authority of touchy officialdom. A young Japanese man sitting near joined the conversation in polite English.

"I advise you to go back," he said. "You can get off at the next station and soon the northbound train will pass. At Shingeshu you can stay overnight at the Railroad Hotel and get your visa in the morning."

The thing to do was to comply, with the best grace possible. Dejectedly, Jessie got herself and Elsie off the train at the next stop and sat in a tiny station in the gathering dusk, wondering if the young man had really known about a northbound train. He had. The train came, and finally, about midnight, she was settling Elsie in a very comfortable hotel room at Shingeshu. As for Elsie, it was all a wonderful adventure. In the morning, they took a rickshaw over the bridge to Antung, on the Manchurian side, got the Japanese consul to issue a visa, and were on the southbound train again, just twenty-four hours late.

Elsie and Archie were in Miss Gordon's school for second grade, while I did kindergarten at home. They took me once to visit. The one-room school was an awesome place, the familiar faces of playmates seeming strangely dignified in that unfamiliar setting. I longed to go to school too, but the next year, Miss Gordon returned to the United States to be married, the families with older children were transferred or went on furlough, and the school ceased to be.

Our station settled into what became the pattern of our childhood years. We three and Huldah Blair were the only ones of school age; the other children were infants or pre-schoolers. Our schoolwork was done at home, and our play confined to such games as two boys and two girls could play, or to such adventures as we could contrive.

It was a quiet world, and small, but a good one. There was the "burrow" that we had one year under a large, flat packing case, in a hole in our stony yard that had been excavated, to be filled later with good earth to make a flower bed. The four of us could just about squeeze into the burrow, which seemed a large, cool, dark and different world, once inside. It had straw in the bottom, and one must enter ceremoniously chewing a piece of the smooth, yellow, slightly sweetish rice straw.

In our back yard there was a chicken pen, and a variety of cages for rabbits and guinea pigs. The hospital had guinea pigs for experimental purposes, and we got ours from there, amusing ourselves with the digging habits of *real* "burrowers," the snub-nosed, tailless, little "reekers," as we called them from the sound they made.

These pets gave us a chance to learn something about animal life. Rabbits always seemed such mild creatures; but we had two large males—one of them probably a hare rather than a rabbit. They had to be kept separated. Each one had a guinea pig that shared his cage peacefully enough; but one time the guinea pigs got out, and Pak, the outside-man, inadvertently returned them to the wrong cages. I can still feel our shock when the hare, after a quick sniff at his enemy's guinea pig, turned it over on its back and killed it in an instant with his long, sharp teeth.

Another moment of high drama, in the chicken pen, was supplied by a marauding weasel. One hen had hatched a large brood of chicks, but the quick, vicious weasel carried them off, one by one. In one case, it did so right under our eyes. We were playing in the back yard, and the hen was scratching and clucking with her chicks near a stack of firewood, when suddenly there was the flick of a shadow from under the wood. The weasel moved so fast that we never even saw it clearly; but another chick was gone.

Then one night there was a terrible commotion in the chicken shed. Dad kept some sticks of firewood by a window of the upstairs sleeping porch, and he let fly with these to frighten away the intruder. In the morning, the hen still had what was left of her brood of chicks, but her head and neck were covered with blood.

At last Dad caught the weasel. He got a trap of local design that had a wire cage at one end, where a live chicken was placed as bait. Nothing would happen to the chicken—nothing, that is, except a horribly harrowing night. The prowler, trying to find a way in, would enter an open end of the other section of the trap, step on a treadle, and let the door drop in place behind him.

One night the trap worked. In the morning, there was the weasel—small, snarling, unbelievably ferocious—and the chicken, near collapse with fright, caged right next to it. We tried to feed the weasel raw meat, but only found that it tore its mouth lunging at the fork that we thrust in. In a few days, although we tried other ways of feeding, the wild thing died. We thought it such a prize that we persuaded Dad to have it stuffed and mounted by a taxidermist downtown.

That stuffed weasel, more than anything else, would always arouse the instincts of our little dog, Tootsie. When we got the weasel down from the top of a bookcase in Dad's study, she would race around the house, simply beside her canine self. Even years afterward, when moths got into the stuffed weasel and Mother had to throw it out, we cut off the tip of the tail, and that scrap still had enough scent to put Tootsie in the wildest of moods.

Usually our world was bounded by the enclosures of the compound, which lay along the ridge of a hill, higher at the end on which our house stood. Once in a while, when a spirit of daring seized us, Archie and I would climb over the back wall behind our house. The climbing had to be done at a certain place, and with considerable care not to dislodge the heavy, black tiles that crowned and protected the mud-brick wall. Once over, we were on the east face of the hill, a steep country of overhanging trees and projecting roots, precipitous drops here and there, and secret paths that had to be negotiated almost on hands and knees.

We were not supposed to be there. The adventure had the lure of the forbidden, which we expressed by giving exciting names to the places that we explored.

It would look tame and prosaic enough, if it could be revisited now—even had a generation of war and upheaval, followed by another of astounding material progress, not totally altered the old city. But then, those wonderful childhood regions of "over the wall" can never be revisited in fact, but only in fancy.

I recall a different, but related, scene that unfolded one late afternoon. The level, western rays were filtering through trailing branches of a weeping willow in our front yard, and some strains of a hymn I had heard Mother sing kept coming back to me. My battered bicycle on the ground beside me, I stood alone in the quiet of that afternoon world and felt, in a child's way, the fleetingness of time—the *Weltschmerz* of mortality, the piercingly sweet sadness of it all. Truly, "unless you change and become like children, you will never enter the kingdom of heaven" (Matt. 18:3).

Another boyish pleasure was kite flying. The Korean kite was square and flew on one corner, with a rigid stick bisecting it from that bottom corner to the top one and a curved, flexible stick—a thinner sliver of bamboo—arced between the other two corners. When a gust of wind came, or when the flier pulled hard at the string, this kite could partially fold back its wings, as it were, shooting upward or in the direction at which it was tilted at the moment.

The flying of the flexible kite could be developed to a high degree of skill. The stout thread used was wound on a large wooden reel, quite heavy and hung in such a way—with a central axis held in one hand and an off-center hand grip at the opposite reel-end in the other hand—that the reel could be swung, and the kite reeled in at an amazing speed, or the reel could suddenly be turned on end, letting the thread whip out in free fall. For fighting, the thread, or at least a considerable piece of it near the kite, was dipped in glue and passed through powdered glass. This made it a bit stiff, but when it could be crossed, taut, against the thread of another kite and pulled to saw back and forth, the other kite was cut away, to go drifting helplessly and ingloriously down the breeze.

We did some kite fighting on our own, Archie and I, but our biggest thrill was to perch on the tiles of the back wall on a long, late-spring evening and watch a fight in progress between some of the *real* fliers. These were usually not boys; they were young men. From the top of the wall, we could see them below, down on a wide street by the open sewer ditch. They would be fifteen or twenty yards apart, each with a knot of admirers and kibitzers around him. Looking the other way—high, high up in the western sky—we could see their kites, watch them dive and twist and turn in an aerial dogfight as the skillful reel-handling of the fliers maneuvered them.

Sometimes the fight would end in a draw, and the kites would be reeled in when it was almost too dark to see. Other times one would be cut and would fall away into the sunset, perhaps to be picked up by some eager boy and to fly again. Our compound, with its trees lifted above that part of the city, caught quite a few derelict kites, which we sometimes were able to salvage, occasionally getting a big, excellent flier. Sometimes a boy who owned one would come to recover his treasure, and we would pass the kite over the wall and be rewarded by a broad smile.

The widest world of adventure was opened to us in those years by our bicycles. Archie had an American Ranger—a big, heavy affair with marvelous attachments—which he had won by writing to every relative and friend we had in the United States, persuading them to subscribe to the American Medical Association's *Hygeia* magazine. What a proud day, when his reward, the bicycle, at last came through the Japanese customs and was uncrated!

My "wheel," by contrast, was a veteran: a small-sized, stripped-down vehicle that was several years older than I. It had been passed from one family to another, with almost every child in the station learning to ride on it. It represented the minimum in equipment: no mud guards, no brake of any kind—one just held back on the pedals, as there was no coaster-brake, or, for sharper braking, jammed his shoe against the front tire.

Down the hill we would go, through the front gate of the compound, past the entrance of the new dispensary, where it was being built, across the market place—almost deserted if it wasn't market day—and on and on, by one of the roads that led into open country. A favorite ride was along the Egg Hill Road, which ran, after some three miles, past the foot of a symmetrical, egg-shaped hill that had a small lake or pond by its base. There might be a skin of ice on the pond in winter, even, rarely, enough ice for some precarious skating.

Dad had a wonderful pair of shiny skates that clamped onto his shoes, the runners curling up over the toes in a graceful arc. We would hear the ice hiss and, in thin places, crackle ominously under those runners. Of course the day came when Archie, as a teenager with his tubular hockey skates, would criss-cross around Dad's wonderful, silver runners, but that was later, when the world had already lost a good deal of its magic, or changed it for a different sort of excitement.

We usually stopped our bikes at Egg Hill, but one hot spring day, we went on. We followed the road for miles, further than we had ever known it to go, and came at last to the river. What a thrill, to lay the bikes down and rest wearily on the bank, watching the flow of muddy water, shrunken in its course at that time of year, but seeming as broad and as mysterious as the Mississippi!

It was the same Nak Tong, the river down which, about 1900, the timbers for building the first missionary houses in Taegu had been floated, while Dr. Johnson, in a canvas boat, had paddled vigorously to snare them and bring them to shore. It was the river on which the goods of the early missionaries, including the first piano seen in that part of Korea, had been brought up from the coast, making the nearest approach possible by boat to Taegu.

Our childhood was between the times—the rugged early pioneering of the late nineteenth century and the unthought-of upheaval and progress of the latter half of the twentieth century.

∽ ∽ ∽

Meanwhile, Arch's expanding medical work kept him busy. He was in the time of his early maturity, his beginning and middle forties. Beyond the immediate concerns of the general hospital and the efforts in behalf of lepers, other projects were interesting him. Always preoccupied by the problem of tuberculosis, a problem that war conditions in Korea were later to lift to the first level of public need, he translated to Korean, between 1924 and '25, a pamphlet on the cure of tuberculosis. It was first printed in serial form in the *Christian Messenger*, a weekly newspaper of the Korean Church, and later as a small book.

In 1926 Arch went to Tokyo for a meeting of the Far Eastern Association of Tropical Medicine, formed six years earlier. It was an opportunity to meet leading doctors in the field from all over the Far East and also to enjoy lavish hospitality.

The Japanese government, playing host for the first time to this new association, was anxious to impress the visitors with that nation's own advances in the science of medicine as well as with the beauty of the country. After the week of the conference—mornings for scientific meetings, afternoons for visits to hospitals and other institutions, evenings for banquets and social affairs—the delegates had free, first-class railroad passes for two weeks to take them all over the islands.

Arch would not take so long away from home and duty. After two days, he turned in his pass and "came down to earth once again," as he put it, crossing the Japan Strait second class to Korea. He arrived in Taegu with some wonderful souvenirs of Japan in his suitcase, including a silver napkin ring with his name on it and the graceful silhouette of Fujiyama. That napkin ring always had, for us children, a mystic aura of authority and wonder.

In late August of the same year, Arch went to Peking for the biennial meeting of the China Medical Association. Invited to read a paper on hospital evangelism, with particular reference to the program in Taegu that was registering such extraordinary success, he was also much interested in listening and in observing trends in medical work in the much larger and more widely spread mission installations of China. From the conference, he brought home two strong emphases, both of which would be reflected in his own work.

The first of these was the prevention of disease. The conference had underscored public health measures for that purpose. Arch had been thinking about such a goal, seeing in it a prospect of more effective service and also of regaining a lost initiative in Korea. As he wrote to Dr. Brown in New York a few weeks later, commenting on the conference:

> While the sick people come to the mission hospitals for relief, . . . we no longer have the prestige gained by being the only or principal institution for healing in any given district. This prestige can to some extent be regained by becoming pioneers in prevention of disease, just as we were first in the cure of diseases some years ago.

Specifically, Arch was thinking of a prenatal clinic and of baby welfare. Several years would pass before he would find the means and time to translate these thoughts into reality—but it was part of his make-up to be always turning over in his mind projects that were more than he could yet realize.

The Peking Conference also discussed "devolution" in medical work, which was a second emphasis that Arch brought home from it. The term was in vogue in those days. As the national churches grew in strength, proponents said, the missions should be transferring to them responsibility for projects and institutions the missions had initiated. Arch was heartily in agreement. More attention should be given to devolution in Korea, he thought. In effect, the Taegu Hospital would be the first Presbyterian hospital in Korea (Severance, in Seoul, being a union institution) to have a board of directors composed of an equal number of Korean Christians and missionaries—although this step, like the baby welfare clinic, would not be taken until after Arch's furlough.

As the furlough date approached, he was busy with the completion of the new dispensary building. At last, a scant month before our family left the country, it stood ready. Off the gleaming central corridor, rooms opened on both sides. For the first time, there were separate facilities for the principal specialties: for surgical consultations and treatment, for obstetrics and gynecology, internal medicine, pediatrics, and eye-ear-nose-and-throat. There was also an x-ray room and darkroom, a laboratory, a drug room, waiting rooms, and the necessary offices. The next thing would be the preparation of enough physicians to staff adequately all of the specialties.

At the same time, Arch was preparing for his furlough in another way. It seems strange in the present perspective, two generations later, that up to that time no mission hospital in Korea had undertaken to keep its doors open during an extended absence of its missionary superintendent. Arch devised a plan to change that pattern. Taegu would not ask for a replacement for him during his furlough. The staff, which under Arch's leadership had developed a real *esprit de corps*, would carry on just as if he were there. Monthly reports would go to him in the United States, and he would keep as constantly in touch as the slow boat-mail could manage.

He was ready to attempt a delicate balancing act, leaving the day-to-day operations to a staff in which he had confidence while still maintaining some oversight from afar. It was a bold scheme. Not ready to step out altogether, not by a good many years, he was to a degree making a declaration of independence from the doctrine of the indispensable Westerner.

## 14

## Romance, Tragedy and Opportunity of Leprosy Treatment

IN 1924 THERE WAS a celebration in Taegu. Word had gone out from the London headquarters of the Mission to Lepers that the fiftieth anniversary of its founding by Mr. Wellesley C. Bailey should be suitably observed. In Taegu seven years had passed since that memorable fall day in 1917 when some three thousand people, seated row on row on mats spread across the level ground and up the slope, had witnessed the dedication of the first three buildings of the Taegu Leper Hospital. Much had happened in those seven years.

Arch, dealing principally with the American Committee of the Mission to Lepers, and with its diligent and genial secretary, William M. Danner, had been pressing ahead with expansion. A gift from the Parkersburg Missionary Federation of Parkersburg, West Virginia, had enabled him to erect a different type of living quarters—a two-story brick building consisting simply of four large rooms, two on each floor. The construction was Western-style, with wood floors and with stoves for heating, rather than the flu-heated floors of the earlier, Korean-style buildings.

The concession to national custom, however—both practical and economical—was that the twenty patients lodged in each large room unrolled their bedding at night and slept on the gleaming wood floor. No furniture was needed beyond a row of lockers on one wall for them to stow bedding and personal possessions. By day they sat on the floor cross-legged, in the posture so natural to them from childhood and so painfully awkward to us Westerners, accustomed to our chairs. When they entered, the patients left their shoes at the door, which reduced the labor of cleaning and kept the wood polished to a beautiful shine. As washrooms and hygienic facilities were located elsewhere, the dormitory building was kept simple to an extreme.

For the Taegu Leper Hospital, the timing of the Mission to Lepers' fiftieth anniversary was just right. Not only was the Parkersburg Building just finished, the Japanese Government of Chosen had also made a grant of Yen 7,700 ($3,850), with which Arch had been able to enlarge the hospital's small dispensary building and greatly improve its facilities.

These advances were dedicated in an anniversary ceremony that followed closely the pattern of the 1917 celebration. Again, the highest Japanese officials of the province were there, including the governor, who said in part in his fervent address:

> Among many dedication ceremonies I am grateful for the opportunity of attending this, the most important one.... My wish is that all those on the outside now afflicted with this dreadful disease may have an opportunity to enter the hospital for treatment and that a sure method of preventing the disease may be found.

The governor's wish was far from achievable at the time, although the Taegu Leper Hospital was able to add, in the following year, a companion dormitory building on the women's side of the campus. The Anderson Memorial was given by the Princeton, New Jersey, Auxiliary of what had by then become the American Mission to Lepers—and Arch continued to press ahead constantly on treatment of the disease.

As a young, single doctor on his first assignment to Taegu, he had purchased that small, one-room house, not more than a shelter for six leper boys and men, to have a place to live out what was left of their lives. Then chaulmoogra oil treatment began to be explored. Arch wrote about that in 1925, in a pamphlet that he called *Romance, Tragedy and Opportunity of Leprosy Treatment*. The remedy was ancient. As he noted:

> In the treatment of this disease there has been known for many centuries to the peoples of Asia a valuable medicament called, in the Indian vernacular, "Chulmoogra." In other countries it has other names. The Burmese call it "Kalaw"—in Assam it is known as "Lemtam." In China its name is "Ta Feng Tzu." The history of this drug dates back to time immemorial.

The "Romance" of Arch's pamphlet was a legend, recorded by Joseph F. Rock of Burma, telling of a Princess Piya of northern India, back in the remote times before the Buddha, who had contracted leprosy. The five princes and four princesses, her brothers and sisters, took her on a trip deep into the jungle and left her there in a cave with a very narrow entrance, stocking the cave well with all kinds of provisions.

It happened (as, of course, it would happen) that living in the same jungle was an ex-king, Rama, once ruler of Benares, who had abdicated his throne when he developed symptoms of leprosy and had gone into voluntary exile. Rama lived in the hollow trunk of a great jungle tree. For some time he had subsisted chiefly on the fruits and leaves of the kalaw tree, which had wrought a marvelous cure in him. Not only had his symptoms of leprosy disappeared, but he also felt stronger and better than he had ever felt when surrounded by the luxury of his palace.

One day a tiger, prowling near Piya's cave, was attracted by the scent of a human being. It tried frantically to enter the cave. Piya, horrified, gave a piercing scream. Rama heard the cry and noted carefully the direction from which it came, and the next day he discovered the cave.

"Who lives in the cave?" he shouted.

Piya answered, and courtly greetings were exchanged. She told the stranger her story, but was too shy and modest to come out. So Rama succeeded where the tiger had failed. He squeezed into the cave and carried Piya off to his hollow trunk, where he fed her the fruits, roots and leaves of the kalaw tree. She, too, was soon cured of leprosy and began to bear Rama a series of sixteen pairs of twins, giving him thirty-two sons. So marvelous, it would seem, was the virtue of the kalaw tree.

English physicians traveling in the Far East learned rather early of the use of this efficacious drug, and an oil, *chaulmoogra*, began to be extracted from the seeds of this species of *hydnocarpus*. The problem was that trying to take the oil by mouth provoked violent nausea, and injecting it subcutaneously frequently produced abscesses. In 1920 Doctors McDonald and Dean, working in the Philippine Islands and applying the chemistry of the oil, produced a preparation of mixed ethyl esters derived from it. They found that these could be injected in four parts, with one part of camphor oil to lessen pain and promote absorption. Given as a deep intramuscular injection, the substance seldom produced an abscess.

The results were most encouraging when injections of from four to nine cc were given twice weekly, with the smaller dose given at the beginning and gradually increased according to the age, health and strength of the patient. Early cases could frequently be arrested after as little as six months of treatment, although often the treatment had to continue for several years.

In Taegu Arch took up eagerly the chaulmoogra oil treatment of leprosy. He was glad to use the ethyl esters, when these were provided without charge by the Japanese government. In the later 1920s and early '30s he began to conduct some experiments on his own with use of the whole oil. It was widely thought that plain chaulmoogra oil, in large doses, would have a toxic effect on the human system, because such effects had been shown in experiments with rabbits. Arch was not convinced, noting that rabbits commonly had difficulty assimilating fats. He selected patients having no complication except Hansen's Disease (the more technical and less prejudicial term for leprosy), and began, under strictly controlled conditions, to administer to them rather large doses of whole chaulmoogra oil, combined with pure olive oil—three parts chaulmoogra to one part olive. Why olive oil? Because of its nutritional value and because it is easily absorbed by the tissues of the body. One idea Arch was busy introducing to the regimen of the Taegu Leper Hospital was that recovery from the disease could be aided by making a patient's general health as robust as possible.

The results of whole oil treatment proved heartening. Arch found that the oil received directly from Thailand seemed to be purer and to produce less irritation than that obtained from India or Japan. He started his selected patients on lower doses, gradually increasing the amount of the chaulmoogra-olive mixture they were given. Meanwhile the most careful check was kept on these patients, watching for the least sign of toxic effect, which might mean that their doses should be reduced again.

A modified sedimentation test of the blood, developed by Dr. Muir of India, was run frequently. The test indicated the patient's resistance, increased resistance meaning that an increased dose could be given. At the same time, an accurate and detailed clinical chart, on which Arch placed more reliance than on the sedimentation test, showed a record of temperature, pulse, respiration, and so forth, helping him and his assistants keep a constant watch for any symptom of toxic reaction. Where there was no contra-indication, the dose went up one cc every two weeks.

In Tokyo in 1931, Arch read a paper to an audience at the Imperial University, before the fourth annual meeting of the Leprosy Association in Japan. In the paper, titled "Massive Doses of Chaulmoogra Oil in the Treatment of Leprosy," he reviewed other methods of treatment and then reported on the experience at the Taegu Leper Hospital. Of its four hundred patients, 266 were receiving twenty cc or more of the chaulmoogra-olive mixture twice weekly, and of these, 107 were getting thirty cc, with the dose still being increased.

None of the cases, Arch reported, had shown even the first manifestations of a toxic effect, such as loss of appetite, nausea, and vomiting; nor was there evidence of any kidney irritation, also thought to be an effect of too-large doses of chaulmoogra oil. Occasionally an abscess would form at the site of injection, but this was due to infection and not related to the size of the dose. One assistant, who took greater care than others with injections, could report having given 10,408 of them with only one abscess.

Beyond use of the oil, Arch reported very satisfactory results in the improvement of his patients. This was not easily measured and scientifically tabulated because, in dealing with a disease like leprosy, improvement was at best slow and uncertain. Nevertheless, he was convinced by results that his theory was sound: the more chaulmoogra oil that could be absorbed by the body, the brighter would be the prospects of an early arresting of the disease.

The conclusions expressed in Arch's paper were significant for his time. Up until a few weeks before Pearl Harbor, he continued to order and receive large consignments of chaulmoogra oil from Thailand. The treatment of Hansen's Disease has long since left such methods behind; but it was chaulmoogra oil, in Taegu, which first turned what had begun as an asylum, simply a place of refuge, into a leprosy hospital.

By the mid-1920s, with the capacity of the hospital at four hundred, about fifty patients were being discharged each year with the disease apparently arrested. Arch was eager to get early cases, in which the prognosis was much more favorable. Such cases might be treated and discharged, making way for other patients to be received.

At the same time, the problem was how to steel oneself against the wretchedness and need of those who were sunk far down in the disease. This was particularly harrowing in the case of women lepers, because of the outlook for them. As Arch wrote in a report in 1922, using the "editorial we," as he always did:

> We have been puzzled, perplexed and worried often during the year because of women lepers, who have come seeking admission to the Leper Hospital when there is no room. Not that we have not had to turn away men lepers, for we have, and many of them. The women present a difficult problem, because soon after a new applicant arrives from the country, the men lepers at liberty in this district become aware of her presence and then sit in wait for her. If she cannot be admitted and is turned away, these villains at once kidnap her, and from then on her life is hardly to be compared to that of a dog.

In general Arch kept pressing for getting early cases. A number of patients with very advanced cases were housed in older, Korean-style buildings at the back part of the property. It would wring the heart to visit that section—to have seen what a ghastly ruin disease could make of the human form, created "in the image of God."

Yet, incomprehensibly, the image was still there. Many of these patients, who had nothing left in this life, were already living by faith in a life to come. Crippled, maimed, blinded, an unearthly light would come over their wasted faces—as I have seen it—when Dad spoke to them of their Savior Jesus. It was an extreme, radiant vindication of life over death.

The treatment of the leprosy patients involved a tremendous amount of work. The report for one year, 1926-27, showed 37,843 injections given. In addition, some two-thirds of the patients had some kind of external ulcer resulting from the disease, and these had to be dressed daily. That year 72,124 dressings were done. At least, in the treatment of these ulcers, the local anesthesia, which is a characteristic effect of the disease, was merciful. I vividly recall seeing some of the most appalling, open sores imaginable being dressed, while the patient never twitched a muscle because he could feel no pain.

Leprosy is not highly contagious, but rather to a low degree infectious—similar to tuberculosis, only lower. The bacillus causing it, *mycobacterium leprae*, first isolated and identified in 1874 by Norwegian scientist Gerhard Hansen, seems to be transmitted only by prolonged contact with a person suffering from the disease in the "open," or communicable, phase. Is it a disease of the tropics—is climate a factor? Perhaps so, although cases occur well outside the tropics.

Indeed, in the Middle Ages, leprosy was a scourge in far-from-tropical Europe, until the most drastic segregation virtually eliminated it. It appears probable that malnutrition, crowding, unsanitary conditions, and the general wretchedness of dense populations in underprivileged areas have more to do with the spread of the disease than climate does. Now, in the second decade of the twenty-first century, the use of several antibiotics has brought leprosy largely under control. It is still a problem, notably in India, but in 2012 the estimated total of cases globally was down to 180,000.

In Taegu, Arch set out to do all he could for the living conditions of patients in the hospital. This meant bathing and general sanitation. He pressed the city authorities to build a pipeline from the city water system to the leper hospital. On the campus, to replace the more primitive facilities, he planned a group of central service buildings. They would include a dining hall, kitchen, laundry, washrooms, bathrooms, and toilets, all with running hot and cold water.

Improved living conditions also meant better diet. To accomplish this, an institution operating on a very slender budget would have to produce more of its own food. The patients were receiving a daily ration of two parts rice and one part barley, with a small amount of soy beans, some fresh vegetables part of the year, fish once a week, and occasionally a little rabbit meat. This last came from a few rabbit hutches tended by the patients themselves.

Arch began to conceive the idea of radically expanding such activity into a sort of model farm. There couldn't be much agriculture—the hospital had only a modest amount of land—but a department of animal husbandry might be developed, and so it would be, although not yet.

Animal husbandry could be almost more valuable in another way than in supplementing diet. Among the worst results of leprosy were the unseen ravages of mind and spirit. To realize that one had fallen victim to the most loathed and hated of all diseases, to be ostracized by society, put out by one's own family—to see love and family affection turn to revulsion—planted a cancer in the soul. Let the hospital give these lives, tossed out like potsherds on the refuse heap of the world, something useful and meaningful that they could do. Let it prepare them, some of them at least, to go back one day to their agrarian society, healed and taking with them a skill and knowledge that would give them even a little extra that they could offer; and, above all, let it point a way toward healing their crushed and alienated spirits.

This last was, uniquely, the Christian side of the hospital's ministry. From the time patients were admitted, they began to hear the Christian message. They did not hear it from foreigners, except occasionally, but from the Korean pastor who served the Leper Hospital Church and, most convincingly, from their fellow patients. From the early 1920s, the hospital had included on its staff a fulltime pastor, and soon afterward the patients who were Christians were organized into a church. It even came to have a missionary society. What the patients in a leprosy hospital could do in the way of missionary work might seem quite little, but the society found at least two expressions for its purpose.

It organized the approach to be made to new patients, to bring the Christian message personally to each one and encourage them to believe; and it gathered offerings, out of the poverty of these people who had almost nothing in this life, to contribute toward carrying the Gospel to sufferers from leprosy on the outside. In 1927, Arch reported that average weekly contributions per patient were slightly over one US cent. Yet, partly due to the efforts of this Society, and partly to the ministry of the pastor of the hospital church and to other forms of witness, the time came when among lepers of the province, there were ten Christian groups of fifty to eighty members each.

The last building Arch had the satisfaction of seeing completed at the leper hospital in this term of service was the chapel. Like the rest of the campus, it was simple and functional, with just a few touches to set it apart from other structures. Made possible by a gift of five thousand dollars from the American Mission to Lepers, the construction was done in the summer of 1927 and the chapel dedicated that September.

The first floor had classrooms, used for Sunday school and also for the day school in which younger patients received primary school instruction. In addition, there were offices for the administrator and the pastor, and a meeting room for the elected members of the church's session. The second floor, with a higher ceiling, housed the chapel and auditorium. It had Gothic-arched windows at the ends and direct access by a wide, external flight of steps.

Worshippers sat cross-legged on the floor in the traditional manner, affording an excellent economy of space. Down the center of the room ran a low, movable partition, separating the men's section from the women's and preserving the strictest propriety. For the reassurance of guests who might be nervous about close contact with the patients, the speakers' proscenium had a back section, glassed off and accessible by separate stairs. The glass panes could be slid open when a guest wished to speak to the congregation.

This leper hospital church gave an extraordinary witness. In the winter of 1926, Arch had an opportunity to visit a leprosy colony established by the Japanese government on Little Deer Island, off the southwest coast of Korea, and to confirm an unusual story. The Little Deer colony had been set up ten years earlier and, to keep the virtual inmates from escaping, equipped with a high, barbed-wire fence and guard stations for the soldiers who patrolled the place. When the first buildings were completed, the authorities instructed police to find and send to the colony two lepers from each county of the southern provinces.

In the county of Taegu, the police reported that they could find no lepers and asked permission to take two from the hospital, which was still a small establishment. This was odd, considering the long waiting list at the Taegu facility, even at that time. But at length Arch agreed, and two Christian patients were selected to be sent.

One of them, Chang Cha-sun, had a Bible. Reaching the Little Deer colony, he and his companion found about 130 others already there, among them five or six fellow Christians. Chang Cha-sun read from his Bible, interesting others in the colony in the readings; but the superintendent, informed of this, forbade the Christians to gather for Bible study or worship.

A shrine was being completed in the colony, and soon the "National Spirit of Japan" would be brought to reside there. That autumn a Shinto priest and Japanese policemen accompanied the National Spirit from the capital in Japan, and as evidence of the spirit's presence, his tablet was placed in the shrine. Every leper had to bow before the tablet, and Chang Cha-sun, the Christian, had to conform. Bible study, however, was carried on in secret.

Then came a change in officials overseeing the colony. The new superintendent made a tour of inspection of the Taegu and other Christian leper institutions. He was amazed that these institutions had no barbed-wire fences or pickets—that instead they had long lists of applicants waiting to be admitted.

On his return to the government colony, the new superintendent declared religious liberty. The Christians could meet openly, and they were soon reinforced by the arrival of others from the Taegu district. Patients at the Taegu hospital sent them about twenty Bibles and hymnals. Not long after this, a high officer from the Government General, on visiting the colony, left a present of two hundred yen ($100) for the lepers. A cow was bought and slaughtered for a feast and a few musical instruments purchased, and then the balance of the present, surprisingly, was turned over to the Christians to buy more hymnbooks and Bibles.

From that point on, Christian services were held in the shrine each Sunday. The superintendent even invited a Japanese pastor from the Korean mainland to come and preach. After doing so for some time, this pastor was able to arrange the transfer to the colony of a patient who had some preparation as a preacher as well as knowledge of the Japanese language for official contacts. This young man, after something of a struggle, won acceptance by the Christian lepers and served them faithfully for three years, until he died.

The changes in the leper colony were striking. When Arch visited Little Deer Island, in December 1926, he found that of 250 lepers in the colony, two hundred were Christians. The military guard was gone, and the deserted guard stations were falling apart. The Tablet of the National Spirit remained, respectfully protected in a small room, but the rest of the shrine had become a Christian church, and there was peace and harmony in the colony.

The Little Deer colony eventually grew very large. In the Japanese government's effort to round up all lepers and eliminate the disease from southern Korea, the colony housed, at its peak, some five thousand patients—probably the largest institution of its kind in the world.

After his visit that December, Arch saw a chance to accomplish two purposes at once. One of his problems was what to do with the "burnt-out" cases in his hospital. These were more-or-less advanced cases in which the disease, whether as a result of treatment or simply in taking its natural course, had reached a point of stabilization. These cases were apparently arrested—there was no evidence of any danger of infection to others—yet the ravages of the disease had already left deformities that meant the patient could not be returned to society. Although without reason, horror of the disease would keep such a person ostracized. The only course remaining was to give him or her shelter and food and, if possible, a useful occupation, as long as he or she lived.

Arch's problem was that in his relatively small hospital the patients with burnt-out cases occupied spaces that could be used for treating earlier cases and returning them to the outside world. Little Deer, backed directly by government resources and designed more as a colony than a hospital, might agree to take many of these people with burnt-out cases and ease the problem for Taegu.

At the same time, such transfers could serve a greater purpose. These patients would all have been in the Hospital for two or three years, at least. By that time, most of them would have become staunch Christians. They might receive their transfer as a mission to carry the hope of the Gospel to fellow patients in the government colony.

# 15

# Treatment Stations—a Bright Hope Eclipsed

IN THE EARLY 1920S, Arch conceived a bold idea for carrying the fight against leprosy into the field. The success of the chaulmoogra treatment was encouraging, particularly in cases that were dealt with early in the progress of the disease. If somehow all early cases in a given area—say, in North Kyung Sang Province—could be discovered and brought under treatment, if those in the infectious stage could be isolated, if healthy children could be separated from affected parents, couldn't leprosy be stamped out altogether in that area in a matter of years? In his annual report of the Taegu Leper Hospital for 1923-24 Arch wrote:

> The ever-increasing number of patients being dismissed as apparently cured makes us long to be able to place the benefits of the modern treatment within reach of every leper in the Province. It has long been our dream to send out a qualified assistant who would visit regularly once a week each of six large towns in the Province, holding a clinic and administering treatment to all the lepers in and around each town. By this means, hundreds whom we could never care for in our institution could be treated, patients needing hospital treatment could better be selected, and those discharged as free from symptoms could be kept under observation and further treatment administered, if desirable.
>
> It will always be financially impossible to care for more than a fraction of the lepers in this Province by gathering them into institutions. But what a great and beneficent work could be done by making the modern treatment easily accessible to all! Such a program, if inaugurated, would inspire us with new enthusiasm in our task and would bring the day near when our dream of ridding the country of this baneful disease might be realized.

Here was the essential idea of a new plan of attack. By the following year, 1925, Arch had developed it further. He had realized that, given the situation—the twice-weekly frequency of treatments and need for careful control of each case—the type of mobile clinic suggested in his 1923–24 report would not answer the problem.

The result was a more carefully worked out plan for ten treatment stations, to cover the province. This plan was the essence of the pamphlet that he prepared that year and that has been reviewed, in part, above: *Romance, Tragedy and Opportunity of Leprosy Treatment*. In the pamphlet, after relating the legendary Romance of Rama and Piya, Arch went on to outline what he saw as a looming real-life tragedy, in his province of southern Korea:

> The Taegu Leper Hospital is located in the capital of North Kyung Sang Province. At present it accommodates 410 lepers. In this Province, with an area of about 7,300 square miles and a population of a little more than 2,000,000, a recent survey revealed the location of 1,700 lepers. Undoubtedly there are a few hundred not yet discovered. For financial and other reasons, the Leper Hospital has almost reached the limit of its capacity. Two thousand lepers in the province are depending upon us for treatment. Shall they suffer and die without help when there is a well established remedy?

To counter this, Arch went on, in his pamphlet, to offer what he characterized as an "opportunity." This he expressed in terms of the confident assurance that he himself knew, better than anyone, was a long distance from realization:

> The plan is to get all the lepers in this Province under treatment as soon as possible. To this end, Treatment Stations will be established in centers where the greatest number of lepers are located. This will be a comparatively inexpensive method, as the great majority of lepers who will come regularly to the Stations for treatment will continue to live in their homes and be self-supporting.
>
> When conditions in the home, or the nature of the disease, indicate the need of isolation, such cases will be referred to the Taegu Leper Hospital. Patients discharged from the hospital as apparently cured will be kept under observation at the Treatment Station nearest their home, and additional treatment given, if indicated.
>
> As the disease is not hereditary, untainted children of leper parents will be removed to a Home for such children, where they will be properly cared for and permitted to grow up healthy and strong. This Home will be centrally located in the City of Taegu.

> Medical supervision of these Treatment Stations will be provided by a Korean doctor, who will have an itinerary that will make possible a visit to each station once a week, or once every ten days. To visit each of ten stations, the doctor will travel a distance of 322 miles. . . .
>
> At each Treatment Station will be permanently located a nurse, or someone qualified to give the hypodermic treatments. Preferably, the nurse shall be one who, in the early stage of the disease, entered the Leper Hospital as a patient, where he was not only made free from all symptoms, but trained in the treatment and care of the disease.

It was a bold proposal. Arch followed it, in the pamphlet, with a remarkable budget, built on the assumption that the Japanese government would provide the ethyl esters (still being used at that time) for injections, free of charge. The budget included five hundred dollars each, to buy ten sites and erect ten buildings—that made five thousand dollars. Then came an annual amount of only $3,352—to cover the salary and expenses of a Korean doctor, salaries for ten assistants, and minimal operating expenses for the ten treatment stations. There was also an outline map of the province, showing the proposed locations of the ten stations and the distances between them. Arch ended the pamphlet with a final appeal:

> Such an opportunity as this will find its climax either in a great tragedy or a great romance. If treatment is withheld, 2,000 lepers without any hope of a cure will be left to the ravages of the most loathsome of all diseases, which destroys both the flesh and the spirit. As the 2,000 deteriorate, they will gradually spread the infection—hundreds of others will contract the disease—hundreds of children fall victims to their parents' malady—and thus the vicious cycle of the tragedy of leprosy without treatment will go on.
>
> On the other hand, if treatment is made available according to the plan proposed above, a new chapter will be written in the history of leprosy, a chapter full of thrilling interest and with a "happy ending" that might well rival that of any ancient romance. It would mean not only that 2,000 lepers would be given new life and new hope, but the other 2,000,000 inhabitants of the Province would be safeguarded from the contagion of this dreaded disease, and perhaps the first forward step taken in a definite program to "rid the world of leprosy."

For once Arch had a response that actually exceeded his ability to use it. He had appealed for funds for his treatment station program to be sent to the office of the American Mission to Lepers in New York. The funds began to pour in. His pamphlet was taken up and reprinted as an article in the *Hospital Social Service* magazine in 1926. A nurse in the United States read the article and immediately sat down and wrote to Arch. She would like to come out to Korea to help in this program to stamp out leprosy in an entire province of the country.

But Arch was running into opposition from an unexpected quarter. The Japanese authorities had an absolute horror of leprosy. In the early days of their colony on Little Deer Island, the physician in attendance wore hip-length rubber boots, a gown reaching below the knees, and surgical gloves and mask—to protect against any possibility of infection. The government was glad to cooperate in the support of the Taegu Leper Hospital, but it favored a pattern of segregation and was afraid of the treatment-station proposal: such stations, encouraging patients to remain in their own homes, would imperil the health of the community. Further, the authorities argued, many lepers had been put out of their homes. They were vagrants and beggars. If a treatment station were established in a given place, they would tend to cluster around it, putting up shacks and camping in the vicinity, constituting a menace to the healthy community.

Arch pleaded with the authorities. Meanwhile, letters from Executive Secretary Danner of the American Mission to Lepers began to arrive, pleading with him. Couldn't he do something to get that treatment station program going? Money was still coming in. People were asking about it. Professional leprologists in other parts of the world were interested.

Arch wrote back with chagrin that Dr. José Rodríguez, former physician-in-chief of the Culion Colony in the Philippines, had made a personal trip from Kobe to get first-hand knowledge of the plan, and that Dr. Gushue-Taylor of Formosa, while touring Oriental countries to investigate leprosy problems, had sent a request for an appointment to survey the Taegu project.

The chief objection of health authorities of the Government of Chosen in Seoul was that the local communities would vigorously oppose the establishment of leprosy treatment stations. At last, they agreed to what Arch was then asking for: the establishment of three stations as test projects. If the tests turned out as they feared, he would give up the program; but if all went well, he could proceed. In November 1926, he wrote to New York that permission had been secured. In a second letter two months later, he reported: "We are now selecting sites and hope to commence work on buildings as soon as cold weather passes."

Then came a hurdle he hadn't figured on. Although the central government authorities had given their permission, the head of the provincial department of hygiene would not. This petty official was already vexed, as it seemed. It was his duty to escort official Japanese visitors from Seoul or Tokyo to the Taegu Leper Hospital, and he disliked hearing them exclaim over work for which he could not take any credit.

Arch wrote to Danner in May, "I have told him that we would turn the whole work over to him any day, if the Government would back him and produce the support."

The gesture was safe enough, as both Arch and the official knew. Government was glad to have the work done under private auspices, even if these were Christian, with no more responsibility for the officials than to approve the sending of an annual subsidy.

To block establishment of treatment stations, which would be one thing more that he would have to take admiring visitors to see, and yet not to oppose his superiors in Seoul, the provincial head of hygiene declared that the Koreans were objecting to putting leprosy treatment stations in their communities. Arch countered the objection with a move both decisive and face-saving. In the village of Koon Ee, where he hoped to place the first station, he arranged to have a petition circulated by the villagers themselves. The petition was an expression of thanks to the superintendent of the Taegu Leper Hospital for his intention to start a work of treating leprosy in their district.

The stratagem worked. Arch had written to Danner that spring (1927):

> It is a great disappointment to us to be thus held back by one petty, jealous official, but we are determined that full approval will be secured before driving a nail.

That fall nails were being driven at Koon Ee, and in the spring, just before he left on furlough, Arch had the immense satisfaction of seeing the first rural Leprosy Treatment Station of the province go into operation.

Three years later, in March 1931, Arch went to Tokyo to the Imperial University, for the fourth annual meeting of the Leprosy Association of Japan. At that meeting, as commented above in chapter 14, he read a paper on "Massive Doses of Chaulmoogra Oil in the Treatment of Leprosy." At the same meeting he read a second paper, "Country Clinics or Dispensaries for Treatment of Lepers," which included a report on the three years' experience gained by that time at the Koon Ee Station. This experience, considered to be highly successful, had revealed some interesting facts. The actual number of sufferers from leprosy in that area was much higher than conventional surveys would reveal. In the Koon Ee district, the police had reported twenty cases, but the treatment station came to have seventy patients on its roll.

Nor had these patients migrated from other areas, as the authorities had feared would happen. The treatment station had been careful to secure a copy of the police registration of each patient, to prove that he or she was a permanent resident of the district.

Treatment given at the station was further proving the effectiveness of chaulmoogra oil as a remedy. When patients were treated in a hospital, some argued that a major part of the improvement was due to better diet and improved health conditions. Undoubtedly these were factors. But Koon Ee gave an opportunity to demonstrate the effectiveness of chaulmoogra oil, unaided by other treatments. The clinic's patients received bi-weekly injections of the oil. Apart from these, they continued to live under the same conditions as before, with the same food, work, and habits. The clinic gave them no money, clothing, or food. Under these circumstances, it could be reported that "all early cases have shown a decided improvement, some being entirely freed from all symptoms, while ten to fifteen percent of more advanced cases have also been greatly benefitted."

At the same time, the rural clinic threw into relief one of the particular problems of the treatment of leprosy: the psychology of the patient. The revulsion with which society looked on the disease meant that people who were stricken by it, or suspected they had been stricken, would often hide their symptoms and go to any length to avoid discovery.

The first symptom of leprosy is usually loss of sensation in a part of the skin, accompanied by a certain degree of depigmentation. The progress of the disease, if untreated at the outset, is inexorable. In early cases, it can be arrested, and symptoms may disappear altogether; but if the person affected does not receive treatment, the lesions gradually become more serious. The disease attacks either the skin or nerve fibers, or both; if the skin, lumps called nodules form and may become open ulcers. If the nerves, the fibers are gradually killed, bringing pain at first, then loss of all feeling, and finally loss of bone and flesh, which wither away when there is no nerve to vitalize them.

Obviously, the hope of controlling the disease through treatment stations was to get cases at an early stage. The general pattern was to bring all cases under biweekly treatment, taking the early ones on Mondays and Thursdays, and the more advanced cases on Tuesdays and Fridays. The station assistants used the remaining days for keeping records and making biopsies—microscopic examinations of tissue to detect the presence of the leprosy bacillus. These assistants, themselves former patients whose cases had been arrested, had been trained at the Taegu Leper Hospital. There, most of the work of giving injections and dressings, making laboratory tests, etc. was done by the patients themselves, under supervision, giving some of them an opportunity to develop considerable skill.

A substantial problem remained: how to induce the undiscovered cases, those who had noticed a suspicious symptom but could keep on hiding it for some time yet, to come in for treatment. Some did come, while not admitting to their neighbors where they were going. On clinic days, these sufferers would make elaborate preparations: the men, for going to market or to cut wood in the hills; the women, for going to gather wild herbs and roots. Others would not come at all.

There was the case of a young woman from a well-to-do family. When she contracted leprosy, her husband, a law student, brought suit for divorce. Still, she couldn't bring herself to face the fact of her disease. Her father came to the treatment station, loitered there for a long time, and went away without speaking to anyone. In four or five days he was back, but only ventured to speak, finally, when the doctor was present. Even then, he waited until most of the patients had left.

"Doctor," he said, almost in a whisper, "could you come to my house to examine my daughter? She seems to have a skin disease."

"Bring her here to the clinic."

"Please, Doctor, lower your voice," the man broke in excitedly. "Don't let anyone hear you."

"All right," the doctor shrugged, "just bring your daughter on the next day that I am here."

He did. The young woman came, wrapped up from head to toe, only one eye visible. When it came her turn to be examined, she said tremblingly, "I have an unclean disease," and began to sob. But she had made her breakthrough. From that time, she didn't miss a clinic day, and because her case was early and she was young, the injections soon began to take effect, and her symptoms to fade and disappear.

Arch's plan was that early cases be cared for, as far as possible, at the treatment stations. When laboratory analysis revealed the presence of the bacillus, the cases were considered "open" or "infectious," and the danger of infection to others was greater. He tried to segregate those patients for treatment in the hospital. The advanced cases, those with evident deformities—who might still be infectious or might be "burnt out," where the analysis no longer showed the presence of bacillus—would be sent to the government colony on Little Deer Island, to be cared for indefinitely.

As trained personnel became available to help carry the load, Arch might eventually have established his complete chain of ten treatment stations in the province. A second one was set up at Uisung early in 1931, and a third was coming into being soon after. But by that time, the winds of Japanese politics had changed direction. In Tokyo the militarists were settling themselves in the saddle. Officials who were too pro-Western were being replaced, and others, reading the large-writ handwriting on the wall, were busy falling in line with the new doctrine: Japan supreme, governing her "Greater East Asia Co-Prosperity Sphere." Arch's chain of rural treatment stations and the uncared-for leprosy victims of North Kyung Sang Province would be among the casualties of the militarists' rise to power.

# 16

# Our Last Family Furlough

"Arch, there's no way we could afford that! Not all five of us—two cabins and such a long voyage! Where would the money come from? It's a wonderful idea, I agree, but not for us. We're too many."

"Now, Lawssie, . . ." It was one of those rare moments. He put his arm around his wife, drew her close. In his affectionate mood, he would sometimes drop the familiar Jessie and use, whimsically, the middle name she used to have, that Robert and Catherine Rodgers gave their baby girl to preserve a family name since forgotten—Lawson—Jessie Lawson Rodgers. Arch liked, teasingly, to revive it, but make a diminutive out of it—Lawssie—sometimes sounding the *s* as a *z*.

"Lawsie dear, the board lets us use a travel allowance now. Instead of paying our passage across the Pacific and to New York by the most direct route, they will give that to us in cash, if we can get ourselves there in some other way. So, why not go by the ports?"

"By which ports?"

"Shanghai—Hongkong—Saigon—Ceylon—Djibouti—Suez."

"I see. You have this all figured out, as you always do."

Sometimes Arch could be annoying, exasperating, even—he was so sure of himself, having everything worked out in mind before he said anything. Still, she had to admit that just the names of those faraway places had an intriguing sound.

"Not all figured," he was answering. "We have plenty of time to sit down together and plan the details, just where to stop and what to see. You know about those things better than I do."

Probably she did. Her schooling had been broader than his, and now, for the last four years, she had been teaching the children at home, using the wonderfully illustrated Calvert School materials that came from Baltimore. But how . . . ?

"How about the money, Arch? It would surely be a lot more expensive."

"We have enough saved up, along with the travel allowance, if we use the least expensive way."

It was a wonderful prospect. Jessie had dreamt about something like that—only dreamt. She went upstairs and brought down the globe they had bought from a family that was leaving and that she found useful for the children's lessons. Wonderingly, she traced with her finger a sea route from Japan, down the coast of China and Indochina, around the Malay Peninsula and across the Indian Ocean, then up the Red Sea and the Suez Canal to the Mediterranean. The Mediterranean, the "Roman Lake" of Augustus: it was the gateway to Antiquity and to Europe!

"And on this side," Arch was saying, "right here is the Holy Land. We might meet up there with Gordon and Myra."

Gordon and Myra—so they were in this, too! She might have known someone of his family was part of Arch's plan.

As it all turned out, Gordon and Myra would be coming to Korea for a brief visit. Gordon had been doing well in his practice in Orchard. He and Myra would be in Taegu for two weeks. Then they would be going on around the world, using the Dollar Steamship Company of the United States. Jessie got the plans—those Arch already had in mind—in pieces. Gordon was chipping in five hundred dollars, so that Arch and his family could make the same voyage he and Myra would be making, although not in the same ship.

Arch was clear on that. He and Jessie and the children would use a less expensive steamship line, so the money could go further. Did he have that picked out, too? Well, he had learned that the French company Messageries Maritimes had a ship, the *Sphinx*, making a similar passage about the same time as the Dollar Line ship. They could book second class on the *Sphinx* and save quite a bit.

"Jessie, you know I'm relying on you," Arch said, as the trip began to take shape. "For our family, this is a once-in-a-lifetime opportunity. We'll have just this one furlough trip together. By the next one, the children will be grown up and gone away to college."

That was a sobering thought. The term of service in Korea was seven years, then a year's furlough. Theirs had been due in 1927, but they had agreed, in support of the mission board's budget, to extend their term by a year and make it 1928. Elsie would be turning twelve for this trip "home" and Archie going toward eleven, with Don a little over nine. They would be old enough—especially Elsie and perhaps Archie—to get a lot out of such a trip and, as Arch pointed out, it would happen just this one time.

Jessie did her part. Teaching the children at home, she herself had learned much, poring over the Calvert School's color reproductions of great paintings and its photographs of classical statues and buildings. Now there would be a chance actually to see some of these, among the monuments and museums of a few cities of Europe. Eagerly, she assembled the materials that she had, and planned with Arch where they could realistically hope to go and in what order.

∽ ∽ ∽

The French line's *Sphinx* hauled anchor in Kobe in early March, steaming south toward the tropics. A chief port of call, naturally, was Saigon, French Indochina (now Vietnam); after that stop, every cabin and berth was filled. Rounding the Malay Peninsula, the *Sphinx* came within a degree or two of the Equator. A stout canvas tarpaulin was spread above the deck for shade. I remember it all as great fun—when we three had eaten at the children's serving and the adults were below in the dining hall—running and jumping on the springy canvas!

We understood none of the French language, which maybe contributed to our getting into occasional scraps with the French kids. I remember vividly my pride and satisfaction when, one evening, Archie got one particularly troublesome boy down on the library floor and pummeled him soundly until some adults came and stopped the lesson. Archie was old enough for that. For myself, I made friends with an English boy, and we only did such things as haul down the French tricolor on the ship's stern, in order to put up a home-made flag of our own design. We were in the process of doing that when an irate French sailor interrupted us.

In the galley, the cook did his own coffee-roasting for passengers and crew. The rich, pungent aroma of coffee being roasted!—when I smell it anywhere I am again on the deck of the *Sphinx* steaming through the tropics. No air conditioning in those days, we crossed the Indian Ocean with portholes open, straining for a breeze. One day a flying fish flew right through one of those portholes, and plopped on the floor of the dining hall. A French waiter promptly scooped it up on his tray and bore it off to the kitchen. Another day I found myself the center of unwelcome amusement, when a freak wave splashed through an open port in that same dining hall and drenched me where I sat.

So we came to Djibouti, at the entrance to the Red Sea, and then to Suez, where we left the *Sphinx* and rode across the desert by car to Cairo, to see such sights as the real Sphinx. What a blinding glare of sands around the Pyramids! After Cairo it was back across the desert, this time by crowded train, and on to Jerusalem. In stony Palestine we three children began collecting some of the stones and writing on them, to remember all of the places we saw.

I was the bearer of a zipper bag that was soon half full of stones, though I don't remember them, except a smooth one or two from the shore of Galilee. We kids went swimming in the storied sea, furtively, because we didn't have proper bathing suits. How good and cool the water felt!

After Palestine another ship of the same French line took us through the Mediterranean to Marseilles. That wasn't the plan, but some error had been made and there was no reservation to go via Beirut, Constantinople, and Athens to Naples, as the tickets said—so it was Marseilles instead. Stromboli, in mid-Mediterranean, was a sight to remember, when our ship passed close by the tiny island—nothing more than the upper part of a volcano, sticking out of the water and pouring smoke from its top. Long after it fell astern, as dusk came on, we could see the column of smoke and, from the crater, the ruddy glow on the under side of it.

From Marseilles, it was by train down the Riviera to Naples. Mother and Elsie made up lists of things to see. For my nine years, Naples to London seemed largely a succession of museums, stone corridors of various sorts, aimlessly wandered through. In Paris, I did leave my cap at the foot of the Dying Gladiator (an eloquent marble in the Louvre actually thought to be a Dying Gaul, copy of an earlier Hellenistic work) and had to go back to find it. That was one statue I remembered.

∽ ∽ ∽

To Arch's credit, the family made that trip, and made it together. He respected a broad education and resolved that his children should have it. When the family arrived in New York in early June, he and Jessie had no plan as to where the furlough year would be spent. After a few weeks with her parents in Ridley Park and with her siblings, living nearby, he took all of us to Ontario for a return to the country and relatives of his boyhood.

There, on the farm of Aunt Beck, his father's sister, he could again drive a team of horses in the haying season. We children drank the water, tasting of minerals, that the windmill pump brought up from a deep well, and splashed delightedly in its coolness. Uncle George, no longer well, mostly sat in an armchair on the verandah, but even Archie was given a share in the work. They had him leading the team of big farm horses that pulled a rope, where it went over pulleys up into the barn to haul huge fork-loads of hay from the wagon to the lofts. There the men, including Dad, were waiting to distribute it.

Of an evening sometimes, with the work done, Roger, the hired-man who lived in a neat cottage down the path, would get out his bagpipe and walk up and down skirling it in his front yard. The distance seemed just right for the adults to enjoy and be stirred by that evocation of *auld* Scotland, as the sky turned rose and dusk came across the fields.

After Ontario we had lodgings at Chautauqua, the beautiful summer conference center near the western end of New York State. A large home had been turned into a sort of rooming house for missionaries and church workers. For adults there were stimulating lectures and fine music; for us children, a club with all sorts of fascinating activities; and for all, the lush beauty of the tree-filled campus and Chautauqua Lake lapping at its edge.

Then, happily, a way opened for our family to be in Princeton, New Jersey. Payne Hall, a small apartment building since known affectionately to many Presbyterian missionaries on furlough—later both Archie and I and our families would be among them—was new then. We had apartment D-3. That year, Dad decided he would do his utmost to send his sons to Princeton University.

On this furlough there was little time for study—a prime objective of the furlough year. Arch did manage to get in about a month on x-ray readings and diagnosis at the University of Pennsylvania Hospital in Philadelphia. He needed this because Spencer Hoyt, his younger missionary colleague in Taegu from 1922 to 1927, had resigned. Dr. Hoyt had done some specialty work in x-ray, and there was as yet no Korean technician fully trained to take his place. During a second month, Arch commuted to New York City, sitting in on staff conferences at New York Hospital and viewing surgery at Presbyterian. Apart from these stints, his energies were focused on fundraising.

It had been thirteen years since he, a young, single missionary doctor returning to his Taegu assignment in 1915 after that first furlough, had begun to plan and to sketch a new hospital building. The old, cramped, two-story, tile-roofed structure he inherited—poorly constructed and already outdated—was still in service. Over his years in Taegu and his extended health leave, 1918–20, Arch had dreamt and planned for a building that would be, as first order, fireproof. It would provide the badly needed range of facilities: an up-to-date, sterile operating room; an adequate, efficient kitchen and laundry; patient rooms and wards; offices; and at the heart of the structure, a chapel.

There were many sketches, and there were repeated petitions and overtures. Taegu Station supported them, even proposing that a tract of land that it could spare be sold and the proceeds used toward the new hospital, but the mission board in New York had other priorities.

Arch had come to realize that if the sort of building he was envisioning for Taegu should ever become a reality, the money would have to be gathered, largely, by his own effort—and for that, a furlough was strategic. The board's policy was that missionaries, as they visited churches in the United States that contributed to the mission cause, were to tell about their work, but not to make appeals for their own particular projects. Any promotion that they might do privately, however, as to individual donors, they were free to pursue.

Arch had carefully built up a list of prospects whom he might approach. He felt comfortable with personal promotion, rather than public speaking, and the record of the Taegu medical work, to which he could point, was strong and convincing. By the time his furlough year was up, he had brought together enough funds to assure construction of the long-planned fireproof hospital and, independently, for the central facilities building at the Taegu Leper Hospital as well.

One donor was Howard Winn, an active Christian philanthropist in Kansas City, Missouri. Winn permitted himself the sort of eccentric candor that his position allowed—perhaps even more then than now. Accustomed to being sought out continually for sizable donations, he would fend them off by abrupt and cutting remarks. Arch had learned something of this psychology in dealing with touchy Japanese government officials in Korea. Generally, he managed to stay on the good side of Winn and got extensive help from him for Taegu.

One time he was going to see Winn in Kansas City when a fellow promoter of Christian causes called him.

"Arch, you seem to be in well with Winn, but somehow I've bothered him. How about it if we go together to see him?"

They met Mr. Winn on the sidewalk in front of his home that spring evening. Arch's friend lost no time. "Mr. Winn," he began apologetically, "I was crazy to write you the way I did." Howard Winn didn't smile. "I agree with you," was his short rejoinder.

Arch wanted to take an automobile back to Korea. He had had a couple of Model T Fords, including one of the first seen in Taegu, but felt that they didn't hold up. In addition, spare parts were too hard to come by. If this time he could take back a somewhat more expensive car, it might last for the seven-year term. He suggested as much, guardedly, to Howard Winn.

"Come and see me about it in the morning," Winn said.

The next morning he took Arch to a Cadillac dealer. Cadillac was then building the LaSalle, a smaller vehicle, and there was one, bright red, on the showroom floor.

"Get in and step on the starter," the salesman invited.

Arch did. Not much happened, and he was going to step on it again when the salesman said, "Don't do it! It's already running."

The motor was purring like a kitten. Arch got out and looked the beautiful thing all over.

"Don't worry about the color," the salesman put in. "If it's too bright for you, we can give you a funeral black."

"Do you know how to drive it?" Winn wanted to know. The hand shift was something new in those days, but yes, Arch had tried some of that type.

"Then you can drive it back to Philadelphia; it's yours."

Arch was staggered. Of course, something like that was what he had hoped for, knowing Howard Winn, from the moment they entered the agency. But he was seeing this red LaSalle on the dirt streets of Taegu, seeing it pushing and honking among the ox carts and the droves of pedestrians, seeing it parked by the door of the hospital dispensary.

"Let me think it over," he said. "Let me tell you tomorrow."

That night he prayed to God about it, and, in the morning, had a proposition for Howard Winn. Would Winn swap, and give Arch the black Hudson that he was driving while he took the LaSalle himself?

The philanthropist listened with indifference. No, that didn't interest him. Arch came away without a cent for a car to take back to Korea.

Happily, his disappointment with Mr. Winn was later offset. Mrs. A. P. Schauffler of New York City, a warm friend of missions, gave him a Buick. It was the Silver Anniversary model, a wonderful car. He rigged it with a declinable back for the front seat, to make a car-bed, and with places for an ice-box lunch basket, bedding rolls, a tent, and other equipment for a family junket across the United States on the way back to Korea.

Our family left Princeton in early June 1929, starting toward Taegu. There were tourist cabins then, a few of them, and camps where one could pitch a tent, but no luxuriously comfortable motels. We hit on a camp the first night out and unloaded the Buick. Archie and I were to sleep in the tent, but in the half-darkness we picked the wrong spot, and then a drenching June downpour came on. The tent floor was soon deep in rainwater. Next, we camped over Sunday in a tourist park—uncomfortable and gritty—on the edge of Pittsburgh. After that, the tent stayed folded up. Archie and I slept in the car, while the others used roadside cabins, which usually offered small comfort, at best, in the sticky, mosquito-ridden heat.

A visit with the Fletchers in Nebraska provided an interlude. It was hot there, too, with the parched, searing heat of a Nebraska summer, but we kids didn't mind terribly: there was a pony from Uncle Gordon's farm to ride and cousins to play with.

Then, beyond Nebraska, we had an unforgettable week in Yellowstone Park. I learned by heart the evening *spiehl* of a park ranger, who sat his horse before a semi-circle of log seats at the bears' feeding ground at Old

Faithful and poured out information, mixed with comic anecdotes, while we watched the bears come lumbering out of the woods for some evening scraps. That was material for me to regale adult audiences for months afterward, whenever I could get a hearing.

On, then, to the West Coast, to Korea, and Taegu. We arrived in August. The compound was deserted, everyone away for the summer. Excitedly, we children raced from one end to the other in the still heat, exploring every corner, calling to one another about every remembered spot; but a change had come over it all, a subtle change we were not adult enough to analyze.

We had been in the United States for a year, had been in public school with scores of other children. We would re-adjust to life in Korea, but Taegu station would not again be for us the quiet, sufficient childhood world it had been. In fact, all three of us were going away to boarding school that fall, to the PYFS (Pyongyang Foreign School) in the north of the country.

# 17

# Crowning Achievement

MAHN BO-KI SHE NAMED him—"Ten Thousand Blessings." The baby *was* ten thousand blessings to her, a lone woman. Kang Si was our cook through most of my childhood years. She had been just a woman from the country, simple and ignorant, married to a no-good husband, and she had one child, a daughter, the light of her mother's life. The child was a good girl, and intelligent and attractive. With some help, her mother managed to put her through primary and middle school, which meant she could make a "good" marriage for her.

So, all had gone smoothly for Kang Si. A marriage was arranged with a family from Andong, and a year later her daughter was expecting a baby. She wouldn't use the hospital facilities, which she might have used. The baby was born in the compound gatehouse, where Kang Si lived. It was a boy, and her cup was filling: there would be an heir.

Then, suddenly, when the baby was a week old, Kang Si burst right into Jessie and Arch's bedroom one early morning. She was beside herself. Her daughter was abruptly ill, feverish and irrational. Couldn't the Doctor please help her!

He went, of course, but he couldn't help much, not back then in 1925. Puerperal fever carried off the young mother in a day or two, and Kang Si was alone—more alone than she had ever been. The cry of her heart was the name she gave the baby boy, a name of all her longings—Mahn Bo-ki, Ten Thousand Blessings.

But how could she care for him? In Korea there was very little cow's milk, fresh or canned, and less knowledge of how to use it in infant feeding. When a baby's mother had abundant milk and could nurse him for six or eight months, he did well. When her undernourishment, disease or death shut off from him this supply, usually he died.

Naturally, Mahn Bo-ki's case was different. Jessie gave Kang Si milk from their cow, taught her how to prepare a baby formula, and guided her in feeding the little fellow, as he grew old enough to take supplementary foods. The years passed. Mahn Bo-ki became a schoolboy, grew into a tall, strapping youth. Conspicuous among his schoolmates, he grew startlingly tall for a Korean boy of that time. Neighbors and friends said that it was natural—he was growing like a Westerner, because he had been fed Western style.

It was about then that Pearl Harbor came. When Jessie and Arch were under house arrest and about to be repatriated, Kang Si came stealthily to the back door one night. She knew they must be leaving soon. Perhaps there would be things they could not be taking with them—anything the Doctor might not need would be just fine for Mahn Bo-ki. "You know," she said proudly, "he can even wear the Doctor's shoes."

Arch saw him once after that, in Seoul in 1946, after liberation. He was in music school, playing in the school orchestra and still standing almost a head taller than his classmates. Years later we heard of him once more. He was conducting what was, at that time, the National Symphony Orchestra of Korea.

Mahn Bo-ki, in his babyhood, had given a strong push to a Baby Welfare Project in Taegu Hospital. It was one of those projects that crowded into Arch's busy mind, and was turned over and over there for some years, before time and means could be found to give it expression in reality. The first recording of it in a specific way was in a letter written to New York in 1926, shortly after Arch had come back from Peking from a meeting of the China Medical Association. The emphasis there on preventive medicine had stiffened his resolve to launch some effort in that direction, as part of Taegu's medical program.

Why not become, as he wrote,

> pioneers in prevention of disease, just as we were first in the cure of disease some years ago. . . . In the city of Taegu, for instance, there is a great need for Baby Welfare work. . . . We hope to erect a small building, where people may come and secure milk, fresh and canned, properly prepared according to formula, to suit age, weight, etc. of any baby. At the beginning, Korean nurses under foreign supervision would be responsible for preparation of all bottles and milk, and this would be a fine training for them. They would, in turn, teach the mothers who came for milk, until they could do the work properly in the home. We hope to get a considerable supply of milk from missionaries, as most of us have cows on the hill, and some money for the building, which will not cost more than two or three hundred dollars.

That was Arch, with his "editorial we" and his perennial hopefulness of doing just a little more than he could do. Every cent that could be raised was then going into the dispensary building fund, and the next year, the new dispensary was going up. It was all he could manage—to get the dispensary finished and occupied—just before leaving on furlough in 1928. The "two or three hundred dollars" for a milk station was not found.

Instead of that, however, the way was cleared for something more complete—which also was typical of how Arch worked. A few months after his return from the United States, he launched a Baby Welfare project—not with just a milk station and a food laboratory, but with a well-baby clinic in addition. Infants were enrolled and checked regularly by the hospital pediatrician in a weekly clinic. The mothers listened to short lectures and watched demonstrations on the prevention of disease, on feeding schedules and all aspects of baby care. There was a pre-natal clinic and special instruction for expectant mothers; and this program was possible because the new dispensary had been built and the old building was available for such use.

The one who really made the baby clinic run was Nurse Li Yoo-boon. They had had a merry time joking about her in the hospital and the station. In 1924, Claire Hedberg, RN, newly arrived missionary superintendent of nurses in the Taegu Hospital, had set up a school of nursing. Government recognition could not be secured, but the plan was to use staff doctors and give as complete a course of instruction as possible. Then the graduates would take the government examinations and, if they were fortunate, might receive government licenses to practice.

Miss Hedberg took in a starting class of five girls—but the course was new, and long and hard, and one by one her students dropped out. In the spring of 1928, she made carefully proper and complete preparations for the first graduating exercises of the school of nursing. There would be a reception for the graduating class, with all of the trimmings. Then it almost had to be postponed, because, as Miss Hedberg announced to the station members the day before the graduation, the graduating class had gotten a touch of dysentery. The Class of '28 was only one—Nurse Li.

She proved to be worth a whole class. The staying power she had shown before graduation continued to be her special mark. For well over a decade after it was organized, she carried the major part of the baby clinic work, with valuable counsel and help from Mrs. Sue Adams, RN, and Mrs. Helen Chamness, and with Jessie's constant backing. Even after Pearl Harbor, when Ned Adams, Jessie and Arch, the only ones left in the station, were under house arrest, the Japanese let the clinic continue to receive milk from the station cows, and loyal Nurse Li, still carrying on, had a means of keeping in touch.

Along with getting milk from the compound and other clinic supplies from the city, she secured and slipped in to Arch and Jessie the things they needed. The last night before they left to be repatriated, she came to the back door in her uniform to say goodbye, and Jessie gave her, as a remembrance, a package of silver spoons.

The baby clinic's pattern was to follow for three years the children who were enrolled. After that, they were "graduated" in a formal little ceremony of the type that parents the world around delight in, the pre-schoolers also entering in with solemn faces. By World War II, over two hundred children had received graduation certificates. It was a small operation; most such efforts were pitifully small, in comparison with the people's need. The best that one could do was to point the way.

After Nurse Li's Class of '28, the school of nursing carried on, turning out a small class each year until Miss Hedberg resigned in 1934 to be married. It was her effort and organizational ability that had sustained it. For some years, there was no school. The hospital had to depend on graduate nurses who were trained elsewhere, who directed and taught raw nurse's aides. When Ella Sharrocks, RN, another missionary nurse, joined the staff briefly in 1940–41, it was possible to re-open the school, only to have it closed again during the war years.

After Liberation Day (the term loyal Koreans used for August 15, 1945) the school of nursing at last got government recognition. It was one of the first to be sanctioned by the national health department of South Korea's provisional government. Graduates could be given their titles without having to qualify in separate government examinations.

∾ ∾ ∾

Returning to Taegu in 1929 from his furlough in the United States, Arch seemed ready to realize his dream of a fireproof hospital. For fourteen years he had planned and worked toward it, and with his strenuous fund-raising in the furlough year the funds were in hand. One might have thought that he couldn't get started fast enough, seeing the foundation dug and the walls going up. But his psychology was different. This was what he had longed and worked for. Now, at last, it was within his grasp, and he was going to do it right. He couldn't allow any detail to be overlooked.

On furlough he had joined the American Hospital Association, so that he could use the association's library and "service bureau." Now he stacked his desk with twenty mini-libraries covering a range of subjects: laundries, incinerators, elevators, dumb-waiters, flooring, lighting, operating-room equipment, hospital colors—whatever he could think of. This would be a modern medical facility, thoroughly the latest word in every way, within the funds that had been scraped together to create it.

The plans that he had sketched and resketched were still being studied. Early in 1930, he began excavating foundations. At the same time, Edwin Campbell, a missionary who also had training as an architect, came down from Syunchun to spend three months in Taegu meticulously drawing detailed plans and ironing out the wrinkles. By the end of that year, the brick walls were up, and concrete floors, as well as the flat slab of the concrete roof, were in. The iron window frames were in place, and the electrical installation, which had been done along with the concrete work, was finished.

It might have seemed that the final goal was only a few months away. Arch himself wrote confidently to New York that plumbing would be installed in the coming winter. Painting and so forth would be finished in the spring—equipment would go in—and then, "we [will be] ready for the dedication in the late spring."

Yet, at all costs, he was going to see it done right. Instead of a few weeks, the plumbers were months in the building. Meanwhile, of the money that Arch had pulled together, dollar by dollar, more than three thousand dollars was lost when the Japanese yen dropped in exchange value. He began a long series of entreaties, got the backing of the mission, and finally received this amount from the board in New York, two years later, in compensation for the loss in exchange.

After the plumbers came the plastering and the floors. A polished terrazzo type of floor had been decided on, with different colors for different rooms and services mixed into the flooring material. Private rooms would be green, semi-private brown, and the wards maroon. But the cement that was available wouldn't take the colors. At last, after innumerable tests, Arch found a type of cement from Manchuria, containing magnesium, that would do what he wanted done.

On the hospital staff and in the station, people were getting impatient. It had been a year and a half since construction began. Why couldn't the building as it stood be occupied and put in service, leaving the finishing touches until later? Arch wouldn't work that way. He had waited too long for this. He could wait a little longer. Through another entire year, he and Jessie worked, selecting colors, supervising painting, checking every small detail, while all the time he was carrying the full load of both the general and the leper hospitals.

In fact, the effort was intensified. There had been two years of drought and crop failure in the province. The current account of the hospital showed a deficit, and Arch was resolved that this must be wiped out and there must even be a small surplus, before the move to the new building could be made.

Late that year, 1932, Jessie was joined by Helen Henderson in the task of making bedspreads and curtains. Helen, the sister-in-law of Harold Henderson of Taegu station, had just lost her husband in Manchuria.

Lloyd Henderson was traveling alone with his "man." They had put up at a tiny inn, and it was the dead of night, when Japanese police roused him. The Japanese had pushed into Manchuria the year before. The policemen declared that it was not safe—there were bandits abroad. Lloyd must get up and go back to a town he had come through. He objected, but the police were adamant. It was on the way back to the other town, while Lloyd rode through the darkness in the front of his ox-cart, that he was suddenly attacked and shot. His Korean companion, very reluctant to talk, would say only that Lloyd died there in the cart. Of course, the Japanese authorities said that it was bandits, but neither the US consul in Manchuria nor any other American ever saw Lloyd's body, and many wondered.

In those years, Japan was beginning to probe in the Far East, feeling its way toward expansion and conquest, pressing to get the Westerners out of its "Greater East Asia Co-Prosperity Sphere." The technique of planned incidents, sent up as trial balloons, was a recognized one. A few years later, there was the *USS Panay* on the Yangtze River, strafed, bombed, and sunk by Japanese planes in December 1937, while the Japanese government claimed that their pilots could not distinguish between US and Chinese flags at 300 meters. Such arrows would point eventually to Pearl Harbor.

After Lloyd was killed, Helen Henderson and her two children moved immediately to Taegu. It was October 1932. To keep busy, she began to help Claire Hedberg and Jessie with the finishing touches at the new hospital. The terrazzo floors gleamed and shone. In each room and in the corridors, colors had been carefully blended and harmonized. On the second floor, over the main entrance, the children's ward was adorned all around the walls with a band of pictures of animals and birds, which a Korean artist had skillfully copied from plates of the *National Geographic* magazine. Above the children's area, on the third floor, was something new in Taegu: a small maternity ward. Going to a hospital for delivery was still a novel idea for expectant mothers. It would take some vigorous, prolonged selling to keep occupied the four beds of the maternity ward.

On the second floor, in the heart of the building, was a small, attractive chapel—a memorial to Dr. James Adams, Taegu station's pioneer, given by his widow. The dark wood pews and dark woodwork behind the pulpit breathed serenity, while on that woodwork was spelled out in gilt, in the Chinese ideographs read by all educated people in Northeast Asia, in the Korean Hangul script, and in English, this text: "My house shall be called a house of prayer for all peoples" (Isa. 56:7).

Finally, almost three years after ground had been broken, the building was ready. All equipment was installed, even the huge cylindrical washer and steam mangles of the laundry, themselves a great "sight-see" for ever-curious visitors. The curtains were in place, and colorful chintz covers and pillows adorned the wicker furniture of the "solaria," visible at the end of each hallway.

Helen Henderson admired it all. "Now," she said brightly, "if there weren't any patients coming in, wouldn't it stay lovely?"

Arch picked the Korean New Year, in February 1933, to dedicate the new building. It was an auspicious date, and it was also a time when the patient census fell off to a minimum. Everyone who could possibly go home did so. There would not be many patients to move from the old, tiled-roof hospital to the new one.

Many people had shared in putting up the building. Dr. Robert E. Speer, board secretary, wrote a note of thanks to one donor. His note was a testimony that Arch prized for its content, and much more for the man who wrote it, one of the world-wide Christian mission's great statesmen. Dr. Speer wrote of the medical work,

> It is thoroughly good work medically, in the midst of an area of great need, and from the point of view of its missionary spirit and evangelistic method, it is, I think, one of the most remarkable and effective hospitals in the world. I do not know of more than three or four other hospitals which, it seems to me, are its equal in the matter of tireless living and fruitful evangelistic work.

When at last the building was completed and dedicated, Arch sent a message of appreciation to the board's officials in New York, enclosing copies of a photograph of the new building that a Taegu newspaper had run. The letter went to George H. Trull, secretary for Special Gifts, but one of the pictures was for Dr. Cleland B. McAfee, who had succeeded Dr. Brown as Korea secretary. Dr. McAfee answered in his enthusiastic way:

> Your letter of March 30th to Mr. Trull has been passed around to the offices and I have received the excellent picture of the Hospital intended for me. I doubt if the Queen of Sheba was much more surprised when she saw Solomon than I was when I saw this picture. The half had never been told me. I think no one realized that the Hospital would be so impressive and give such promise of effectiveness as it does. We have few such buildings anywhere in our missionary equipment, and we will hope for a continuance of your own strength until you get it on a good and

permanent foundation. The Lord bless you richly and reward you for the sacrificial service which this building represents.

~ ~ ~

Adequate staff for the expanding medical work was a problem that Arch worked at continuously. Back in 1930, when construction on the new building was just beginning, he received an unexpected reinforcement. Dr. Walther Kaltefleiter, known in our family conversations as "the German Doc," was one of those hard-up international wanderers to be found everywhere in the world. From Shanghai, he had come up to Pusan on an agreement to work there with a Korean doctor, but the agreement fell through, and he was left without support, living with a Japanese family in Pusan. That was not far from Taegu. The Japanese health authorities got in touch with Arch, and soon Dr. Kaltefleiter joined the Taegu Hospital staff.

As he was a foreigner and alone, that logically meant that he should move into our guest room. Mother was not enthusiastic. The German Doc was a bit eccentric. He wore long underwear, wrist-and-ankle-length, right through the roasting heat of Taegu's summer, and his manners showed the clipped precision of German discipline. When introduced, he clicked his heels as if he were on a parade ground; but always he was unfailingly polite. Finding himself in the intimate Christian community of Taegu Station, he did his best to fit in. At prayer services, he took his turn at reading the Bible—evidently not familiar to him in any language—in stiff, precise English. Courteously, he broke off smoking cigarettes—consuming pounds of Japanese candy in the effort. It was that fall that Martha Bruen, our neighbor and Mother's close friend, died of cancer. After her death, Dr. Kaltefleiter moved next door, with Mr. Bruen, only to leave Taegu the following year, when Harry Bruen also left on furlough.

Poor "Pu Hai-ri"—as Dad affectionately called our neighbor, using his Korean name—he was not made to live alone. A year or so after he came back to Taegu from furlough he began to squire Claire Hedberg around, she being the hospital's only missionary nurse. In its early years, the hospital had had a hard time holding on to missionary nurses. In a span of eighteen years, from 1905 to 1923, there had been five of them, two of whom resigned to be married—but Claire had stuck. For eleven years she did a capable job of supervising nursing service and of directing the hospital's small school of nursing, serving cheerfully under the handicaps of the cramped, antiquated building.

Yet, now that Harry Bruen was escorting her here and there, the conclusion seemed inevitable. It was. In September 1934, with the new hospital in use only a year and a half, Harry and Claire were married. The ceremony was simple and quiet, conducted in the "Alpha House" where the single women lived, with just the members of the station and a small number of Korean friends. I was there, feeling some adolescent curiosity and self-consciousness. Elsie and Archie had left that summer, to return to the United States for college.

Harry Bruen was sixty when he married again, although Claire was a good deal younger. Pu Hai-ri's many Korean friends approved. Martha had given him two daughters—both grown up now—but no son. The friends' approval was joyously vindicated, a year-and-a-half later, when a son, Harry Jr., was born.

∾ ∾ ∾

At the hospital, Arch was very aware that a modern building was not enough. If the work were to keep pace with developments in medical science, even modestly, it must be organized into departments, each headed by a well-trained specialist. The most urgently needed of these departments were x-ray and clinical laboratory.

For the first, the very man was available. Suh Bo-ki, as a young secondary-school graduate, had taught Korean to Arch's associate, Spencer Hoyt, and Dr. Hoyt had used him as a helper and taught him a good deal about x-ray technique. Now, in 1930, Suh went to the University of Pennsylvania Hospital in Philadelphia to study for a year in the Department of Radiology. Scholarship help came from the ladies of the Pennsylvania Medical Missionary Society, the same organization that had come to Arch's personal aid with a cottage for our family, when he was just out of Trudeau Sanatorium in 1918.

Mr. Suh would be one of the Hospital's most loyal staff members, as well as a strong supporter of its Preaching Society. Returning to Taegu after his study, he would take charge of x-ray on through the 1930s and through most of the war years, until a Japanese supervisor would oust him early in 1945. When the American military government would be set up in South Korea, Suh Bo-ki—with his good English and urbane manner—would serve with it for three years and later with the YMCA and in other capacities, until called back to Taegu Hospital in 1956 to a busy and considerably expanded x-ray department.

Y. B. Moon, the hospital's laboratory technician, was the next to be helped by a scholarship from the Pennsylvania Medical Missionary Society, after Suh's return. He went to Philadelphia in 1932 to study for eighteen months in the University of Pennsylvania's William Pepper Laboratory of Clinical Medicine. In effect, earnest, scholarly Moon never seemed to get enough of studying in his specialty. A college graduate to begin with—Union Christian College, Pyongyang, later functioning "in exile" in Seoul—he added to his Philadelphia studies three months in Seoul and Tokyo. Then came sixteen more months in Tokyo and a few weeks, after the war, in the US Army's 34th General Hospital in Seoul, topping it all off with eighteen months and an MSc from the Harvard School of Public Health.

Moon never broke his connection with Taegu Hospital. Quiet, steady, and unspectacular, through the war years he was permitted to carry on, even serving as hospital superintendent for a time. Later, as the head of an expanding department, he launched the venture of a school of medical technology as a branch of the hospital program, doing his share to fulfill the teaching function which Taegu Hospital came to stress.

L. W. Whong, MD, was another who came to be bound up with Taegu Hospital. It was in 1939 that Arch got in touch with him. He had been in the United States, receiving his full medical education, thanks again in part to help from women of the Pennsylvania Medical Missionary Society, and he was looking for a place in Korea to practice and pay back his indebtedness in service.

Dr. Whong was a northerner, but the opportunities in his own city, Pyongyang, didn't appeal much to him. He decided on Taegu, adopting the south, although he never lost the certain drive that seemed, at that time, more characteristic of the northerners in Korea.

After two years, World War II broke out and Dr. Whong was jailed immediately by the Japanese authorities. They suspected and feared his natural qualities of leadership, as well as his connections with people in the United States; but after five months they let him out. From then on through the war he did much to hold the hospital together. An appointee of the Japanese police nominally supervised it, but Dr. Whong's was the real leadership.

When the war ended, the US military government stepped in. Dr. Whong was virtually recruited, sent off to the United States to study public health, and brought back to Seoul to be put behind a desk. He couldn't take it. He was a clinical doctor. Behind the desk, his spirit wilted; his nerves went awry; his weight went down.

Arch, back in Korea and also assigned to Seoul, met his colleague there when he was almost ready for psychiatric treatment and managed to persuade the Army to shift him to a clinical post, suggesting Taegu. That was how Dr. Whong went back to Taegu Hospital. He was deeply interested in the spiritual purpose of the facility, as he had been from the beginning.

When a small church was organized in the hospital itself, to minister to the staff and to ambulatory patients, he was elected its first elder.

When the Communists invaded from North Korea, initially driving deep into South Korea, it was Dr. Whong, as acting superintendent, who directed the emergency transfer of most of the hospital staff and equipment to temporary quarters deeper inside the Pusan Perimeter. Y. B. Moon stayed behind in Taegu with about a quarter of the staff, to help care for the wounded there. Then and through the chaotic years that followed, Dr. Whong did much, with very little in the way of equipment and supplies, to give leadership to the institution.

In a letter from an earlier and happier time, a year before Pearl Harbor, Jessie described an outing she and Arch took with the two young couples: Dr. Whong and his attractive wife, a graduate of Ewha, a women's college in Seoul, and Mr. and Mrs. Moon. Such an outing was a rare sort of experience, and memorable.

Leaving behind the August heat of the city, they drove up into the mountains, then left the car and continued by a path through fragrant pine woods, along a tumbling mountain stream, to an inn near the ancient Buddhist monastery of Haeinsa (hi-EEN-sah). The place—now a tourist destination—was famous for its sequestered beauty and for its library of Buddhist texts inscribed on more than 81,000 wood printing blocks, each measuring some twelve by twenty inches and covered with beautifully carved Chinese characters done in reverse for printing—an astounding achievement.

That evening the party of six went to see the monastery by moonlight. They had been in a festive mood; now the haunting beauty of the mountain woods and the graceful, timeless curves of tiled roofs in the moonlit clearing quieted them. Y. B. Moon, who had a fine voice, sang in English a hymn he had selected to learn. After returning to the inn, they sat for a long time in the moonlight, while the talk flowed along, sometimes in English, sometimes in Korean, until at last, reluctantly, they went to their rooms.

As Jessie wrote, it was one of those interludes, of which there are too few, when heart touches heart—among the most real moments of life.

# 18

# "Dr. Fletcher, Praise, Grace Pavilion"

THE VILLAGERS GAPED. THEY had never seen such pigs. They *had* pigs—scrawny, razor-backed creatures with small, vicious eyes—that kept up a ceaseless grunting around the refuse heaps and open sewers of their villages. But the huge, sleek animals they were staring at could hardly be identified as the same genus.

Then there were the chickens: pure-white Leghorns, which were reported to produce a fabulous number of eggs; and Rhode Island Reds, as big as geese. Beyond them, rabbits: big, soft-eyed Chinchillas, not in little, straw-thatched hutches but in long rows of pens, arranged in several tiers and ingeniously designed to keep the animals clean, comfortable, and healthy. Finally, there were the pigeons—big White Kings from California, the males strutting and puffing up their feathers.

It was all quite a "sight-see." Down below, on the sunny slope of this south-looking knoll, was a barn. The villagers were familiar enough with cows, and with caring for the oxen used in plowing and hauling, which were a measure of any farmer's wealth. But even the barn was full of novelties for them, so unusual were the Western notions it incorporated.

This was the animal husbandry department of Taegu Leper Hospital in the middle 1930s. The man behind it all—poking his close-cropped head into the corners, keeping a watchful eye on everything, although his voice, when he spoke to the men and boys doing the work, sounded mild and kindly—was the Rev. O. V. Chamness.

Vaughan Chamness of Taegu Station was an "evangelistic man." Like others with his mission, he had his district assigned to him for rural itineration and church visitation, but he also loved animals. Further, as a junior missionary in those days, Vaughan gravitated to Arch and became a sort of spiritual disciple. That was how he began working in earnest on developing Arch's idea of a department of animal husbandry. This would give many of the able-bodied among the leprosy patients—and most of them, as early cases, were in that category—some useful, outdoor work to do, a good thing in itself. Such exercise meant better health, better morale, and a quicker recovery.

Also, the department would provide fresh meat, milk and eggs, improving diet while reducing operating costs. And, finally, it would give the patients whose disease was arrested a valuable training that they could take with them when at last they might leave the hospital and return to society.

Vaughan wrote to the US Department of Agriculture in Washington and got blueprints of modern, scientifically designed hog pens, chicken houses, and the rest. He and Arch, both from farming backgrounds, enthusiastically laid out the buildings of a miniature model farm on the little knoll at the back of the leper hospital property. With help from the American Mission to Lepers, they then built the real farm—neat, white buildings with dark green trim, contrasting oddly with the mud-walled, straw-thatched houses of a village only a hundred yards away. Meanwhile, Vaughan ordered the stock—Berkshire pigs from England, chickens, rabbits and pigeons from California, Holstein cows from Japan. Some of these he brought back with him when he returned to Taegu from furlough, watching and tending them personally on the long Pacific crossing.

No surprise that the villagers who visited the place gaped and that, most of all, they stood in awe of the immense, black Berkshire boar, which the leprosy patients fed until it grew to prodigious size. All through the hospital, the male patients were organized into work squads. Each man had an assignment according to his health and ability and according to his trade before he was struck by the dreaded disease.

There were fifty or more different tasks, ranging from assisting in the laboratory and treatment rooms—at which some patients became highly skilled—through painting, carpentry, road building, cleaning, sweeping, to the many jobs of farming, cultivating intensively the hospital's few acres of farm land, caring for some four hundred fruit trees in the orchard, and tending the animals and poultry. For women patients, there was plenty to do of the sort of thing they had been accustomed to before they came to the hospital—cooking the food, washing and ironing, mending old clothes and making new ones—as well as the more specialized tasks of preparing the thousands of dressings required by the hospital clinic, assisting in the clinic and laboratory, and teaching in the day school. Among the patients were children and young people, many of them with little or no schooling.

The community cared for itself. It was divided strictly into two halves, the sexes kept segregated, but each half did its appropriate type of work for the whole. In 1931 the central service building was completed. An original plan had called for several buildings, but in the end the services were combined in one. It was two-story, with a large dining room upstairs, separated by cabinets into men's and women's halves reached by separate outdoor stairways at opposite ends of the building. In the center of the dining room, bringing up huge loads of steaming rice, barley, and soybeans from the kitchen below, was a marvelous device—a hand-operated dumb waiter.

The ground-floor kitchen was also a marvel, something that never failed to cause Japanese visitors to suck in breath between the front teeth in the characteristic hiss of surprise and admiration. The Japanese visitors were always great admirers of cleanliness and efficient regimentation. Here they saw huge, iron kettles with hollow jackets in which super-heated steam could be circulated. The kettles, with heavy wooden lids raised and lowered by ropes and pulleys, were capable of cooking enormous quantities of rice or a fragrant blend of rolled barley and soybeans, maintaining an exactly controlled temperature and dumping over to spew out their contents when precisely done. Steam was used also to sterilize bowls and brass chopsticks and spoons, and to provide hot running water for the washrooms, showers, and laundry located on the ground floor of the service building.

Just before the structure was completed, Arch wrote to the American Mission to Lepers, with perhaps-pardonable hyperbole, that when the service building went into use, the Taegu Leper Hospital

> will be the most Sanitary and Efficient Treatment Hospital for lepers in the whole wide world. This may sound boastful, but it is every word true. Every leper will wash his face and hands under a faucet with running water. Every leper will bathe his body under a shower with running hot and cold water. Every leper will eat rice that has been steam cooked. Every leper will eat from dishes that, after every meal, are sterilized by steam.

The Japanese officials, as noted above, held in high respect anyone engaged in leprosy work, their respect enhanced by their horror of the disease. In this the Imperial Family led the way, setting a pattern with its personal support of leprosy institutions. At the time of the coronation of Emperor Hirohito in the fall of 1928, a number of leprosy workers in Korea were decorated with the Blue Ribbon, equal to the Sixth Order, by His Imperial Majesty.

Arch was one of the missionary physicians to receive this honor, although since he was on furlough at the time, the actual presentation was made a year later by Governor Masayoshi Inamuro of North Kyung Sang Province. The governor said, in his brief presentation speech:

> It is a most pleasant honor and duty to have the privilege of presenting you with this very honorable decoration of Japan, the "Konju Hosho."

> You have been in this land, which is very different from your home country in climate, custom, and in every respect, since 1909. Seventeen of those years you have served as director of the Taegu Leper Hospital. During those years you have always treated the poor lepers with deep and gracious love and sympathy.
>
> Not only the lepers, but all who know you in your work hold you in high esteem and reverence for your great sacrifice and most earnest work, mingled with great human love. I believe that it is for this reason that this great honor is being conferred upon you this morning.
>
> I sincerely hope for you everlasting good health. I also pray for future augmentation and accomplishment of your work, until the disease of leprosy is eradicated from this district. . . .

In the early 1930s, the Empress Dowager of Japan gave to each of the three mission leprosy institutions in Korea, from her personal funds, a gift of one thousand yen a year for five years, to which her son, Emperor Hirohito, added another five hundred. Arch saved up the money that came to Taegu, 7,500 yen in all, and used it to put up another two-story, brick dormitory housing eighty male patients, designed on the order of those already built. He designated this one as an Imperial Memorial.

In those years, Arch received another recognition of his leprosy work, which touched him more deeply than Japan's highly regarded *Konju Hosho* award. As his arrival in Korea in 1909 had coincided with the silver anniversary celebration of twenty-five years of Protestant missionary effort in the country, the twenty-fifth anniversary of his own arrival coincided with the jubilee year of a half-century of Protestant missions, which occurred in 1934.

The leprosy patients wanted to do something fitting to mark that occasion. Out of their poverty, current and former patients of the hospital collected a fund. It took them a while, but they got together enough to erect, on their own initiative, a tiny, red-brick building at the entrance to the hospital grounds.

Set in a grove of dwarf pine trees, it was done in American Colonial style, with green shutters at the windows, and was surrounded by a low, white picket fence. Most of the interior was given over to an attractively furnished reception room, with an adjoining small kitchenette where the traditional welcoming cup of tea could be prepared for visitors to the hospital.

Actually, the idea of the patients had been that this little "guest house," Oriental in its concept but so thoughtfully Western in its realization, could be a place for the Doctor and his wife, when visiting the hospital, to rest or even spend the night. In fact, the crowded schedule at both hospitals left little time for such relaxation, but the guest house was useful as a reception room, and the sacrificial devotion that had built it gave it a treasured meaning.

As a part of the Autumn Thanksgiving Service in 1936, the small building was dedicated. The patients had placed over the door a granite slab with an inscription in the classic Chinese ideograph that read: "Dr. Fletcher, Praise, Grace Pavilion."

At this time, the Japanese government in Chosen was intensifying its own efforts to deal with the leprosy problem. The facilities of the Little Deer Island colony were expanded. Then the police announced that in late November 1935, a number of whole settlements of lepers would be eliminated, one of the largest being in the environs of Taegu City. The people who lived there, in wretched shacks and hovels, supported themselves in large part by sorting refuse and rounding up tin cans that could be sold for a few "sen." Among them was a group of Christians, founded through the efforts of the leper hospital church, which, in the self-supporting tradition of the Korean church, had managed to erect its own small chapel.

With more efficiency than humanitarian concern, the police moved in. Men, women, and children were rounded up, herded onto trucks in the sort of scene becoming familiar in the wars and totalitarianism of the twentieth century, and hauled off to the Taegu leper hospital, as a distribution depot. Then kerosene was liberally poured around and a pall of black smoke began to rise, hanging over that quarter of the city, as the deserted shacks and the chapel burned to the ground.

The leper hospital, wrote Arch, was "literally alive night and day with lepers, police and officials" that week. Some 400 people had been rounded up, between sufferers from the disease and their children, and 250 of them were designated to be sent to the Little Deer colony. None wanted to go. The colony was well-organized and efficient, but there was little kindness to temper efficiency, little regard for the patient as a human being, and less hope of ever leaving once a person had been enclosed there.

The 250 were separated in the leper hospital chapel in Taegu. Bright lights played on the exterior at night and armed police patrolled, to see that no patient escaped. That last night before the long truck ride to Little Deer Island began, the pastor of the leper hospital church spoke long and late to these people, trying to get through to them a message of comfort and hope.

It was the Gospel in stark simplicity. This world, in effect, was ending for them. Could they believe that these things were really the shadows, the Insubstantial, and that beyond gleamed the untrammeled Reality? Could they believe in Love?

The Taegu leper hospital was asked to take 150 of these dispossessed patients. Some old, Korean-style buildings could be repaired and about fifty lodged there. There was really no place for the remaining hundred, but Arch felt they could not be turned away and the government was ready to provide their support if he would squeeze them in. The more difficult problem was that about fifty of this group were children. These children, born of leprous parents, were "untainted," or at least had been born so, though the probabilities of their contracting the disease were high. They must be separated from their parents and carefully controlled, to watch for the appearance of any symptoms.

For two years and more, Arch wrestled with this problem, meanwhile making shifts to accommodate the children as best he could. Finally, a small gift came from Miss Anna Williams of Chicago. To this, he and Jessie decided to add a gift of their own. Their children were grown up and back in the United States in college.

They sold their summer cottage at Sorai Beach and combined the proceeds with Miss Williams' gift to build a modest children's home segregated from the rest of the hospital, where untainted minors could have a promise of growing up to healthy adulthood. Younger children were cared for by housemothers and taught primary school in the home, while the older ones walked to a public secondary school in the city.

Year by year, after 1935 and until the attack on Pearl Harbor diverted all of the Empire's energies to destruction and conquest, the local Japanese police continued their annual round-ups of leprosy victims. The scene on the Taegu leper hospital grounds was repeated: bright lights flooding the chapel, mounted police watchfully patrolling, while a wretched group waited for deportation to the last stopping-place. After that first year, the Preaching Society of the general hospital was more prepared. The members collected a small sum among the staff and filled paper bags with cookies and fruit.

On the last night of waiting, for those going to Little Deer the general hospital staff put on a program with motion pictures, music by a choral group of nurses, readings from the Bible and an exhortation by one of the hospital evangelists. With each of the bags of cookies and fruit went a copy of one of the Gospels. It was a moving invocation of "the peace of God, which passes all understanding," expressed by the Apostle Paul (Phil. 4:7).

By 1941 the patient census at the leper hospital was nearing seven hundred. Thirty-five buildings, large and small, housed the patients and provided for their needs, while another fifteen included residences for non-patient members of the staff, the children's home, and the animal husbandry buildings.

Then the war closed in. Through it the leper hospital kept going. Prodded, perhaps, by fear of the disease, the Japanese government maintained enough support to provide for the patients, with strict economies. All help from abroad was cut off. Providentially, Pai Chung-won was serving as business manager of the institution. Pai had been a policeman, a Korean serving in the Japanese police force in Korea before he came to work with Arch in the leper hospital. He had a strong sense of discipline, tempered by his Christian faith and anchored in his loyalty to that cause, to which he now dedicated himself. The war years were very lean ones, but Pai held on, and held the hospital together.

After liberation the US Army provided some help and modest progress was made. That was shattered by the Communist invasion from the north. At the first sweep southward of the Red forces, their guns came close enough to be heard plainly from the hospital grounds; but just there the advance was stopped.

Administrator Pai held on. On the side, after the armistice, he began to take an active part in local politics, heading the Taegu City Council for several years. He even ran for mayor and for national assemblyman, although without success. Through it all, for more than twenty-five years, he continued his dedicated service to the Taegu leper hospital.

# 19

# Sorai Beach

Sorai Beach—it is an enchanted name and place, one that I must evoke for a few pages, even while the place evoked is no longer there. Whatever reality may be left is inaccessible for now, shut away in North Korea.

The story of Sorai Village, improbable cradle of Protestant Christianity in all Korea, and of H. G. Underwood's discovery of Sorai Beach has been told in chapter 7. It was an ideal spot for summer rest and recreation. The blue bay sparkled, ringed and protected by a scattering of offshore islands. Clear water and the long, level beach shelving gently out to sea invited swimmers to splash for hours. Nights were warm and loaded with stars. When there was no moon, the water would sparkle with phosphorescence, each breaking wave a line of cool fire. Of course there were storms, violent, tempestuous winds driving before them torrents of drenching rain. A fearful surf would beat in on the rocks of the headland; but when the storm was past the sea would lie quiet again, grey and still, seeming transparent at the horizon, as one sometimes saw it at dawning. All of the moods of the sea were there, but a sheltered sea with land meeting it, hills and rocks, headlands and shimmering white dunes with wisps of coarse grass growing in them.

Over the years Underwood's bold vision of a Sorai Beach Association had been fulfilled. Other missionary families had built cottages, springing up in an odd assortment of sizes, shapes and styles—according to what each owner fancied as appropriate and what he or she could afford. Dad, having visited Sorai a time or two, put up a cottage for our family. With enterprise, and characteristic frugality, he bought a Korean pavilion, one that measured ten *kahn*. The *kahn* was a square about eight feet on a side, so determined by the convenient length of heavy beams that were jointed into the tops of pillars at eight-foot intervals to form these squares. The beams, in turn, supported the structure of the heavy, tiled roof. They were mostly left natural, just the bark removed and a little shaping done here and there, the surface polished by exposure and wear. We children would sometimes climb up and sit astride those beams to enjoy a different perspective.

When Dad bought the pavilion, its tile roof and framework of beams and pillars were disassembled, hauled by ox-cart to the site at Sorai that he had purchased, and there put back together. The rest was simple. A half-basement was excavated to accommodate elementary kitchen and bathroom facilities and cook's quarters. Predictably, although rarely, this part of the house could be near-ankle-deep in water after a torrential rainstorm. Above, carpenters installed a wood floor, wood clapboard for outside walls and, between bedrooms, thin-wood partitions reaching as high as the cross beams to give a measure of privacy, while air circulated freely under the ponderous tile roof. That roof was a comfort. It might leak when the wind drove rain up under the tiles, but it couldn't blow off, as lighter, corrugated-iron roofs sometimes did in the Sorai gales.

Around the sides, a minimum of glass was used. There were shutters—whole sections of the side walls, starting about window height and hinged at the top, which could be lifted and propped open at various angles by shutter sticks. In the dining-living part of the cottage, the lower wall sections could be let down as well, to extend the floor out to a surrounding rail. It was a simple arrangement, not private, but absolutely delightful in fine weather.

When the weather was not fine, the box had to be shut up tight, as tight as could be managed. Small windows set in some of the shutters gave an impression of portholes in a storm-battered ship as the rain sluiced down them. Apart from these, the interior was dark and could be damp if a storm was prolonged, but we of the younger set didn't mind. The storms, like so much else at Sorai Beach, were full of high adventure.

We children had a small boat, an open type, rigged with a gaffed mainsail and a jib, in which we sailed the bay and came into intimate contact with the sea in some of its more sheltered moods. There were a number of such boats, as simple and as various in their design as the cottages that lined the hill, and the owners, missionaries or their children, proudly formed the Sorai Yacht Club. We held races each summer, a series of them, prepared and managed as professionally as the older members of the club could contrive. A few of the missionary men, such as Dr. H. H. Underwood (son of the pioneer H. G.), gave guidance and stability to the sport, and it became a passion among us junior yachtsmen.

Dad was never much interested in boating. He had grown up on a farm, miles from the sea although not far from the north shore of Lake Ontario. Further, his vacations were short. Mother would go up to Sorai for six or eight weeks with the three of us, but Dad would not take more than two weeks off from the hospital. When he joined us, he found swimming and playing golf on the Sorai Beach Association's improvised links more congenial than bobbing around in a small, open boat.

One time he was game enough to go along with us on a "cruise" to one of the islands. Unfortunately, the breeze died soon after we left our beach. Dad had to man an oar, teamed with Archie, for a three- or four-mile row under a burning sun. Elsie and a girlfriend had the other pair of oars, which meant that my job was just to sit in the stern, hold the tiller and steer for the island. Happily, a bit of breeze came up for the voyage home.

Boating aside, Dad was fond of Sorai Beach and as enthusiastic, in his reserved way, as anyone about the beauties of the place and especially the cool breezes, when he had been enduring the full heat of summer alone in our Taegu house. In the later years of the Sorai Beach resort, roads were improved, and the trip to Sorai became quite easy. Earlier, the trip had been an adventure in itself.

My recollections do not go back as far as the days of the "Sorai steamer," a little coastal tub that used to wallow along near the shore between the ports of Chemulpo and Chinampo, but many people had vivid memories of its scant and stuffy accommodations. For one of the jocular Sorai songs, to the tune of "Funiculli, Funiculla," one resident supplied this stanza:

"Some say the trip to Sorai is delightful,

But that's a lie; but that's a lie.

You know, yourself, that it is simply frightful,

And so do I; and so do I."

A few in the community objected that it was not quite proper for a group of missionaries to roar out joyously, "But that's a lie"; but no one questioned the truth of the assertion—no one, at least, who remembered those actual voyages.

On one trip to Sorai, our family and the Bruens, traveling by car, put up for a night at a Japanese inn. Dad and Harry Bruen decided to enjoy the relaxing luxury of a Japanese bath. "Pu Hai-ri" had been through and was drying off as best he could with one of the inn's diminutive towels when, abruptly, the door opened and there stood the Japanese landlady. Dad was in the deep wooden tub where he could just submerge, but Pu Hai-ri was caught. Embarrassedly he tried to cover himself in some decent way with the tiny towel. The landlady, not at all embarrassed, stood smiling and bowing, obviously amused at the antics of the foreign gentleman. As an attentive hostess, she had just dropped by to see that her guests lacked nothing.

Even at Sorai Beach, a missionary physician found it hard to relax altogether. People got sick and needed attention, sometimes at awkward hours. Dad again took the initiative to get the matter organized. A small, rustic dispensary was set up, and missionary physicians and dentists took turns keeping it open for a short time daily. Sometimes Korean doctors vacationing nearby shared in the project, and a nurse was employed, so that service could be extended to villagers of the surrounding region as well as to the missionary community.

There were systems and mechanics necessary to operating a summer community that came to include eighty or ninety residents, but our younger generation was oblivious to these complications. For us, it was enough that we had comradeship and that the sea was always there, with its constantly changing fascination.

When out on the bay the breeze died and the water grew still and glassy, the sea washed into one's soul, gentle and subdued as it could be. Sunrays would burn down slantingly, below the surface. I could see them, leaning over the side of the boat while my reflection looked up at me and the slack sail slatted with the lazy rise and fall of long, slow swells. Then might come a shower of rain. It would approach from far away across the water with a puff of breeze, puckering the surface, reaching us at length with its cool breath, and pushing the boat briefly while it brought big drops that spattered the sails and pocked the surface of the swells, a drop leaping up from the water for each raindrop that fell.

We were not skilled mariners, but how we loved that bit of ocean trapped in the circle of bay and islands and trapped in a circle of boyish hearts! Once we took an overnight cruise across the bay, six or eight of us. We pulled up on a strange beach near sunset and, after eating part of the picnic fare we'd brought along, anchored a few cable lengths off shore to sleep in the boats. In the early morning, we climbed a headland to look around on a strange countryside and down on our toy boats, drawn up on the beach below.

Later, with a morning breeze, we went gliding up the coast, close in to shore, feeling like Vikings, or like the later Spaniards, coasting the unfamiliar shores of the New World. The coastline broke off in a point. Beyond it, across a narrow channel, were the hills of one of the larger islands, which the Sorai Beach community knew as "Clam" for its outline as seen from there. Leaving our boats anchored in a well-protected cove, we splashed ashore and climbed over part of the island.

In one place, we were running headlong down a slope, leaping bushes and boulders, shouting and laughing, when the runners ahead suddenly stopped short. Panting, the rest of us piled up there in a group. Directly at our feet, the slope was cut away; wind and water had bitten a chunk out of the hill. At what seemed to our excited imagination as an awesome distance, far below us, the waves frothed and broke on a stony beach. It was the seaward side of the island. The swells were larger, the breakers more majestic, and beyond, at the edge of vision, stretched the straight blue line of the open sea.

When we got back to our boats, they were high and dry. Tides on that part of the world's shores are large. We had left our boats in perhaps four feet of water, but that had vanished, and the whole cove was empty. Fortunately for us, the water's floor there was smooth, with rounded stones covered by a good layer of sea slime. We found that our boats slid quite easily and were soon in navigable water again. They were flat-bottomed, with retractable centerboards, a design suited to frequent beachings.

There was still excitement ahead, when we came again to the narrow channel between the island and the mainland, and found that the tide, still ebbing, was running hard with an ominous swirling over a stony bar that stretched across the channel. Several attempts to pole our boats across against the tide convinced us that, as far as we were from home, the safer course was the wiser one.

We drew in close to shore by the island, jumped out, and waded and hauled the boats, not without tugging and straining, through the shallow, rushing water that poured over the bar. Then, the long sail home—heeling over merrily with a good breeze on the beam, brisk enough to wet us a bit with spray—before we made Sorai Point and pulled down our sails in our home berth.

The boat Elsie, Archie and I had was an old one called *Veteran*, bought from another family, for which we pooled Christmas money from relatives in the far-off "homeland." The year before we bought her, she had won the trophy in the Sorai Yacht Club races. Of course we raced her again, with Archie, who had picked up some knowledge of sailing, as skipper and Elsie and me as crew. With absolute earnestness, we sailed that boat, and again *Veteran* came through, winning the trophy in a long and close series of races.

It was our great moment in boating. That trophy, which the Underwoods had donated, was a replica in miniature of a Korean fishing junk, made entirely of brass, with a wash of silver on the tall, square sails. The winning skipper had the privilege of keeping the trophy all year and of having his name and the name of his boat engraved on the sail. Though we competed again twice after that, until our brief summers of childhood and early adolescence ended and Elsie and Archie left Korea for college, our luck was not so good. *Veteran* was outclassed. She had to compete against a couple of newer boats, built on a better design.

This must be all for Sorai Beach. The evocation of old, happy days is generally a requiem. For this one, the Thirty-Eighth Parallel cuts across Korea some miles south of Sorai Point. The deserted cottages will long since have been dismantled for re-usable material. I know of no one who has been able to return, leaving the Sorai Beach Association a far memory.

## 20

# Donkey Egg

DAD HAD A "DONKEY egg" story, a Korean folk tale that he used to tell us when we were little. Farmer Kim wanted to go to Seoul for a try at the civil service examinations, thinking he might become a grand public official, but it was too far to walk, and he had no donkey. About then, along came a shrewd merchant who offered him a marvelous price on a donkey egg, the last he had left. Kim bought it and kept it carefully in a warm place for many days, but the thing wouldn't hatch and wouldn't hatch.

At last, keen fellow that he was, he began to suspect he had been tricked. In a fit of anger, he picked up the donkey egg and threw it over the wall of his *mahdang* (walled yard). Then, just to make sure, Kim leaned over the wall to see where the egg had smashed. What he saw, out of the corner of his eye, was something small, grey, and furry, scurrying across the rice paddies toward his neighbor's house. Kim rushed out the gate and arrived, gasping for breath, at the neighbor's porch.

"Have you seen my donkey? Which way did he go?"

The neighbor listened with wonder to the story of the donkey egg. His own animals had never been produced that way. In fact, his she-ass was about due. He got up and went around to the walled *mahdang* with Kim and, would you know? There was the she-ass with not one shaky-legged little grey foal, but two! So Kim was right. The neighbor gave him the second foal, and after he had raised it, he rode off to Seoul on it. What did he care that some of his friends said his neighbor's she-ass had borne twins, and that all he had seen scampering off across the rice paddies was a startled rabbit?

The story tickled Dad, and he didn't mind repeating it. It pleased his farm boy's "savvy" about such things as animal breeding, and he liked foolish Kim's not really proving as foolish as his neighbor.

Dad had an affectionate nature, and a sense of humor, although a lot of people didn't suspect it. He did his part at home when he could. He would help Mother with our baths when we were small; and then, while we splashed around and, one by one, got out to be dried beside the little kerosene stove in winter, he would get his harmonica and play one tune after another from his brief repertory. The sounds of that harmonica are woven all through the web of my memory.

Dad loved to sing, too, joining in with a vigorous bass if someone supplied the melody. He sang the bass of the hymn "Now the Day is Over" with such gusto that for years we children thought the bass harmony was the melody. A few of the hymns were his favorites. I can see and hear him yet, of a winter day, walking up and down between our dining and living rooms in Taegu, with the warming sun coming in the south windows, singing,

> "Just a few more days to be filled with praise,
>
> And to tell the old, old story . . .
>
> I'll exchange my cross for a starry crown
>
> Where the gates swing outward never. . . ."

In his months at the Trudeau Sanatorium, Dad had learned the importance of relaxing, out of which, as out of every other part of the daily routine, he made a small, methodical ritual. When he came home from the hospital at noon, he liked to have lunch ready and then, after maybe a round of "gobang" (an adapted board game) or some such with one of us, he would settle down in his Morris chair, put his head back and, in a few moments, be breathing deeply. No alarm was needed to wake him up. After just a matter of minutes, as surely as if something had touched off a bell inside of him, Dad would wake with a start, look at his watch, jump up from the chair, and head off down the gravel front walk toward the hospital and a two-o'clock operation. Each day the movements and timing were the same.

For exercise, he liked to play tennis on the not-too-bad court the station had made at one end of the compound. After we learned to play, Archie and I used to take him on together, with us using the doubles lines on the court and him the singles. He had a frustrating serve: a sudden, jerky ball that would occasionally come slicing across the net to bite in one corner of the service box and hardly bounce at all. When it went in, he was delighted and would chuckle out loud, though he made a show of hiding the chuckle behind his hand. He didn't use the serve much on me, but Archie was older and fair game.

Of course, Dad's days of satisfaction in that respect dwindled rapidly. He was proud to see how tall Archie was growing and proud to be beaten by him before Archie got through high school.

Why do they call it "adolescence," and why is it gone so soon? Those brief years are certainly far from "carefree" or "pain-free," even for the happiest among us, but they leave a golden mist, a bitter-sweetness we never quite know again. A time came when I saw the Taegu hills through that mist, when the childhood scenes started to take on a different meaning. There were longer vistas and larger issues; and it was a time in Korea when the issues were sharpening. We tried to talk knowingly about them. Then off we Fletcher children went to America and college, trading what we'd known for a bright new world that was altogether different.

At the railroad station, when it was my turn, Mother and Dad saw me off on the northbound train, going up to join a party taking the Trans-Siberian Railway for Russia, Europe, and the Atlantic. Mother's goodbye was warm and affectionate. I was the last, and they would be alone after that; but Dad just took my hand with a strong squeeze. He was like that. He didn't put his arm around my shoulders or anything such. But it was the first time, I think, that he had ever given me his hand.

I felt that I was beginning to be a man, and I felt the warmth of his goodbye ("God-be-with-ye"). All of that went into the travel diary I began to keep.

∞ ∞ ∞

In Korea, as in much of the world, shadows were deepening. Like others, Dad kept busy and kept hoping. After their push into Manchuria in 1931, the Japanese were busy consolidating the new Empire of Manchoukuo as a puppet state, while preparing their next push into China. One summer they tried whipping up anti-Chinese feeling among the Koreans, spreading stories of Chinese atrocities against Koreans in Manchuria. Down at Sorai Beach a Chinese grocer who called himself E. D. Steward (his main business was in Seoul) was in danger of his life. Missionary men took turns doing guard duty, although without weapons, to protect him and other Chinese of the community. When the situation got more tense, they rushed the Chinese down to the cove, put an outboard motor on our little *Veteran*, the boat most conveniently available, and carried them up the coast to a point of comparative safety.

It was tremendously exciting and dramatic, and we didn't heed the exhaust-spatters of the motor on the freshly painted stern of our boat. We also didn't heed the ominous way in which this fragment fit the sinister pattern taking shape under Japan's military party—any more than, as boarding school kids, we read the whole meaning of the blackouts and air-raid drills in Pyongyang. Then, a few solitary planes would drone overhead and the searchlights would finger the night sky until they could pick up the planes and nail them in crossed shafts of their beams.

Later the "China incident," beginning in 1937, further bared the Japanese military's naked will to conquer. Japan's East Asia Co-Prosperity Sphere had no discernible limits. The military rarely let slip any suggestion that Western interests in Southeast Asia and the Pacific might eventually be taken over, but within its secrecy it knew what it was about. Blackouts and other measures were intensified to key up sentiments of the civilian population to a wartime pitch. In quiet Taegu, Mother and Dad, sitting by a small iron stove in an upstairs room to conserve fuel, wrote to us in the United States about these things. They wrote guardedly, of course, as everyone did.

ᨀ ᨀ ᨀ

In June 1937, Mother and Dad returned to the United States on a furlough, which marked the end of Dad's fourth term of service in Korea. This one had been an eight-year term: the lean years of the Depression had obliged the Board of Foreign Missions to ask everyone abroad to lengthen terms by a year. Elsie, Archie and I drove out to Nebraska in a second-hand Studebaker that a helpful minister had picked out for Dad. The car, turned over to us ready for the road, perplexed Archie for the first fifty miles or so by swerving consistently to one side. At length, it occurred to us to check the tires. They were inflated to about thirty-five pounds in one front tire and fifteen in the other!

Meanwhile Mother and Dad were having their greater automotive thrills. Uncle Tom and my cousin "Bub" (Archibald Carrol) had met them on the West Coast in a new Chevy. Bub had grown up in Nebraska. He took the curves in the Rockies as if he were negotiating the flat Plains, then gunned the Chevy's engine up to eighty miles an hour on the straight stretches, which meant more back in 1937 than it would now. Uncle Tom kept emphasizing that the car was equipped all around with blowout-proof tires, while Bub would take one hand off the wheel to wave at the marvels of the mountain scenery. Dad was just back from eight years of honking his way among pedestrians and ox-carts on Korea's dirt streets and roads. He hunched down in the back seat, gripping the robe rail for balance and swallowing aspirin. When at last they entered the western end of Nebraska, Uncle Tom eyed the flat, dusty fields shimmering in the heat of late June. "This," he declared fondly, "is real country."

That year slipped away quickly. We revisited Canada as a family and then spent a happy August at Ventnor, New Jersey, right next door to the cottage where I was born. In September it was back to college, Elsie returning to Wilson, a women's college in Chambersburg, Pennsylvania, for her senior year and Archie and I to Princeton. Majoring in chemistry, Archie was going on in medicine in the fall at Columbia's College of Physicians and Surgeons in New York City. I had started out toward medicine, too, but had switched my major to English, deciding on preparation for the Presbyterian ministry. The seminary in Princeton (not connected with Princeton University) is the largest theological school of the Presbyterian Church (USA). We two could live at home that year, as the family had one of the missionary apartments in Payne Hall, across from the seminary. In the spring, Elsie and Archie both graduated with honors, with our proud parents on hand, and after Mother and Dad had seen us off toward our summer destinations, they turned back again toward Korea.

∽ ∽ ∽

Internationally, and in Korea's part of the world, the gathering shadows were growing darker. Japan's military party, in complete control, seemed determined to unify the people behind it and to curb foreign influence. This included cutting to a minimum the activities of Christian missionaries, particularly those accustomed to traveling in rural areas in evangelistic itineration, and requiring certain observances of all Korean citizens of the Empire, Christian as well as non-Christian. That action raised the "Shrine Issue."

Shintoism was Japan's state religion. It centered on the emperor, who stood as not only the head of state, or at least the figurehead, but also as the chief symbol of national religious devotion. Such an arrangement has been promoted and capitalized on by more than one aggressive nation in the course of world history, as witness first century Rome and, with modifications, imperial Great Britain. Adolph Hitler did, perhaps, something of the same, with the revival of Teutonic legend, and Soviet Communism developed a brand of secular mythology.

In Japan it was a simple matter. The emperor was the god-man; religious piety and national patriotism were easily wed. Shintoism used no images. There were pictures of His Imperial Highness here and there, but in the Shinto shrines most often seen were memorial tablets, suitably inscribed. It was the spirit that mattered, the pervasive presence of the spirit of Ama-taratsu, sun-goddess sustainer of Japan, ordained to fulfill the nation's imperial destiny.

Understandably, the Koreans wished to have none of this. For Christians and non-Christians alike, the Shinto shrines were an abomination. The former, for the most part, felt that they represented the glorifying of a mere man as god, "worshiping and serving the creature rather than the Creator," as St. Paul had described and condemned it (Rom. 1:25). The latter cared little about such considerations, but saw in the shrines of a religion foreign to their own culture a symbol of the hated interloper and of his oppression.

For the Japanese military, however, Shintoism was an instrument ideally shaped for its designs. Perhaps some military leaders were really devout Shintoists, or persuaded themselves that they were. Others may have had less piety than craftiness. In any case, Shintoism provided a ground on which to draw together the deepest and most sacred associations of the Japanese people, welding in them a national will to conquer and to fulfill the divine destiny. Such a will could be fanned to fanatical heat.

So much for Japan. In Korea Shintoism had to be imposed on an occupied country. The first to feel official pressure were the schools. In Korea, as in quite a few other parts of the world, the first organized schools, and some of the best were those associated with Christian missions. In time, the Japanese colonial government developed its own school system. That forced the Christian schools, if they were to survive, to seek "designation" by government education authorities, which meant that while they were not incorporated into the government program, their graduates would be recognized and their certificates accepted as valid.

In the 1930s, the government began to bring pressure to bear on these Christian schools, such as requiring that history be taught by Japanese teachers acceptable to the government department of education. That would ensure that Korean students received a proper Japanese slant on world affairs past and present. It was a familiar tactic, an essential early step toward controlling the minds of the people.

Quite early, Japan had imposed the teaching of the Japanese language in all schools in Korea, and later only Japanese was taught. When we children were small, for example, we had a Korean tutor for a while who taught us his language out of a primer. A few years later, Mother wanted to get one of those primers, and there were none to be had. The Korean language was no longer being taught; Japan was doing its best to relegate Korean to the status of a mere folk language.

Then the shrine issue became acute. All "designated" schools must, on certain national holidays, take their entire student body to the nearest state shrine. The government said that this was only a patriotic observance, a mark of respect for the emperor. The children would go, and at the proper times they would bow. In the Orient, one bows to show respect. Children often bow to their parents and to other adults. This was not a form of worship that would do violence to anyone's conscience.

But what should the Korean Christians think of it? Some few saw nothing to be concerned about. They included people who had been to the United States. Was this any different from laying a wreath at the Lincoln

Memorial or taking off one's hat when the flag went by? But a majority of Korean Christians considered it an abomination, because it was linked to a false religion and because it was imposed by the conqueror. What united piety and patriotism in Japan was bitterly opposed by both piety and patriotism among the Christians of Korea.

Being in medical work, not educational, Arch did not find himself directly involved in the problem. Further, he held that it was an issue that the Koreans themselves must decide. The Westerner came out of a different culture; acts and symbols might mean something else to him or her. Further, if things got too hot, she or he could simply leave and go home. The Korean Christians must go on living under Japan.

One day Jessie was visiting a rather well-to-do Korean family. The small son had just come home from school and was brought in to greet the visitor. When he knew who she was, he struck a swaggering pose. "There is no god but Ama-taratsu," he recited; "she's better than all of them."

The Japanese authorities made a remarkable effort to put over this point. Japanese police and plainclothesmen in Korea were everywhere, keeping a particularly close watch on the Christians. By the mid-1930s, they were sitting in Bible classes and church services, making notes and watching for questionable statements that might call for a grilling in the police station or even for a spell in prison. As the shrine issue grew acute, the police refused, in 1936, to allow the Presbyterian (USA) Mission to meet, unless discussion of the issue were ruled off the agenda. On the other hand, they went to great pains two years later to rig an action by the General Assembly of the Korean Presbyterian Church. Delegates to the assembly found themselves accompanied by detectives and police. A motion declaring that it was right for Christians to attend shrine ceremonies was carefully prepared and at the proper time the police saw to it that it was made and seconded from the floor. Missionaries attending had been warned in advance that they should have nothing to say, and no discussion was permitted. In the voting, no negative vote was called for. Some voted in favor, most abstained, but it didn't matter: the motion was declared carried.

By this time, the pressure was extreme. Shinto shrines, large and small, had been placed everywhere. The largest and most impressive was erected on South Mountain, outside Seoul, reached by a great flight of white stone steps and housing a most important spirit, who had been brought from Japan with much pomp. Myriads of Koreans were forced to climb the steps and bow before the tablet of the spirit. Myriads hated it as the place where they were robbed of one of the most precious possessions a person has: self-respect.

The Japanese authorities never issued a blanket order to all Korean Christians to go to the Shinto shrines. Instead, they singled out pastors and other potential leaders, and for these, resistance meant the horrors of a Japanese jail. Many of the delegates to that General Assembly meeting of 1938, for example, never got there. The police told them in advance how they were to vote or else go to jail, and their answer was to choose jail.

Robert T. Oliver describes the experience of evangelist Kim Yun-sun, already imprisoned eight times before he was thirty because he opposed shrine worship. Finally, under torture, he agreed that it might be permissible, but when they released him Kim was remorseful. His integrity had been violated. He went back to the police and declared that he still held his original views.

This time, after six months of holding him incommunicado, the police told Kim's wife to take him away; he was dying. She found him on the frozen ground outside the prison door. This was November in northern Manchuria. Kim's Korean jacket had slipped up, leaving his bare skin against the ice, but he was too weak to pull it down. His wife nursed him slowly back to health, and then the police came for him a tenth time. This time, he got sixteen years at hard labor, although long before his sentence was out, Japan fell and the Communists took over in Manchuria. Perhaps evangelist Kim survived; possibly he escaped to South Korea, as others did. More likely, he was set free years earlier by the Lord whom he served.

# 21

# A Heartbreaking Mess

THE HAND GOD TAKES in human affairs is rarely sensational; more often it may seem imperceptible. In Korea, at this juncture, many would say that God used a slender slip of a woman, a young Afrikaner descended from Dutch Protestants who settled in South Africa more than three hundred years earlier. Quiet, intense, dedicated, she was very simple in her approach.

Miss Aletta M. Jacobz was not sponsored by any denomination. She came to Korea with her traveling companion, Miss Marais, in the fall of 1939 in a personal ministry to missionaries. It was a testimony to this remarkable young woman that she was able to sit down with ministers and theological professors, with men and women old enough to be her parents, who had spent a lifetime teaching others about the Christian faith, and to open their eyes to a meaning of the Bible directly and personally for themselves.

That was the essence of her method: to take certain verses of the Bible and re-read them and think about them until the thrust of the thought went inward, and the falterings and failures of personal inner life stood out sharply against the answer of God for each one.

So much for the person and her method—simplicity itself. The inexplicable was the spiritual power of God, which appeared to clothe itself in this unlikely instrument, choosing this precise time to bring a quickening of revival to Christian missionaries in Korea. For many this was not easy. The higher a person has climbed, the longer may be the way down to humility and real self-emptying; but that was the way Miss Jacobz pointed.

In the plan of God, as she herself would have said, her own ministry was brief. After a few months in Korea, she returned to South Africa. A year and a half later she died of exposure in an open boat in the South Atlantic, when the ship in which she was attempting to cross from South Africa to America struck a mine and sank.

Miss Jacobz came to Taegu Station in November. The insights and experiences gained by members of the station during her visit soon began to be passed on to their Korean colleagues. Meetings for spiritual self-examination and revival were organized in the different institutions. In Taegu Hospital, it was February when these were held among the staff, taking advantage of the usual lull in hospital activity that came with the Korean New Year, when everyone tried to be at home. Dr. M. B. Stokes of Seoul, a Methodist missionary, led the meetings.

Miss Jacobz' method seemed unlikely to succeed, particularly among Asians, because it was based on a recognition of one's failings and a frank confession of them before others, as well as before God. These things must be cleared up, she held, if the channel were to be opened completely for the peace and power of God to fill the human heart. But such confession and public making right of old wrongs went against the prevailing culture. It was sure to mean loss of face.

At Taegu Hospital, in the meetings led by Dr. Stokes only a qualified success had been achieved when, on a Friday afternoon, Arch stood up before his staff. Falteringly, the restrained Scotch Canadian farm boy, who had lived half his life in the Far East, began to speak to these people, *his* people, about some of the inner struggles and subtle sins he now recognized in his relations with them. He had never talked to the staff in this way before. His voice choked and tears blurred his eyes; but the effect on his listeners was electric. Old scores began to be cleared. One person after another stood up to acknowledge wrongs, some of them seemingly trifling, others more serious, but all of them matters that had been impediments to happy, effective living as Christians.

On the last evening, a Sunday, they went on until nearly midnight, singing the hymns that had taken on new meaning for them, telling of what God had said to each one. Nurses, laundry workers, doctors, evangelists, floor-washers all seemed to have had a particular experience. What some sensed, perhaps, in that February of 1940 was that in God's providence this was not only setting right the past; it was preparation for what was to come.

War had broken out in Europe, war on a major scale. The Korean patriots saw, perhaps more clearly than others wanted to see, the vortex of direct conflict toward which Japan and the United States were inescapably moving. Suppressed excitement was running high. None of them seemed to doubt that the Western democracies would win, and surely that would mean liberation and national restoration for Korea.

It was a heady dream, and there were many patriots who wanted to be ready for its realization. Their center of operations outside the country was in Shanghai, and their leader was the doughty Dr. Syngman Rhee, aging but still vigorous. He had spent a dedicated lifetime working for Korean independence, even in the darkest years.

Arch had no contact with the Korean patriots. There was nothing he could have done for them, and any relationship discovered by the Japanese would have put an abrupt end to his own service. Some of his staff must have had contact, however. In winter the old hospital building wasn't used, because patients were fewer and the charity cases, who normally were cared for there, could be accommodated in the new building. Yet more than once, in the dead of night, Jessie and Arch saw what appeared to be lights in the top floor, and one time they heard a car engine start up abruptly and drive away. They pretended not to notice—that was safer for everyone—but they did see chairs set around and candle stubs on a table in the top floor of the old building.

Then, about May 1940, the druggist at the hospital died. He was a thoroughly reliable man and had been in apparently good health the afternoon before, when he left work. Suddenly, he was dead. No one seemed to want to comment on the cause of his death. Little was said, but a startling number of people assembled for the funeral and carried his body on their shoulders a great distance—a sign that he was known and honored much beyond what had been thought while he lived.

On June 1 something else happened. Arch had been working at rebuilding the dispensary. It was put up in 1928 to house the outpatient department with laboratories and x-ray, and consulting rooms for all of the specialties. The work had soon outgrown the structure, and for several years, Arch had been planning to continue using the building as it stood, but at the same time to complete excavation of a full basement and also add a second floor above the existing one.

This would make, in effect, a three-story outpatient building connected on all three levels with the fireproof hospital. And with this, Arch promised himself, he would desist from building—at least unless someone gave the money for an isolation building for tuberculosis, that he still dreamed of. As it was, Taegu would have one of the most complete and modern hospitals in Korea.

The dispensary additions were nearly finished. It had been a struggle to get building materials and permits for importing essential equipment, but at last those things were in place. Carpenters were finishing the final details of the second floor, and plumbers in the basement were completing installation of the heating system, while the busy ebb and flow of patients and staff on the first floor continued as usual. Soon the new units could be opened for service.

June 1 was a Saturday. Shortly before noon, Jessie left the hospital to go home and look after lunch preparations. With her children grown and gone, she had in recent years been giving almost full time to the hospital, supervising laundry and supplies, and had a neat little office on the ground floor of the main building. Before she left that lunchtime, however, she was upstairs. She opened the door connected to the new second floor of the dispensary and looked down the long hallway. The smell of fresh wood and of paint and glue met her nostrils. The glue was made from fish entrails, which Korean carpenters boiled up in a black pot that was always coated thick with it. It was a good smell, mixed faintly with the fresh wood. She noted with satisfaction that the doors down each side of the long corridor were hung. Wood shavings lay scattered on the floor. There was no one in sight.

Jessie hadn't been home long when Arch came up the sloping gravel walk with his usual quick, decided step. He did everything that way, even walking, as though anxious to finish that and get on to what was next. At one o'clock on Saturday, all of the dispensary staff left for the weekend, and only a minimal force remained on duty at the hospital. A little later, at home, lunch was nearly finished, and Jessie and Arch were enjoying the chance to relax.

But something seemed to be different.

"That's odd," Jessie thought vaguely; "I didn't remember this was market day."

Every fifth day, when market was held, the big square below the hospital would fill with people, and all day long the vendors' calling and shouting would reach the house like a roaring of distant surf. Then suddenly her mind focused on the sound, and she sat up straight.

"Arch, do you hear that? It sounds like it's coming from the hospital!"

He had already heard it and was making for the door. Outside, there was confused shouting and a crackle of flames. Grey smoke poured from the direction of the dispensary, mostly hidden by summer foliage of the trees. Arch was off at a run, with Jessie following as closely as she could. When she got within sight of the new upper story, it was completely ablaze.

It was a heartbreaking mess they had to clean up late that afternoon. The firemen had gotten there quite promptly and had hauled their hoses through the hospital building to fight the fire in the adjoining dispensary, filling the corridors with mud and water. Although the hospital was fireproof, terrified relatives and friends had carried all of the patients out onto the lawn in front of the building, adding to the confusion.

Staff and firemen had even attempted to remove a good deal of the hospital equipment, causing needless damage. And of course the drugs and equipment of the dispensary, what could be saved, had been dragged out and dumped helter-skelter. Jessie's little ground-floor office in the hospital was piled high with them. Arch was everywhere that afternoon, rushing back and forth, trying to keep some order in the salvaging, but to little avail. Now began the job of cleaning up, and of adding up the loss.

The fire, which was out in a few hours, had completely gutted the dispensary building. Nothing was left but the brick walls and the blackened joists of the first floor. The new second floor had been full of new supplies and equipment. Arch's pride and joy was there, an ice-cube machine, something that had not been seen in Korea. It could turn out all the ice a modern hospital might need, and was the gift of the church in Norristown, Pennsylvania, which also contributed Arch's salary. All of that was gone.

Much of the dispensary's supply of drugs had been lost and indispensable equipment damaged. The hospital staff had planned happily on putting into service a completely modern outpatient department. Instead, they would have to go back and crowd somehow into the little old dispensary building erected back in 1913 and converted some time ago into a baby clinic and charity outpatient department.

The most depressing thing for Arch was that little hope could be held out for rebuilding. The executive committee of the Korea mission acted fast. One member wrote to New York as soon as he saw an account of the fire in the local newspaper, even before he received word from Arch. The total loss was estimated conservatively at 120,000 yen, and the executive committee quickly put through an action requesting that the board make available that amount from its Fire and Marine Insurance Fund. There was even talk that more should be spent and the dispensary rebuilt with the same fireproof steel and concrete construction that the hospital had used.

The board granted the money, but it was all wishful thinking. Japan was working fervently, getting ready for Pearl Harbor. New buildings were out; no authorization could be secured, and no permit for essential materials.

Why had the building burned? The Japanese police usually investigated such things with severe consequences. Their "investigations" were dreaded; but this time no one was arrested. Inquiries seemed to be scarcely more than perfunctory. Arch realized that there was nothing to do but be quiet and go on.

Two facts seemed dubious, though. The fire had broken out in the unused, almost finished top floor on a Saturday, just after everyone had left the building for the weekend, and it seemed suspiciously to repeat a pattern.

The contractor was a German, J. Weber. That same spring, he had finished a hospital for the Salvation Army, built near the railroad about two-thirds of the way up to Seoul. As the building was being completed, and before it was occupied, fire had broken out, destroying a considerable part of it.

Arch didn't suspect Weber in the dispensary blaze; what did he stand to gain? One thing was sure: the Japanese were curbing American prestige and influence any way they could. It was a year and a half later that Arch was able just to get permission to do a little remodeling of the old dispensary, to make it more adequate for the work that had to be shifted back into it. The contract was let and work started in December 1941—one job Arch himself wasn't to supervise.

In the interim, anti-American pressure kept mounting. The Methodist board was withdrawing all of its personnel, considering that their presence in Korea, as Americans, would only embarrass the Korean Christians and expose them to further harassment. The Presbyterians decided to keep missionaries on the field as long as possible, although where indicated some should be withdrawn.

The US State Department sent the *S.S. Mariposa* to Inchon to pick up American citizens, and she steamed away in November for San Francisco. On board were fifty adult members of the Presbyterian (USA) mission and fifteen children, more than had ever been on any one vessel before. The Pyongyang Foreign School in the north had opened briefly that fall and then shut down. Most mothers with younger children, as well as adults in poor health, left the country.

Still the unrelenting pressure kept up. On January 30, 1941, Arch had written to William Danner of the American Mission to Lepers:

> As you know, some institutions have been closed.... Our work goes on as heretofore and it is my purpose to stay by the institutions which I have built up from the bottom at no little expenditure of strength and effort. This expression of decision is made because the Lord seems to be very definitely leading me in this direction. Where He leads I hope to follow and what more can I say as to the future?

Soon after came the World Day of Prayer incident. The World Day of Prayer was, and is, observed by Christian women around the Earth. The date was in late February, a day for women to gather and pray for one another and for their world, using a common program translated into many languages. What started the trouble in Korea was that, in that particular year, the program material was prepared by Chinese Christian women in Shanghai. Japan was still engaged in her China Incident. Further, Shanghai was where the Korean nationalist movement had its headquarters. Finally, the very theme of the prayer program seemed seditious. It was dedicated to "The Kingdom of God" and included a prayer for peace among all nations.

Even so, the program was translated into Korean and distributed, and on the appointed day groups of Christian women all over Korea gathered to use it in prayer. Abruptly, early in March, came the government's retaliation. Fifteen missionary women in widely separated parts of the country were arrested simultaneously, some grilled repeatedly about the offensive program, some detained for as long as a month.

Why were they encouraging sedition, teaching ignorant Korean women to pray for peace, instead of praying for the success of Japanese arms in China? And what of this talk of a Kingdom of God that they were promising, instead of the Japanese empire? The women detained were released from jail and some left Korea soon after that. The rest would not be long in following.

There was another disturbing incident that spring. The Shinto shrine pressure had taken on a new form. Japanese authorities were demanding that a simple and rather crude little shrine, just a miniature wood replica with small wooden doors, be set on a narrow shelf on a wall of every home in Korea. So far, the shrines had been confined to public places. Now they were to be in the homes.

The requirement was not extended to the homes of foreigners, but in Chungju the local police demanded that a "god-shelf" be placed in the servants' quarters of the missionary residence there, as it was the home of a Korean family. DeWitt Lowe, MD, and the Rev. Otto DeCamp, Presbyterian missionaries, refused, declaring that the house was mission property and no god-shelf could be tolerated. As a result, it was DeCamp and Lowe who were marched off to jail and later transferred to Seoul, where they were held through the spring and early summer. For those left in Korea, the handwriting on the wall was becoming plainer.

Lowe and DeCamp were still in jail in July, when Jessie and Arch went up to Seoul for a wedding, the last trip they were permitted to make out of Taegu. It was an Underwood family wedding. Horace Grant, eldest son of Dr. Horace H. and grandson of grand old Dr. Horace G., Korea mission pioneer, was being married.

The following month, the Japanese expelled a considerable number of the missionaries remaining in Korea. They were charged with various fatuous misdemeanors but given deferred sentences, with the understanding that their departure within two months would cancel the sentences.

That was how there was a farewell supper in Taegu Station in mid-September. The five remaining members of Andong station were there, and nine who were leaving Taegu, all of them preparing to take the night train to Seoul. From there they would make their way to Shanghai, planning to sail for the United States on the *S.S. President Lincoln*; but the *Lincoln*, as it turned out, had no room. After a month in Shanghai the group got a French vessel to the Philippines, where the Presbyterian Philippine mission asked some of them to remain in the security of that country for the duration of the Japanese-US tension and help with the work there.

Herbert Blair of Taegu, his wife, and some others accepted. The advancing Japanese forces found them in the Philippines not so many months later, interned them, and Herbert Blair died of beri beri in the Los Baños Camp in 1945, only three days before liberation.

In Taegu only Ned Adams and Jessie and Arch Fletcher stayed behind. That October Arch got off one last letter to William Danner, sending it by way of Shanghai. The letter analyzed briefly the problems and possibilities of the situation in Korea. It included two terse and typical paragraphs. One was headed "Our program":

> We expect both hospitals to continue as long as they are permitted to serve as Christian institutions. If and when this becomes impossible, they shall not be leased, loaned or sold to a Christian or non-Christian group or individual, but shall be closed.

As it turned out, neither hospital would be closed. Through the hardship of the years ahead both would carry on, though Arch would not be there. The other paragraph, headed "The Future," ended his letter:

> The future of the work is uncertain in these days, but we feel it is hopeful. We will remain as long as the Lord honors our witness; as long as the doors remain open. Your prayers and cooperation are needed as never before.

That same month Arch got another jolt. The compound was deserted now. He and Jessie had moved into one of the smaller houses, in order to leave their larger one for use as a dormitory for nurses. Ned Adams lived a quarter of a mile away, on an opposite knoll. One morning the "outside man" who was looking after the Bruens' house came over in some excitement to report that the place had been broken into in the night.

Arch went back with him to check. Things were in jumbled disarray, as if they had been ransacked hurriedly. There was a large bundle of cloth goods and supplies inside the back door, giving the impression it had been dropped there by thieves rushing to get away.

Some other indications were suspicious. Special attention seemed to have been given to papers in the study. Bookcases had been moved out from the walls and even two wall-lamps torn out, as if a search had been made for a hidden depository of documents. In the garage, the seats of the Bruens' car had been slashed open.

The "intruders," likely more than one, appeared to be looking for evidence of clandestine activity—presumably espionage. This could only mean that the Japanese authorities were behind what was intended to pass for a robbery. Arch found that very disquieting—to be taken note of as one more sign of the times.

# 22

# Sayonara

Twice in his life, Arch was laid on the shelf, and both times it did him good. There were the months in Trudeau Sanatorium in 1918, and there was the house arrest following Pearl Harbor. This narrative began with the news of Pearl Harbor breaking on Taegu and with Jessie and Arch getting the word that their friend and colleague Ned Adams had been locked up. The police took Arch over to check on the Adams' house and see that the water was properly shut off, the radiators drained and so forth. He found there the remains of tea, which Ned apparently had made for himself in his solitude just before they came for him. He also saw some jumbled clothing and blankets where Ned had rummaged, hunting for a few warm things to protect him in the unheated jail.

As he told it later, Ned put on some long underwear. He wasn't used to it and found it itchy. As the days in jail passed, the itching got worse, but he wasn't going to peel off the underwear for fear the guards might take it away from him. Endurance has its limits, though; at last Ned just had to get that underwear off, and then he knew why it itched him so. Every seam was lined with prison lice.

Ned was about three weeks in jail. At first Arch expected the same treatment, and Jessie said if they were going to take him, she almost hoped they'd take her, too. She had no wish to stay alone in that eerie house, blacked out at night, cut off from everyone. Both of them packed small bags with the bare essentials for prison life and kept them near the door in case the police shouldn't give them much time; but the police didn't come. Later they thought about money. They weren't supposed to leave their own yard, but as no very strict watch seemed to be kept they slipped over to another house where the station safe was located and got out all the money that was left. This they divided. Jessie had made money belts, and both kept the belts constantly on their bodies. Still no order came consigning them to jail—and then they got word on the quiet that Ned was back home. A little later, the police announced that news with evident satisfaction.

Arch and Jessie had a practice of exchanging newspapers with Ned. The two houses had a joint subscription to the *Japan Times and Advertiser,* an English-language paper that the Japanese chose to keep on publishing after Pearl Harbor, presumably to continue printing extravagant accounts of their victories. Jessie and Arch would read the paper and then send it over to Ned via the Korean outside man assigned to take care of the station cows. He was the only person allowed to shuttle back and forth in this way. Later, the outside man would bring back the old papers, several at a time. On inside pages, in the margins here and there, would be brief notes scribbled by the recipients as the papers went and came. Sometimes, as a sort of code, Ned, Jessie and Arch used references to Bible verses that might convey a veiled report on how each was faring.

When two months had gone by, the police abruptly appeared at the door, more of them than usual, and Ned with them. Apparently they were thinking in terms of taking over the houses soon, and wanted to see the disposition of rooms upstairs and so forth. Arch invited them in and said under his breath to Jessie, "Stay here and talk to Ned while I take them upstairs." He was up there a good while, stalling for time while he showed the police every nook and cranny of the place. Meanwhile Ned, wearing a full beard as a relic of his prison experience, talked fast to Jessie, telling her how he had been treated there.

The police were the major harassers. There were three groups of them, the plainclothes detectives, the black-uniformed civilian police, and, most to be feared, the khaki military police. Representatives of one group or another, and sometimes of more than one, would come to the house every day. Looking out an upstairs window Jessie would see a bicycle below, which meant that one of them was there. Arch received them in the front part of the house, unheated all winter. He sometimes broke out in a cold sweat though, trying to answer their questions. He knew he had to be unfailingly courteous, while also choosing his words with care in replying to the endless and often insolent questions they put to him.

When he thought it was the right moment, he would go to a small serving window between the dining room and kitchen and open it a crack. This meant that Jessie should bring in tea. She had some sugar that had been gathered up from the various houses on the compound, and she had used it to make cookies to offer to the honored guests. Their loud, polite hissing over the hot tea and cookies was with obvious relish; such small luxuries were no longer to be had by police underlings in Japan's war effort.

Once Arch was able to work a little stratagem on one of them. He had heard that the Japanese had made a great issue elsewhere of a couple of shortwave radio sets in missionary homes, apparently convinced that if these Americans had receivers, they must also have some type of transmitters. Although his set was only long-wave, Arch disconnected it and put it away. Inevitably, one of the most bothersome of his police questioners asked him about his having a radio.

"Oh, that. I have just a small set, but it's put away; I don't use it. As a matter of fact, I'd like you to have it, if you would be willing to receive it."

The Japanese officer seemed surprised and, under his incommunicative exterior, delighted. He would be back that evening—well after dark, of course—to receive the radio; and so he was. After that Arch felt more sure of at least this one questioner. Another time, though, when the man's probing questions became too troublesome, Arch put in:

"Also, sir, if the chief of police should become very concerned about radio transmission, I could mention to him the set which I passed along to you, not so?"

All through Arch and Jessie's internment, a few Korean friends had occasionally slipped up to the compound under cover of darkness to tap cautiously at the back door and relay news that was going around. Another contact was through Li Yoo-boon, the devoted nurse at the Well Baby Clinic. Milk from the cows Arch helped to look after was carried down to the baby clinic in the dispensary every day in five-pound cracker tins. When the empty tins came back, Nurse Li often slipped into them a little sugar or flour or something else she could get and thought the Doctor and his wife might be needing. Of course the outside man who carried the tins knew of their contents, but no suspicion had been aroused.

Once a grateful ex-patient even entered the compound and came up to the house in broad daylight. The man had spent some time in the hospital for a badly crippled back. Now the police took him for a hunchback beggar and let him in, probably thinking he would serve as an annoyance to the foreigners. Instead, the ex-patient wanted to know what he could do; and when Arch gave him some money, he went and bought a chicken and smuggled it back in his beggar's bag, giving Jessie and Arch a rare treat. These friends and former patients were as happy as anyone to outwit the hated police, even though they ran considerable risk in doing so.

For many US and British subjects, in Korea and other Japanese possessions, internment was a hideous nightmare. For others, and even for some of those who suffered severely, it was a spiritual experience. Jessie and Arch had no real hardship. What they had was uncertainty, along with an abrupt, forced adjustment to a life of solitude and inactivity. They went cautiously around to the other houses, let themselves in and gathered up books and a few phonograph records. There was plenty of time, as well, for Bible study—and plenty of incentive, what with the unsettled nature of things. And then, the simple chores of daily living took time when they had to do everything themselves.

Arch found himself adjusting to it. He even began to find a freedom and an inner peace in this life of simple trust, focused on each day as it came and went. There was no use looking back and no basis for looking forward. The mood to cultivate was rest. For her part, Jessie discovered a text that spoke directly to her out of the Bible that December. It was Isaiah 52:12 (King James Version):

> For ye shall not go out in haste, neither shall ye go by flight: for Jehovah will go before you; and the God of Israel will be your reward.

It seemed a promise that they would go, but calmly and in God's time.

Jessie and Arch came to love a phonograph record, a contralto singing, "Oh, rest in the Lord; wait patiently for him, . . ." With Jessie playing the piano, they would sing hymns together, as they did everything else together, just the two of them. They were probably closer to one another than they had ever been in the twenty-six years of their marriage.

One hymn that they sang began to be a favorite with Arch, who by temperament did not excel in patience. The words are by Bradford Torrey:

> "Not so in haste, my heart!
>
> Have faith in God and wait;
>
> Although He linger long
>
> He never comes too late. . . .
>
> "Until He cometh, rest,
>
> Nor grudge the hours that roll;
>
> The feet that wait for God
>
> Are soonest at the goal."

As spring came on, the compound was filled with beauty. An oasis of calm, its leafing trees attracted flocks of birds, becoming a veritable bird sanctuary. In the previous fall, after the others all left the station, Jessie had dug up flower bulbs from a number of the yards and planted them around the house she and Arch had moved into. Now the bulbs—hyacinths, tulips, dahlias—began to sprout and blossom, and to splash the borders with their rich colors. They were like the kindly Presence of God, gracious and reassuring.

In March the police abruptly took a new tack:

"Do you wish to send a message to anyone in America? We will take the message and send it for you."

Jessie and Arch discussed that proposal, turning it around and examining it this way and that. What were the police up to? Did they want to get something out of them, or hope to trap them in some way? Or might there be a chance that somehow a message really would be sent through? They decided on a carefully innocuous statement addressed to Jessie's father, just to say they were well and were being treated considerately. Of course it never went through; and just what the police expected to gain by the move still remains obscure.

The next month, April, the police had bigger news. There was to be an exchange of civilians. Arch and Jessie would be repatriated, along with all other US and Canadian citizens in Korea. They should be ready to leave in early May.

Jessie stood watching near a front window until she could see that the police were well down the road to the compound gate; then she hugged Arch.

"Can that be? Do you think it's really true—an exchange of civilians? Would such a thing be arranged?"

Arch returned the hug, with both arms around her, making her think fleetingly how he had really grown more affectionate in their solitude.

"It could be, I suppose," he offered rather hesitantly. "In all of this, we're in unfamiliar territory. War makes strange things happen. Who knows?"

"Well, I won't let myself get excited; but maybe we ought to start to get ready."

"Yes, dear," he agreed. "'Not so in haste . . . Have faith in God and wait.' At the same time, we should be prepared, and maybe we'll hear something more."

Now Arch and Jessie began sorting and packing. They didn't know how much they might be able to take with them, but were optimistic and naive enough to hope that things left behind might be protected in some way and might still be recoverable when the mission representatives were able to return. If such a hope seems far-fetched, war was something they hadn't been through as yet.

They spent a good many hours sorting the possessions and keepsakes of two and a half decades spent in Taegu, deciding what should go in the first two trunks, which the police told them they could take, and what in a third, if anything else could be taken, and so on.

A couple of days later, after another visit by the police, Jessie noticed that Arch didn't seem involved in what they were doing; some suggestions she made seemed to go by him unheard. "Let's take a break," she said. "I'll make us a cup of tea."

When they settled at the table with the teapot between them, Arch took a sip and held the cup, looking down into it. Jessie knew he had something to tell her and knew that she needed to wait while he got ready. After a long moment, it came.

"I found out, Lawssie, from the police, that there's a Mr. Oda, a government liaison officer in Seoul, whom we enemy aliens can deal with."

He took another sip and let a second long moment pass.

"And does that have something to do with us now, dear?" Jessie asked.

"Well, it might. You see, after some soul-searching and prayer, I'm wishing to send a message to Mr. Oda through the police to ask that he agree for me to stay in Taegu and to help in any way I can."

"Stay in Taegu—just you?" Jessie knew her voice was trembling. She was trembling all over, especially inside.

"Yes, I wouldn't ask that you should stay."

As he went on, he got up and came around the table to put his hand gently on her shoulder while she turned to him. It was so unusual of him—the *whole thing* was so unusual—and beginning to feel surreal.

Arch continued: "It's important that you go back, now that there's a chance, to see the children and have them see you—to see your family, too. I don't know that Mr. Oda can do anything, but I feel that I should make a try."

The room got very quiet. There were tears in Jessie's heart, but none came to her eyes. She put her hand on his, where it rested on her shoulder.

"Arch, this is so like you. But whoever this Mr. Oda is, the Lord will show us the way."

"Yes, He will," Arch said, "and in the meantime we'll keep on getting ready to go."

That was all. The evening came on, and the night, and Jessie said nothing more about it. Arch, of course, would not—then, nor the following day, either. Jessie fought down a surge of anxiety when, in late afternoon, the principal police officer appeared, accompanied by two others.

He entered rather stiffly, declined Arch's hospitable gesture that he take a seat, and promptly delivered his message: Mr. Oda had said, "No." The policeman himself had wondered that the alien doctor should make such a request, but had conveyed it faithfully to the authority in Seoul. The answer was immediate and brief: No.

With that, the police withdrew. Jessie and Arch had their answer—from the Lord. Jessie felt deeply grateful, and grateful also, as time passed, that Arch was in full acceptance, making no comment and pushing along willingly with preparations to leave.

Predictably, the original date for leaving began to be moved to a later one. It got to be the end of May, and then at last the police said June 2, and stuck to it. They also said, on the night of June 1, however, that no trunks at all could be taken—"only what you can carry in your hands." Early next morning, Jessie and Arch were up and at work. Jessie was also given some verses for that day. The reading for June 2 in *Daily Light*, her devotional booklet of selected Bible verses, was this:

> Thus shall ye eat it: with your loins girded, and ye shall eat it in haste: it is the Lord's Passover—Arise ye, and depart; for this is not your rest—Here have we no continuing city, but we seek one to come—There remaineth therefore a rest to the people of God.

They worked all day and into the evening, trying to sort and repack only the most precious and irreplaceable things, plus what they guessed might be the most necessary things—in a footlocker commandeered from another house and in several small suitcases. What was left they tried to stow in the safest places they could think of.

For some days, the police, in their unfailing daily visits, had been hinting broadly at things they saw in the house that they would like to receive personally. The policeman to whom Arch had given the radio kept badgering him for the keys to his automobile, insisting that it was for the chief of police. But Arch kept refusing; the car was not his, he maintained, but had been given for the use of the superintendent of the leprosy hospital. He couldn't dispose of it personally.

On that last night, the outside man came back after dark, and they gave him what was left in the house of sugar, flour, and other supplies—then worth more than money. Jessie suggested that he come back for some other things in the morning, but fear crept into his eyes.

"No," he shook his head, "none of us would dare come back once you are gone."

It seemed as if they never *would* be gone. They worked right through until after midnight. It was 2:00 a.m. when the luggage was all stacked down by the door and the police came to take them to the station. How many times had they driven in the still of night through the deserted streets to meet some arriving guest, or to see us children off for school after vacation! This time they walked, surrounded by detectives and police, with Hai, the outside man, helpful to the last, managing part of the baggage.

At the station, they saw Ned Adams with his own escort of police and plainclothesmen. They greeted each other restrainedly, but nothing could hide the light that shone in Ned's eyes. He was going to see his wife and family again! After the first three weeks in jail, he had been released to his home, but had to cope, alone, with his solitude. He had caught pine warblers and made cages for them, filling the living room of his house with their warbles and chatter to drive away the loneliness. It was rare to see this species of bird in Taegu; apparently they were migrating and had varied their route.

The acquisitive policeman was still trying to get the keys to Arch's car, but Arch put him off and never did surrender them. Of course it was only a moral victory; the authorities would soon have the car anyway.

There was the usual pins-and-needles wait. At last a whistle shrieked in the night, and the headlamp of the locomotive appeared up the track. The police escorted the three of them to their railway car. They had to manage their own luggage now; "what you can carry" had been the instruction. Arch did it determinedly in two trips, one for Jessie's bags and one for his own, up and across the overpass and down to the second platform—dripping with perspiration in the warm, pre-dawn June air.

One car had been reserved for the repatriates, and they were all there. Among excited greetings, Jessie checked them off mentally. No resident of the mission left in Korea seemed to be missing. All the day before, while she and Arch were sorting and repacking in Taegu, the train had been gathering them up along the line, from Manchuria on down. With her woman's eye, Jessie noticed, while pretending not to, the marks that prison and privation had left on some. She was shocked to see the residual effects of torture on a few of these longtime friends. But now that would be passed, they hoped; at least they had started home.

There was no sleep the rest of that night. Indeed, the sky was greying in an hour or so, and soon the sun was up. They had too much to talk about, all of them—even if the ubiquitous police were there in the train coach, and they communicated some things only by furtive looks and silences.

At Pusan there were more delays, and then they were transferred to a ferry to cross the strait to Japan. Not all in the party knew one another. There were a number of Roman Catholic Maryknoll fathers and sisters and some business people, as well as Protestant missionaries of four or five different missions. On the ferry, the accommodations were comfortable, Japanese style, consisting of a large room with the springy rice-straw *tatami* on the floor. Shades were drawn, and the enemy aliens were not allowed on deck. After twenty-seven hours and the emotional exertion of the past night, Jessie sank down gratefully on the *tatami* and was soon asleep.

In late afternoon the ferry docked at Shimonoseki. From there it was all night by train to Kobe, sitting bolt upright in a third-class day coach. In Kobe they were marched to the immigration building near the station. It had been erected as a sort of barracks and marshaling center for Japanese emigrants on their way to Brazil. The male foreigners were all assigned to the third floor and women to the second. Wade Koons of Seoul became acting spokesman for the group as billets were arranged for. He called aside Jessie and Arch.

"It isn't coming out even," he said. "How about the Underwoods and you and us sharing a room? We know each other well."

There were eight in the Underwood party, including two children they were looking after, so this made twelve. The room the twelve were assigned to was just large enough for a central aisle and six beds on each side, set so close together that one had to climb over the foot of the bed to get into it. But it wasn't for long, as they hoped, and they all were on their way home—so they laughed and joked over the awkwardness of the arrangement.

After all, some of the men had been in jail in Seoul, also twelve in a room, when they were joined by a thirteenth inmate, a young Eurasian *girl*. They decided she should have the cot next to the door and should choose which of the men she might feel least embarrassed to have in the cot next to her. She chose one of the senior missionaries, and they all managed to work out their prison living surprisingly well.

From the immigration building in Kobe, the repatriates could look out and see the *Asama Maru* riding at anchor in the harbor. She was the ship that was to take them all the way to Lourenço Marques in Portuguese East Africa (now Mozambique), where they would meet the Swedish liner *S.S. Gripsholm*, chartered by the US Government, and be exchanged for an equal number of Japanese subjects being sent back from Canada and the United States. After that, the circuitous voyage would continue down around the Cape of Good Hope, across to Río de Janeiro, and at last to New York. The *Asama* was plainly marked with huge white crosses painted on her fore and aft sides and a white illuminated cross bolted to her superstructure, to mark her neutral purpose.

Then the ship disappeared from her berth in the harbor. Eventually an explanation reached them; she had gone to Yokohama. They would be taken to Tokyo to board her there. That meant more days of waiting. Presumably there was some final dickering going on between Japan and the United States through the Swiss about arrangements for the swap of civilians. At last, after an interminable two weeks, the order went around to be ready to move.

On June 17 in the long evening light, the enemy aliens, more than a hundred of them, were lined up by fours and marched to the station to take a night train to Tokyo. On the way they passed a wire enclosure where some Americans, probably GIs who had been taken prisoner, saw them and shouted, "Give my love to Broadway! Tell 'em we'll be back!" Immediately the Japanese guards began shouting too, angrily. The repatriates waved, but didn't call back.

On the train that night, sitting on wood third-class benches, there were others who had been held in Japan, including one missionary who had spent six months in jail in solitary and was just reunited with his wife. All night he kept hungrily munching at the cookies and other sweets she had managed to save and bring him. It had been in his Bible class that Toyohiko Kagawa, peace activist and Christian leader, was converted to Christianity. He kept asking for news about this and that friend, what she had done with different articles, and how she had arranged about the house. She tried to get him to be quiet and sleep, or let others try to sleep, but he was too prison-starved for news of the outside world. Finally dawn came and the train approached Tokyo.

At the station, they learned that they would be taken to the Imperial Hotel for breakfast. One never knew what to expect: this time it was the dining salon of the hotel, still luxurious, with linen, gleaming silver, and roses on every table. The full breakfast menu included juice, eggs and bacon, coffee with sugar and cream! Scarcity and war were shut out behind the Imperial's handsome doors—but not quite. Photographs were being taken. The elaborate spread would show in propaganda pictures how the Japanese treated their enemy aliens before they repatriated them.

At the dock, there was more queuing up and waiting; they seemed to have done nothing else for weeks. Cabins had to be assigned and passengers distributed according to sex and place of origin in the different classes of accommodation. Jessie was put in a second-class cabin with three Canadian women. Arch started out in one third-class cabin with a dozen men, then was moved to another. All were to remain below decks, but they could feel when the diesel engines started to throb and could hear the shouting and running back and forth that meant the vessel was finally casting off. Slowly she proceeded down the estuary and through the harbor toward the breakwater and open sea. And then she halted.

The engines stopped; the anchor chain rattled out. There was no explanation. Many of those on board had been through the horrors of various prisons. Some of the journalists, in particular, had been told they would never get out alive. Would they be taken off now? Was the whole thing just to be a cruel farce for them? Several of them swore they would jump before they'd let themselves be taken off the ship; but nobody came for them. The *Asama* rode quietly at anchor and day followed sunny day—still without an explanation, only rumor.

It had been a week when suddenly, about 1:00 a.m., Jessie woke in her berth. A bright light was shining in the porthole. A voice had just called, "Sayonara." Others answered, and there were steps of several men going down a steep gangway. The other women in the cabin were awake. Cautiously they peered out the open porthole and could see a launch bobbing below. The men from the gangway, apparently shore crew, were just jumping into it. The *Asama* was ablaze with lights and again one could feel the faint vibration of her engines. In a few moments, they began to throb and she was gathering way, making for open sea.

At Hongkong, more repatriates were taken aboard, and at Saigon. The ship never made port, but stood outside the harbors while launches brought out the passengers and conditions below decks got more crowded. Water was one of the main problems. The Japanese rationed it to a trickle, and that only at certain hours of the day; but all of these things were nothing if they could just make it through to Lourenço Marques. No one would really feel free until the exchange had been made and they were completely out from under the Japanese watch.

That day finally came, July 23, with entrance into the Portuguese harbor past a grimy US freighter, flying the Stars and Stripes and saluting the passengers of the *Asama* with the V for Victory, three shorts and a long on her hoarse whistle. Eyes watching her were wet with tears. The *Gripsholm*, tied up at a wharf, had been there for two days. Laboring tugs pushed the *Asama* in front of her, then the *Conte Verde*, a second exchange ship that had joined the *Asama* at Singapore and crossed the Indian Ocean with her, in behind.

Next day the exchange was carried out, columns of Canadians and Americans walking down one side of the wharf and Japanese up the other. Ambassador Grew and Admiral Nomura almost bumped into each other and nodded stiffly. On the deck of the *Gripsholm*, a huge Swedish smorgasbord was greeted by the repatriates with spontaneous cheers.

After more weeks at sea, where strained nerves gradually relaxed and faded eyes regained some luster, and after a stop part way at incomparable Río, every eye aboard sparkled and glistened at the sight of the Statue of Liberty. "I lift my lamp beside the golden door."

One last disappointment awaited Jessie and Arch there. Her father had come to New York City to meet them, but they weren't permitted to see anyone. Arch was still a Canadian and Jessie, when she married an alien under the old law, had lost her US citizenship; so both were transferred directly from the ship to a waiting train and carried to Montreal. Two days later, they were free and back again in the United States, this time to stay long enough for Jessie to reclaim her citizenship and for Arch, with her help, to be naturalized.

∽ ∽ ∽

Living at the familiar house at 414 Swarthmore Avenue in suburban Ridley Park, Mother's parents' home, where we three had spent happy Christmas vacations in our college days, Dad commuted to Philadelphia and took graduate surgery at the University of Pennsylvania's School of Medicine. Later, while the war continued, he went out to Oklahoma and turned this preparation to account, travelling constantly and lecturing on surgical diagnosis to groups of local doctors under a program of the Oklahoma State Medical Association.

Mother stayed behind in Ridley Park. My sister, Elsie, had joined the WAVES and was out at Boulder, Colorado, sweating it out in the Navy's intensive course in Japanese. Her childhood Korean was of only limited help, but her Oriental background was useful. Archie, now an MD, was in the Army Medical Corps, getting ready to go to Europe, although he never did get really close to the action. I was finishing theological studies and just recently married, serving a small country church and preparing to go to South America, following the family's missionary tradition. The US naval chaplaincy was open to recent seminary graduates, but my wife, Martha, and I felt that Christian mission abroad was the kind of service we were called to choose.

By the fall of 1944, Dad was back from Oklahoma. The end of the war seemed to be in sight. He busied himself, off and on, helping in the medical office of the board in New York and planning for hospital rehabilitation, getting ready to return to Korea as soon as the door should open a crack for civilians. It was in early spring of 1946 that the first of those openings finally came.

# 23

# Thirty-Eighth Parallel

ARCH WAS GOING BACK. Many "old Korea hands" had dreamed about it; but he was actually on his way. The State Department had approved a group of ten, the first Protestant missionaries and among the first civilians to be allowed back in Korea. Arch was elected chairman of the group.

The happenings in Korea immediately after the war are now history, some of it public history, some of it little known. The United States and her wartime ally Russia divided the task of disarming the Japanese in Korea, and of maintaining order while a civilian government could be established. The arrangement was to be temporary and many heartily wished it so. Certainly the American GIs on duty there did, anxious for nothing so much as to go home; and presumably the Koreans, eager to know the exhilaration of ruling their own country for themselves. The inscrutable Russian bear, little understood by most of us then, had other plans.

At first a US-USSR joint commission met in Seoul to agree on a method by which Korea could be unified under a central government. As a democracy, the United States knew only one formula for this and found the problem simple—free general elections adequately supervised would do it—but the Russians had a different goal. After two years of deadlocked disagreement, the joint commission had to be acknowledged a failure.

The United Nations intervened, although without Soviet support. In January 1948, a UN Temporary Commission went to Korea, but the Russians refused to allow it to enter the north of the country. The Thirty-Eighth Parallel, originally just a convenient dividing line, had been converted into a barricaded and closely guarded frontier. As a result, the UN agreed that free general elections would be held in South Korea only and instructed its commission to supervise them. The elections were held on May 10, 1948. The national assembly, elected as a result of the voting, met in June and July to draft a constitution and to elect Dr. Syngman Rhee as the first president. On August 15, 1948, the third anniversary of liberation from Japan, the Republic of Korea was proclaimed and President Rhee inaugurated.

That is running ahead of this story and of Arch driving eagerly from New York to San Francisco in April 1946. He knew very little of the details of the situation in Korea, intricate details that he would try to sort out and understand in the months ahead. He didn't even know how he would get across the Pacific, but his faith and hopes were high. It had been four years since the spring of 1942, when he paced around the yard in Taegu, wondering how soon and in what way the war with Japan might end.

My sister, Elsie, was with him driving to the West Coast. No longer a WAVE, she was going back to Korea, too—waiting for orders from Washington, to take up a civilian post in the Public Information Office of the US-run military government. She had been waiting in the East and now thought she might as well wait in San Francisco. Officially, when they finally came, her orders said that she was a "speech re-write editor," although in all the time she spent in Korea, she never really found out what that was.

∾ ∾ ∾

In San Francisco Arch began making a round of offices, tackling with typical vigor the problem of securing transportation. As well as his own passage, there was a large quantity of relief supplies being sent by the Protestant relief agency Church World Service, for which he was trying to help arrange shipment. Still, he had been there only a week when he sent a wire to Dr. Charles Leber, the general secretary of the board in New York:

SAILING TOMORROW FRIDAY VERY SMALL FREIGHTER BOWLINE REEFER ONLY PASSENGER THIRTY DAY TRIP INFORM HOOPER CROSS MOORE AND DODD FAREWELL EXECUTIVE AND OFFICE STAFF.

The little *Bowline Reefer*, carrying US Army materiel as well as the civilian relief supplies, made it into Incheon harbor just four weeks later, after a none-too-direct passage of 6,600 miles. Because the ship was small, she didn't have to anchor outside of harbors and wait for tenders like the larger ships, but could tie up to unload. An Army security officer had kept her cargo of military stores under close guard all the way across, accepting Arch's light-blue civilian Chevrolet as a part of the Army gear with the unquestioning good nature of those who neither know nor care to understand the mysteries of what the Army ordains. At Incheon this officer saw the car unloaded and made sure the tank was filled with gas before he turned the keys back to its civilian driver.

Now this was really it! Arch's footlocker had come in the trunk of the car. He had only to toss in his suitcase, slip behind the wheel and roll away from the wharf toward Seoul. The twenty-five-mile drive through the green countryside of late spring was over a familiar road, and soon he had picked up two GIs to share it with him. What was not familiar was the lack of movement on the rutted road. Virtually no civilian transport was to be seen anywhere. Japan had left in Korea no automobiles or trucks in running condition, and the civilian economy was only beginning to rally from the austerity and shortages of war. Also, the Thirty-Eighth Parallel lay across the life-stream of Korea's economy, dissecting the industrial north from the agricultural south of the peninsula.

As he drove along, Arch noted the signs of poverty and hardship among the population, the pinched faces and shabby clothes, the few and boney oxen, the little shops almost bare of anything to sell. But it was good to be back. He exulted to be on the road to Seoul in spite of all.

Of course, another changed feature of the Korean scene was the presence of the US Army. He would have to adjust to that in the months and years to come. It still seemed incongruous to one for whom Korea and the United States had always belonged to two separate and entirely distinct worlds. He had moved naturally in those two worlds by turns, but never thought how it would be to mix them.

Several times the car was slowed by a roadblock manned by GIs. Now it was their turn to see something new and surprising, an ordinary stateside civilian car with stateside civilian license plates and a civilian driver. They blinked in amazement and asked no questions, just let him through.

At last, entering the outskirts of Seoul, he dropped his GI passengers and headed for Severance Hospital. This union Christian medical institution, which several Protestant denominations had cooperated in developing into one of the best hospitals and the first medical college in Korea, had kept functioning through the war years, entirely with Korean personnel. The building looked shabby and equipment was worn and in disrepair.

The present officers were not in, so Arch phoned Dr. K. S. Oh, ex-president of the medical college and an old friend, and was taken to his home. Dr. Oh's cordial welcome was the first of many Arch would be treated to as he began to get around South Korea. He spent his first night back in the country in Dr. and Mrs. Oh's neat, small, Japanese-style home, and the next day, with their kind help, arranged to rent a room in the neighboring house of a widow.

He had anticipated trouble on the question of living quarters, but was ready to make the best of it. The State Department in Washington, in giving permission to the first missionaries to return to Korea, had used a military expression, "live off the land." No favors were to be expected from the Army, no mess privileges, no billets; they would have to shift for themselves. This, the missionaries were glad to do, having many friends there. They were quite ready to eat Korean food and to find lodging in a Korean home.

So Arch made his arrangements with a Mrs. Crow. She was the widow of an American, who had married her years before and settled down to live out his life in Korea. When the war broke out, the Japanese tried to repatriate him forcibly on the *Asama,* so that they could exchange him for a Japanese caught in America. But Crow, aging and unwell, refused to be separated from his family.

"You'll have to take me out dead," he said. "It's the only way I'll go."

Finally they gave up, and he stayed, but died soon after. His refusal meant no lack of regard for his far-away native land. His oldest son went to the Philippines to join the US Army fighting Japan, but was caught by the enemy and beheaded. Two other children had been on the *Gripsholm,* having been taken under the Underwoods' wing.

Immediately on getting settled in Seoul, Arch set out to call on General Hodge, commanding officer of the Sixth Army Corps, which was carrying out the occupation of Korea, and on General Lerch, the military governor of Korea, as well as on the colonels who were serving as mayor of the city and governor of the Province. His first lesson in the intricacies of what lay before him came when General Lerch informed him flatly that all missionaries allowed to return to Korea would for the present be billeted by the Army and would eat at Army mess halls. Arch protested that the State Department had told him differently. That didn't matter to the military governor, who added, "Furthermore, you're subject to court martial."

One of the first jobs to be done was to investigate the condition of mission properties. The Presbyterian (USA) board had held property in eight centers in Korea, where the stations of its mission were located. Four of these now lay north of the Thirty-Eighth Parallel, where no arrangement could be made to reach or investigate them. Such reports as could be had about the north came from the Korean refugees who were already streaming south in alarming numbers.

When Arch arrived in Seoul the Communists—Russian and Korean— had not yet been in control of the north for a year, but they were working intensively to consolidate their grip. As a result, the people in the north who had lived and suffered for thirty-five years under total domination by Japan found their dream of freedom defrauded. One form of tyranny was being replaced by another. If anyone might doubt this, there was the grim evidence of the refugees.

One refugee pastor told Arch how he had been imprisoned twice, robbed of all his possessions, even his watch and fountain pen, and intimidated. Finally he fled, making the dangerous journey south with his wife and three children, slipping across the parallel and arriving in Seoul with only the clothes that he wore. This minister had studied in Canada and Edinburgh; he was a natural target for the Communists.

Others had similar stories of jail sentences, beatings, the water cure. They told of hymnbooks and Bibles being seized and torn up before their eyes, with the taunting question, "Where is this God of yours? If this is his Word, let him reclaim it." And what cut deepest, what haunted and disquieted the more thoughtful among them even then, in 1946, was that these new persecutors were Koreans; they were their own people, turned Communist.

A few years later, in New York City I listened as Dr. Hahn Kyung-chik, a brilliant Korean pastor originally from Sinuiju, up on the Yalu River across from Manchuria, told a group of us:

> I know my people; they are a gentle and a peace-loving people, a people of scholars; but I have seen how Communism has transformed them and brought out the worst in many of them, and I say to you that if it can do this with my Korean people, then it can do it with any people anywhere.

In South Korea conditions were already chaotic enough. Several hundred thousand Japanese, many of them prosperous and with extensive holdings, had been shipped back to Japan. There was a sort of justice in the way they were sent, taking with them "what you can carry in your hands," as Arch and Jessie had been forced to do. An equal number, perhaps, of Koreans were being returned to Korea from Manchuria, China, and Japan. Such uprooting brought with it the usual backwash of lost moral standards and of a cynical determination to survive by whatever means. Arch set out to survey the situation and, in particular, to get reports for his New York board on the condition of properties in the three mission stations outside of Seoul that could still be reached.

The first place was Taegu, first in accessibility and first in his affections. He took the "Korea Liberator," the one express train then running daily between Seoul and Pusan. There were no taxis or rickshaws and no porters after working hours to carry one's luggage. He walked with a Korean friend to the station. This was the new Korea. On the train, he produced his ticket, for which he had paid four hundred sixty yen. That should have been about $4.60 in US currency at the going rate of exchange, but the military government was obliging the use of an exchange of fifteen yen to the dollar, which made the ticket cost a little over thirty dollars.

Arch settled down in a second-class car, where he soon located two Korean friends from Taegu. The miles were clicking away as they talked. He hardly noticed when the Korean conductor entered, following a US Army officer, until the officer spoke to him brusquely: "Out of bounds." Arch looked puzzled; Army jargon was still rather unfamiliar.

"Out of bounds for all American and military personnel," the officer amplified.

One car on the train was reserved for all such personnel, it seemed, and the Army had not figured out what to do about US civilians not directly under its control. Arch produced his ticket and finished the trip in the company of his Korean friends. Later, when he went back to Seoul, he made the trip *in* bounds, in the proper car and without having to purchase a ticket, but also without the pleasure of talk with local friends.

Friends in Taegu, knowing he would be coming sometime soon, had planned a big turnout to receive him. A telegram that he had sent four days earlier was delivered at the hospital just an hour before his train arrived. Even so, about a hundred people were at the station with triumphant smiles and shouted greetings. It was the first time they and Arch had seen one another in the new Korea. Now, looking out over the crowd, he had to recall in one vivid flash that pre-dawn send-off by the Japanese police four years before.

At the hospital, his emotions surged. At the sights and faces it was hard to keep the voice steady and the eyes from brimming. There stood the blackened ruin of the outpatient building, just as fire had left it four—no, six—years ago. The hospital was still running, keeping up its service as a Christian institution. He was proud of that. He felt proud and grateful for the members of the staff, as he saw so many familiar faces and learned how different ones had stood by the institution through the thick and thin of the war years.

After leaving the hospital for a year under a Korean physician, the Japanese had taken over its administration. They had locked up Dr. Whong for a while, but left the rest of the staff free to carry on. Dr. Whong's jail term was mainly just a warning. He had studied in the United States and had been too friendly with Americans; they wanted to impress on him what they could do to him if they so chose.

Arch looked the hospital over briefly. He had not been assigned to Taegu, although both hospitals there had urgently requested that. For the time being, the overall job to be done in Korea was much bigger. The hospital building and equipment showed the wear of years when no adequate repair or replacement could be made. The laundry, with its big washer and superheated steam mangle, which had meant so much satisfaction to Arch, had fallen into disuse. Shortages of fuel and water had obliged the setting up of primitive hand facilities for doing laundry outside the building. Some other changes had been made, but the hospital had persevered. Arch told himself he should be grateful, and felt deeply that he was.

Up on the compound, other wrenching adjustments awaited him. Our own house, which had been home for so many years, where he had seen his children grow up and had shared with us our last vacation days before we left home for college, was not too much changed at first glance. He and Jessie had supervised the adapting of it as a nurses' dormitory a few months before Pearl Harbor. Now he was more glad than ever for having taken that step. The nurses had stayed on in the house through the war. It had deteriorated. Some windows were broken, a cellar door missing. Paint was cracked and peeling, and the yard, once bordered with flowers, had returned to being a shaley waste; but the damage might have been worse.

Arch went on across the compound, examining, making notes. When he came to the house he and Jessie had lived in through internment, he recalled wryly how they had worked so feverishly through that last day and night, sorting, repacking, stowing things away. Everything was gone. Not a vestige of what they had thought to save was still there. Even the heating plant and plumbing had been completely torn out and dismantled by the Japanese, desperate for scrap iron in the last stage of the war. Windows and doors were broken.

A refugee family from China, a Christian family, was living in the house without authorization. At least they were protecting it from further destruction by looters and vagrants. Others among the mission houses were in worse condition, although provisional repairs had been made on one or two to fit them out as Army billets.

The question in Korea about houses was, who were the squatters and who were the owners? The Japanese authorities had taken over mission property, and in some instances it had been sold, while in others, recovered directly by the US Sixth Army Corps.

But how would the mission recover it from the Army? That was Arch's job to negotiate, not always easy because the Army, reluctantly realizing that its stay in Korea was to be a long one, was beginning that summer to make plans for bringing out Army dependents. Therefore, a lot more housing was going to be needed.

In general, the Army was generous and cooperative. It offered to repair houses and turn them back to missionaries, in return for the right to use others for a year or so. This was a good thing for the missionaries, who were in a bind. The military government's artificial fifteen-to-one exchange rate meant that if the mission had to buy Korean yen and do the repairing itself, the cost would be prohibitive.

That exchange rate raised a blank wall for almost any type of service for the mission. At first, there was talk that it was to be adjusted at least to sixty-to-one, but that hope faded. Then Arch devised a rather ingenious way of getting around it that was legal and cooperative with the government, and that illustrated his entrepreneurial side. He got a license from the officials of the Korean department of commerce, who by that time were in charge, to buy and sell as an importer. He could buy up whole shipments of commodities in Hongkong (newsprint and yarn became his favorites), have them sent to Korea, and sell them there. The purchase was made in US dollars, with payment collected in Korean yen.

It was a devious method, and no doubt wasteful of a mission doctor's time; but it yielded a good supply of yen at a realistic rate of exchange, while staying within the law, and it was typical of the complexities of trying to do the most simple job in Korea after liberation.

On that first visit to Taegu, Arch had a car and driver put at his disposal, letting him ride out to the leprosy hospital. This place, at least, was a solace. As he entered the grounds the hedges on each side of the road were rich and lushly green. Two trellises arching overhead seemed literally buried in roses. The neat little colonial-style guest house stood off the road to the right, with the Chinese characters on its plaque: "Doctor Fletcher, Praise, Grace Pavilion." He noted with satisfaction the evidence of affectionate care.

Naturally, the Japanese authorities, with their morbid fear of contagion, would have given this place a wide berth, but the patients had certainly done their part to maintain it as best they could. Fitting, he thought, that those so afflicted in this life should have been able to survive the war years in an island of beauty and quiet. It gave one a surge of warmth around the heart.

The warm feeling was still there as he toured the grounds, and more than once he turned his head so that his emotion would not be seen. For him this work had always held a very special place. It was Pai Chung-won, the administrator and ex-policeman, with his exceptional discipline and drive, who had held things together through the hard years.

The assembly bell had been ringing, and the patients were all gathered in the auditorium. When Arch entered they stood and the hymn was announced: a Korean version of "All Hail the Power of Jesus' Name."

"This hymn—," Mr. Pai whispered, "when word came on August fifteenth that Japan had surrendered and we knew we were free, the Christians of Taegu gathered and we sang it as we had never sung it before."

After the hymn, there was the Twenty-Third Psalm and songs and recitations by the children. Then an elder of the church, a man crippled by the disease in an advanced stage, stood to make a speech of welcome. Arch watched him and saw again the unearthly light on the elder's wasted face as he had seen it on others in years gone by. Now he was remembering some of those others and looking for them among the people sitting in the church. Not finding them, he felt a pang of realization. After all, it had been four-years-and-a-half. Then words heard by John the mystic on Patmos came to mind, as if he were hearing them spoken:

> And God shall wipe away all tears from their eyes; and there shall be no more death, neither sorrow, nor crying, neither shall there be any more pain: for the former things are passed away (Rev. 21:4 King James Version).

A chorus was singing, a mixed chorus of young people, all of them victims of the disease.

After the program, Arch climbed the little hill with Administrator Pai, to stop at the Home for Untainted Children. The dedicated women who had cared for these youngsters through the lean years brought them out and had them line up for the distinguished visitors, then bow so low that their foreheads seemed to touch their knees. Arch glanced along the row. His physician's eye caught the symptoms of undernourishment in swollen bellies, with thin arms and legs protruding from shabby, patched jackets, trousers, and skirts. But there was no shabbiness in their voices when they threw their heads back and sang. That was perhaps the hardest moment of the day for Arch, as well as the highest.

Next day, Sunday, there was a reception in the Sin Chung Church. Christians from all over the city were there. Writing about it afterward, Arch said,

> As I entered the Church they flocked from all sides to greet me—some of the grandmothers even embracing me. One of them, unable to contain herself, actually danced before the altar. For the first time I was made to understand the religious emotion that inspired David to dance before the Ark for joy.

All of this, Arch insisted, was because he was the first to go back.

> I was simply basking in the warmness of the feeling in the hearts of the Christians toward the Taegu missionaries.

## 24

## Quonset Huts on a Hill

It was good there was some place in the country with warmness. Korea was vexed by problems of a fearful magnitude. The heady, waking dream of liberation was turning into a nightmare. Refugees, inflation, joblessness, the bitterness of the deferred hope of a free national government, with the arbitrary barrier of the Thirty-Eighth Parallel thrown across the country and only ominous rumors coming from beyond it; all of these contributed to what Arthur Koestler identified, in a similar context, as darkness at noon.

Rot was also attacking the moral fiber of the people. Thieving was everywhere. Hats were stolen right off the heads of their wearers, briefcases and handbags slashed in crowded streetcars. Vice was open and those who practiced it, unashamed.

My sister, Elsie, also went to Taegu that summer. She had stopped at one of the houses where a saintly missionary lady used to live. Some Red Cross nurses were using the house, and Elsie was chatting with one of them when there was a terrific pounding at the door. The Korean cook went and looked out, then came running back, her face grey with fear.

"Who is it?" Elsie asked in Korean.

"It's the soldier; he's come again."

"I know who it is," the nurse broke in. "This GI gets drunk and then comes around here and bothers us. Tell the cook not to open the door, whatever she does, and you'd better not go out either until he gets tired and goes away."

He did go away, finally, and Elsie went out to look at a new road the Army had bulldozed, making an approach to the back of the compound. Returning up that road, she met a young woman with a child. She stopped to speak to the child, and when the mother heard this American woman speak Korean, her interest quickened. After a few exchanges she asked:

"Do you know where I can get an American soldier? It's the only way I can live."

Amid such chaos, the Communists were vigorously active in South Korea as well as in the north. The Communist party was still legal then. In connection with her work with the public information office of the military government, Elsie traveled around South Korea with another young woman, Marilea Hanson, who was a "political analyst." Entering the towns, they would seek meetings with groups of different political colors, including the Communists.

Once, in Kwangju, they thought they had gone too far. The only group that seemed interested in a political discussion *were* the Communists. Elsie and Marilea found themselves crowded into the meeting place, a small Korean house, with a group of ardent leftists. The discussion grew heated; the group poured typically slanted questions on Marilea. Elsie was glad to be only the interpreter and glad that, by interpreting, she could give Marilea a little time to find a good answer. The two came out of the confrontation all right, without backing down from their own position and without starting a fight; but they resolved not to get caught in that sort of spot again.

After getting to Korea, Elsie had worked up her Korean well and with an ease that surprised her. As she gained confidence, she used to go around in a jeep and make speeches as well as listen to them. When the Koreans in the smaller towns saw an American woman, a couple of hundred of them would gather around her; but as soon as she began to speak to them in Korean, and with no foreign accent, there would be five hundred.

∾ ∾ ∾

Jessie also was by that time back in Korea. Arch had said goodbye to her in New York on April 8, 1946. A year later, she arrived at Incheon. In Seoul she found that two of the former residences had been recovered and the mission's personnel squeezed into them. Out of town guests were lodged in the basement. In the common dining room, which the wives who had returned took turns running, there were never fewer than a dozen or fifteen sitting down together.

Early in 1948, Arch made an important shift in his approach. The Severance Union Medical College and Hospital was in wretched shape. There were funds to repair and rehabilitate it, but the government's arbitrary exchange rate still barred the way. By invitation from Severance, Arch joined its staff as a professor of surgery and also became executive director, a new post that principally would mean pushing the rehabilitation program.

This was when he devised his scheme for getting licensed as an importer and breaking through the exchange-rate barrier. Other problems were tackled one by one. Progress was painfully slow, frustrations innumerable, but room by room and building by building the decrepit plant and equipment with which Severance had come through the war years began to be renovated.

In all of this, Arch worked closely with Dr. Y. S. Lee, then president of the medical college and hospital. Dr. Lee was the higher authority, but their offices adjoined one another, and cooperation was of the closest.

Arch still had a final, all-out attack to make on two particular adversaries. Some might have thought that in pouring his energies now into a Seoul institution, he was forgetting Taegu and North Kyung Sang Province, which had absorbed so many of his best years. Rather, what obsessed him now was a wider vision. He longed to carry the fight against the two major enemies to public health in South Korea—tuberculosis and leprosy—into a national crusade.

In Taegu before the war, he had initiated the plan, already described, for setting up a chain of treatment stations throughout the province. Working with the central Taegu Leprosy Hospital, they could, he believed, bring under control and eventually eradicate leprosy from North Kyung Sang province. Now the plan he began to advocate was essentially the same, but on an expanded basis. The area to be cleansed of the scourge of Hansen's Disease was not one province, but all of South Korea.

In August 1949, he had an interview with President Syngman Rhee. Dr. Rhee listened with keen interest to the proposal. Here was a man who loved his people and whose eyes glistened with emotion when he talked about eradicating leprosy in his country. Dr. Rhee asked Arch to write the plan down in detail, with cost estimates for each phase of it. The government would give all support possible.

Arch's plan, as he sent it also to the American Leprosy Mission, called for the development in Seoul of a leprosy center for the training of adequate personnel—medical and nursing plus technicians and administrators—to be deployed later throughout the country. The center would also conduct research and carry on a nation-wide campaign of publicity. Throughout the provinces clinics would be established, essentially the treatment stations of Arch's former plan, where early and non-infectious cases could receive diagnosis and treatment while living in their homes.

Beyond these, he envisioned institutions of four types, which might be variously combined in the same locations: (1) institutions in agricultural areas, where infectious cases might be admitted and treated while improving their health and prospect of recovery by helping to produce vegetables, grains, and other farm produce; (2) institutions for training and rehabilitating people with arrested cases, preparing them to go back into society; (3) special colonies where badly mutilated or hopeless patients might continue to live a life as nearly normal as possible; and (4) homes in which children of leper parents, and those who had been closely associated with patients, might be kept under observation, until demonstrated to be free of the disease or otherwise.

Such was the scheme proposed. President Rhee warmed to it. He informed officials that thereafter no government plan for combating leprosy should be approved unless Arch had initialed it. But the Republic of Korea was a poor country. Help for such projects must come from the United States, from the Economic Cooperation Administration, but the ECA was more interested in propping up aspects of Korea's struggling economy than in helping launch a program for the control of leprosy. Perhaps they were right; perhaps Arch was. In a matter of months history would render the discussion academic.

Meanwhile, in his vision regarding tuberculosis, Arch was meeting with more success. The big US pharmaceuticals firm Merck & Co. was enthusiastic about proving the effectiveness of streptomycin in the treatment of tuberculosis. Arch negotiated with them an offer to provide quantities of the new drug free, if a large-scale, clinically controlled program for its administration could be set up in Korea. With his contacts at Johns Hopkins and Penn and from the time of his own treatment at Trudeau he had no difficulty in forming the advisory committee that Merck stipulated. In Korea, the work would be carried on as an integral part of the program of Severance Union Medical College.

Up on the hill behind the college, with a beautiful view out over the city and the surrounding valley, lay an expanse of land where buildings could be erected; but erecting buildings in Korea at that time was a challenge, even if one had money, which Arch did not. It was a struggle to secure any construction materials, as he well knew from the headaches of rehabilitation of the college and hospital.

So he set to work on a different approach. Hunting through the city, he located several Quonset huts in very good condition. They had been set up by the Army for mess halls. On his request, President Rhee had them requisitioned and moved to the hilltop site, where workmen began to adapt them for service as a tuberculosis sanatorium. That was when Arch and Jessie left Korea on a four-month furlough in the United States. It was April 1950. He never saw what happened to the Quonset huts.

Arch did see the completion of his major work, in the brief years between the end of World War II and the outbreak of the Korea War, which was the rehabilitation of Severance Hospital. When he and Jessie went on furlough, that job had been completed. Some of the buildings had been virtually rebuilt inside. New plumbing functioned efficiently everywhere. New asbestos tile flooring shone in the corridors; surgical cases were full of gleaming new instruments. Some thirty thousand dollars of funds contributed by churches in the United States had been spent on updating Severance as a completely modern medical institution.

Sharing in this way, thought Arch, he could multiply himself many times through the skilled hands of young doctors who would train at Severance to serve in many parts of the new Korea.

Then the dyke at the Thirty-Eighth Parallel broke. The Communist waves poured through Seoul. The bloody tide of fighting flooded and ebbed as the city changed hands four times before bullets gave way to endless, inconclusive "peace negotiations." All of that left the outpatient building of Severance a roofless, gutted ruin, and all the rehabilitation work a heartbreaking shambles.

In the first bitter onslaught, capitalizing on the surprise of their attack, the North Koreans came close to sweeping the peninsula. Intent on driving the United Nations forces into the sea at Pusan, they were stopped by determined resistance at the Pusan perimeter. The line held when the big guns were already clearly audible in Taegu. The Taegu Presbyterian Hospital was virtually turned into a military field facility.

After liberation, Moon Han-chik, the skilled and dedicated laboratory technician who had studied in the United States under Arch's initiative, had served as acting superintendent. Later Dr. R. K. Smith, a seasoned missionary and one-time co-worker with Arch, became superintendent until returning to the United States in 1949. Then Dr. Howard Moffett was named to the post. He was a "second-generationer," son of the beloved Rev. Samuel A. Moffett, one of Korea's great missionary pioneers.

Howie and I had known one another well as high school classmates at Pyongyang Foreign School. Now, he had been in charge in Taegu for just a year when the invasion occurred. Howie had served previously in the US Air Force. With the US military in Korea suddenly converted from occupying to combat troops, he was back in uniform.

Dr. L.W. Whong, the long-time staff member of Taegu hospital, became acting superintendent. It was under Dr. Whong's leadership that, with Taegu under threat, most of the Taegu Presbyterian's resources and staff were moved to Tongnai to set up a temporary hospital. The facility returned to Taegu in early October, while the UN forces advanced almost to the Yalu. They were driven back when the Chinese Communists came into the struggle, and later retook Seoul in March 1951.

Arch had no hand in any of this. He and Jessie had left on their brief furlough, taking with them, in effect, as they had when they were repatriated, "only what you can carry in your hands." It seemed ironic that, for a second time, they should have their possessions in Korea swept away by war.

## 25

## A Stone Tablet Set Up Again

ARCH WAS NEVER ABLE to go back to Korea. He had planned to go and wanted to. He was ready to face, with his missionary and Korean colleagues, the appalling task of trying to begin over again in Seoul among the shattered buildings and crushed lives; but when the fighting ended and the two sides were trying to establish a truce, with little hope of real peace—much less a unified Korea—the clock had moved on too far for Arch.

In the spring of 1952, the patients of the Taegu Leper Hospital wrote to him, in Korean script, a letter of appreciation:

> Over here on the "Place of Love and Joy" [a name suggested much earlier by the Japanese authorities in order to dissociate "Taegu" and "Leper" from the institution] we have a lovely flower garden, in addition to our green trees at this time of year. . . . We, like these flowers and trees, withstood all the turmoil and change of the past decade in this land, since you left us. Your first sweat drops of some thirty-five years ago for us have changed into green leaves and beautiful flowers in our garden. The ocean lies between you and us, but through Christ we communicate with each other. We know you have not forgotten us, and we wish you would come over to us to work for us once more.

Arch would be seventy that summer, and the mission board was not willing to send him back. He finished out his time as a missionary doctor behind a desk in New York City, working in the office for displaced persons, helping relocate fellow Christians from Europe who were victims of World War II. When he retired, his colleagues gave him a party in the offices of the Board of Foreign Missions at 156 Fifth Avenue. But predictably, he couldn't stay retired. For five more years, he continued to serve intermittently as the board's acting medical officer, commuting to "156" from a small apartment in upper Manhattan. In December 1957, he retired definitively.

During this time, the Manhattan apartment saw a good many visitors from Korea. The few Korean keepsakes that two wars had left to Jessie and Arch—the pictures and the brass bowl and candlesticks—had a chance to blend with conversation in the mellifluous language of Korea. Especially, the two "old Korea hands" were always eager for news of Taegu. They heard how the outpatient building, more than a decade after that disastrous fire, was replaced by a modern unit with greatly enlarged facilities, as well as a dining hall and a nurses' dormitory. A children's hospital was added near the main hospital building, the "fireproof hospital" Arch had worked so hard to erect.

At the head of each department was a well-trained, fully qualified specialist, in every case a national. Arch had shared in helping most of these heads get their training; their success was really his greatest satisfaction.

Among them was Dr. Suh, the radiologist. He was the son of Suh Bohki, for whom Arch had gotten a scholarship back in 1930 to study x-ray technique at the University of Pennsylvania. The son got the full medical course his father was not privileged to have. Then he went on to graduate study in radiology, qualifying under the stiff examination of the American Board of Radiologists, before he returned to Taegu Hospital to work with his father.

Severance Hospital in Seoul, still in the process of being rebuilt at a new location, had on its staff an able young doctor as head of the department of bacteriology: Dr. Joon Lew. He had received help and encouragement from Arch while adding to his MD a PhD in infectious diseases at the University of California—in the field of Arch's old antagonist, leprosy. Since Dr. Lew had gone back to Korea, a philanthropic gift was in the process of turning into reality another of Arch's projects for Seoul: the establishment of a center for teaching and research focused on that disease.

In a quiet valley some miles from Taegu a dedicatory stone tablet had been set up earlier with a capstone carved in lines suggesting an ancient Korean tile roof. The stone was erected at the site of the leprosy treatment station that Arch established at Uisung. Grateful patients made the dedication there in the front yard of the small treatment building.

During World War II, the Japanese military authorities knocked down the tablet and threw it aside, even chipping away Arch's name to obliterate the memory of a Western missionary. That war passed, the Japanese left, and then the Communist war convulsed the Korean countryside.

In a region full of refugees, however, a group of the Uisung victims of leprosy established a colony in the hills near Tamni. Treatments were resumed. They put up a tent church, and hunting in the hills, they found the defaced dedicatory stone and set it up again on its original spot. Although the Chinese characters of the inscription on the front had been chipped away, war and hatred and stone chisels could not wipe out what it declared, and still declares. On the back is written:

> Men have various sufferings among which disease is the saddest, and leprosy the most fearful of diseases. Those afflicted with leprosy had to leave home, abandoned by parents, brothers and sisters, family and friends. They were miserable. But God's love is great. Dr. A. G. Fletcher [these characters still remain], the Superintendent of Taegu Presbyterian Hospital, has established a treatment station for us in our district. He has helped us with Gospel and drug. With our deep appreciation, we hereby dedicate to him a stone to remember him and his work forever.

On the grounds of Aerakwon, the institution in modern Taegu carrying on, after a century, the leprosy work initiated by young missionary Arch in 1913, the stone tablet bearing his name stands in a place of honor.

# Postscript

I HAVE TWO FINAL scenes etched lovingly on my memory.

On his definitive retirement, Dad had moved to California with Mother, to Westminster Gardens, a beautiful campus for retired Presbyterian missionaries, located in Duarte, outside of Los Angeles. Although it was a long move away from my family's home in New Jersey, my work at the time enabled me to drop in occasionally for a visit.

On this morning, Dad was dressed and sitting near a wide window in a sunroom of the nursing section. His mind had been failing, as well as his body, as he neared his eighty-seventh birthday. While I sat with him, the door opened. A delegation from South Korea that was being shown around was stopping by, wishing to greet Dr. Fletcher. There were introductions. He looked vague, but managed a few phrases in Korean, even trying to stand in spite of their protests. They stayed just a few minutes, then took leave with deep, respectful bows. I noticed among them a rather striking woman, beautifully dressed, with a touch of Korean style in the lines of her full silk skirt.

It was only a moment later that suddenly the door flew open again. It was the Korean lady rushing in, her face contorted with emotion. She crossed the room, crying out, "AH-bu-ji! AH-bu-ji!." "Father! Father!", and threw her arms around Dad, clinging to him where he sat.

A moment more, and she stepped back. Regaining her composure, without even a nod to me, she walked quietly out the door and was gone, hurrying to rejoin her group. She had been a young nurse at Taegu Hospital, as I learned, when last Arch was head of staff there—before Pearl Harbor, some thirty years earlier. Her outpouring of emotion spoke eloquently of what he had meant to members of his staff.

*Ahbuji*! Father! Only a few months after that encounter, he died.

∾ ∾ ∾

I was able to go back to Korea just once, some twenty years later. Elsie, senior partner in her travel company, arranged the trip, accompanying Archie and his wife, Huldah—Huldah Blair, our childhood playmate at Taegu Station—and my wife, Martha, and me. In Taegu we stayed in a handsome, multi-story hotel above a teeming street of the city of two million, trying to remember our childhood Taegu, with its small sea of thatched and tiled-roof houses sheltering not more than seventy thousand people.

One end of the Taegu station compound had survived. There was the Blairs' house, much as Huldah remembered it. The young doctor and family living there invited us to come in and look around. On the second floor, at the front, was what had been Herb Blair's study. The window above the front door remained, and beside it his old-fashioned, roll-top desk, just as he had left it. Huldah was so glad, and much moved, to see it.

What was our end of the compound had been swallowed up, completely covered by the gleaming complex of buildings that now constituted the Dongsan Medical Center—part of the economic miracle that is the Republic of Korea, and a tribute to my friend Howie Moffett, his associates, and Korean Presbyterian enterprise. Going up a short, steep street, we tried to calculate where the gravel path used to be that led from the hospital grounds up to our front door. At the top of that street now was the entrance to a multi-story dormitory for students of the Dongsan Medical School.

We entered the stainless-steel-and-glass-walled lobby, deciding that right there we might be standing above where the dining-living room of our house was located. Memories of that room flooded in: winter sunlight slanting through the south-facing windows, with Dad striding up and down, singing:

> "Just a few more days to be filled with praise
> 
> And to tell the old, old story . . .
> 
> I'll exchange my cross for a starry crown,
> 
> Where the gates swing outward never;
> 
> At his feet I'll lay every burden down
> 
> And with Jesus reign forever."

Yes, Dad—dear, dedicated, indefatigable Arch—faith affirms that in an unimagined, unimaginable reality, you are—and Jessie with you—as GOD IS—and it is full of light.

# Illustrations

Photo 01. Arch Fletcher (left) with younger brother Dave, Ontario, c. 1888

Photo 02. Fletcher children, top left to right: Gordon, Tom, Arch; bottom: Olive and Dave, Ontario, c. 1898

Photo 03. Fletcher brothers in Nebraska, top, Tom and Gordon; bottom, Arch and Dave, c. 1905

Photo 04. Archibald and Gordon Fletcher, together in medical practice, Nebraska, c. 1906

Photo 05. Archibald G. Fletcher, MD, age 26, Sioux City, Iowa, 1908

Photo 06. Jessie Rodgers (left) with sister Elsie, Philadelphia, Pennsylvania, c. 1908

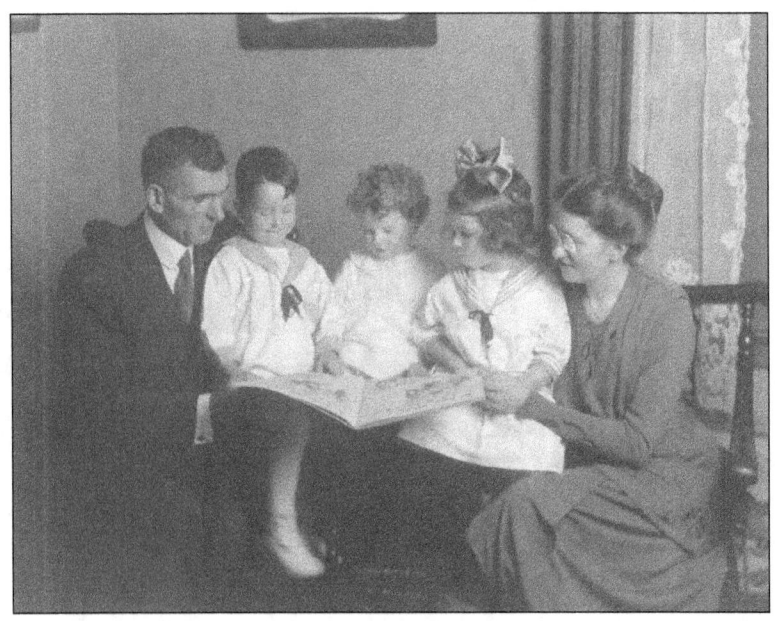

Photo 07. Archibald G. and Jessie Rodgers Fletcher, with children Arch Jr., Donald, and Elsie, 1920

Photo 08. Archibald G. Fletcher, MD,
in his medical coat, Korea, c. 1910

Photo 09. The Presbyterian Hospital, Taegu, 1937

Photo 10. One of the seventy three rural churches established by the Taegu Presbyterian Hospital by 1937

Photo 11. Hospital Evangelist preaching in a village, 1937

Photo 12. The Rev. K. W. Kim, first Christian and first pastor of North Kyeung Sang Province, 1938

Photo 13. Part of the Taegu Leprosy Hospital compound in winter, c. 1937

Photo 14. View of the Taegu Leprosy Hospital in the hills outside Taegu, c. 1938

Photo 15. One of the dormitories, Taegu Leprosy Hospital, c. 1938

Photo 16. Dr. A. G. Fletcher urges a mother with leprosy to allow her children to enter the home for disease-free children

Photo 17. Taegu Leprosy Hospital, 1 ½ miles outside Taegu, providing care in modern dormitories for 660 men, women, and children in 1938

Photo 18. Hog house and dairy barn of the Taegu Leprosy Hospital, providing fresh meat in the production of hogs, rabbits, pigeons, and chickens, 1938

Photo 19. Black Berkshire boar at the animal husbandry facility, Taegu Leprosy Hospital, 1938

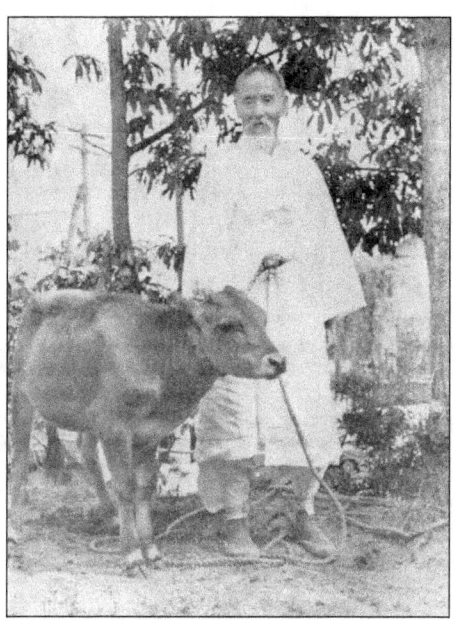

Photo 20. Farmer Pak, an enterprising farmer and active church member, Taegu, 1938

Photo 21. Korean child, giving the church the gift of a goat, from his grandmother, 1938

Photo 22. Dr. A. G. Fletcher and a group of healthy children whose parents are being treated for leprosy, c. 1938

Photo 23. Dr. and Mrs. A. G. Fletcher, in Korean dress outside the Guest House, built with contributions from leprosy patients to honor their 25th anniversary in Korea, photo c. 1937

Photo 24. Presbyterian Hospital in Taegu, established 1899, grown to a seventy-five-bed hospital by 1938

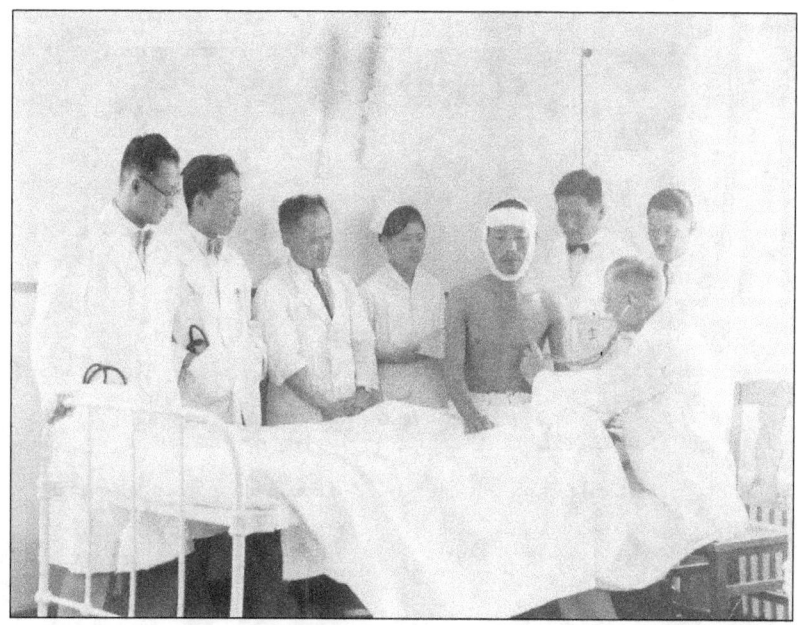

Photo 25. Dr. Fletcher and hospital staff making ward rounds, Taegu, c. 1937

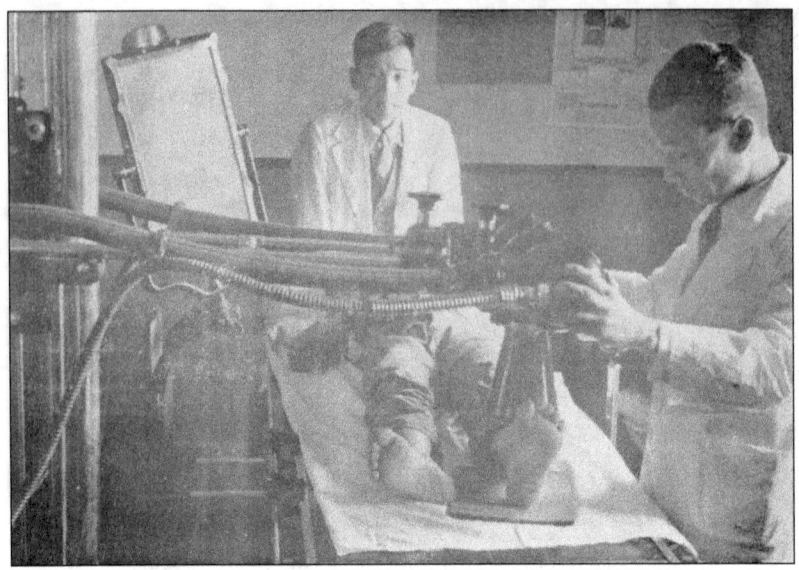

Photo 26. The x-ray department of Taegu Presbyterian Hospital took 1,307 images and gave 1,231 examinations and treatments in 1937

Photo 27. Medical technicians' course, Taegu Presbyterian Hospital, c. 1938

Photo 28. Students in the laboratory, Taegu, c. 1938

Photo 29. Laboratory technicians' course, Taegu, c. 1938

Photo 30. Free night clinics as outreach of Taegu Presbyterian Hospital, c. 1938

Photo 31. Taegu Hospital Baby Clinic Nurse Li Yoo-boon and Mothers' Club president, c. 1938

Photo 32. Graduates of the Baby Clinic wellness program, c. 1938

Photo 33. A. G. Fletcher in Taegu with visiting Toyohiko Kagawa, the famous Japanese social and labor activist and Christian leader, November 1939

Photo 34. Portrait of Archibald G. Fletcher, MD, around the time of his presentation of medical papers in Tokyo, 1931

Photo 35. Dr. L. W. Whong and family, Taegu, c. 1953

ILLUSTRATIONS 227

Photo 36. Dr. L. W. Whong and Mrs. Whong at his Ordination ceremony, Taegu, 1955

Photo 37. Dr. Archibald G. Fletcher serving the Board of Foreign Missions in New York, after his retirement from the Korea Mission, c. 1960

Photo 38. Archibald G. and Jessie Rodgers Fletcher in retirement, New York, 1963

Photo 39. Archibald G. and Jessie Rodgers Fletcher at Westminster Gardens, California, 1968

Photo 40. Dongsan Medical Center today, with the original "fireproof" hospital seen in the lower left, Taegu

Photo 41. Stone tablet in modern-day Aerakwon, recovered and re-erected to commemorate the ministry of Dr. Archibald G. Fletcher

www.ingramcontent.com/pod-product-compliance
Lightning Source LLC
Chambersburg PA
CBHW070311230426
43663CB00011B/2077